EARLY CHILDHOOD EDUCATION SERIES

Sharon Ryan, *Editor*

ADVISORY BOARD: *Celia Genishi, Doris Fromberg, Carrie Lobman, Rachel Theilheimer, Dominic Gullo, Amita Gupta, Beatrice Fennimore, Sue Grieshaber, Jackie Marsh, Mindy Blaise, Gail Yuen, Alice Honig, Betty Jones, Stephanie Feeney, Stacie G. Goffin, Beth Graue*

For a list of other titles in this series, visit www.tcpress.com

(continued)

The States of Child Care

Building a Better System

Sara Gable

FOREWORD BY
Marcy Whitebook

Teachers College
Columbia University
New York and London

Published by Teachers College Press, 1234 Amsterdam Avenue, New York, NY 10027

Library of Congress Cataloging-in-Publication Data

Gable, Sara.
  The states of child care : building a better system / Sara Gable ; foreword by Marcy Whitebook.
    pages cm. — (Early childhood education series)
    Includes bibliographical references and index.
    ISBN 978-0-8077-5474-0 (pbk. : alk. paper)
    eISBN 978-0-8077-7258-4 (ebook)
    1. Child care—United States. 2. Child care services—United States.
  3. Child care—Government policy—United States. 4. Family policy—United States.
  5. Welfare state—United States. I. Title.
    HQ778.63.G23 2013
    362.70973—dc23   2013030703

ISBN 978-0-8077-5474-0 (paperback)
eISBN: 978-0-8077-7258-4 (eBook)

Printed on acid-free paper
Manufactured in the United States of America

20 19 18 17 16 15 14 13   8 7 6 5 4 3 2 1

The difficulties in shaping children's policy stem not only from the sentiments that attach to the issues but also from a cultural reluctance to make children's needs a public responsibility.

—Hillary Rodham, 1977

Contents

Foreword

In the United States, an under-resourced and poorly conceived early childhood system shortchanges children's learning and well-being, strains family budgets, and fuels the poor pay and inadequate work environments of most early childhood practitioners. Sadly, this is true despite more than a half-century of advocacy dedicated to secure the right of all children and families to access equitable, high-quality early childhood services that value and reward those who teach young children.

Over the last several decades, our early childhood system has grown larger, more diverse, and more complex, yet it has remained severely under-resourced, creating daunting obstacles for those of us who embrace the charge of improving it. The slogan of the 1990 Worthy Wages for Child Care Campaign captures the dilemma we still face today: "Parents can't afford to pay; teachers and providers can't afford to stay. Help us find a better way."

In *The States of Child Care: Building a Better System*, Sara Gable guides us toward that better way by helping readers understand how today's early childhood system in the United States came to be. She provides us with the obvious as well as not-so-obvious context that has given rise to our American system, laying bare the ambivalence, fragmentation, and tensions that prevent those who rely upon and provide the services for it from uniting their voices more effectively for change. Sara's sober account of our history exposes the roots of our tenacious problems, never descending into what she labels "doom and gloom." Rather she uncovers the underlying dynamics that obfuscate divisions among natural allies, such as parents and practitioners, and fuel the illusion of a well-functioning child care market. In doing so, Sara gives voice to the perspectives of parents, practitioners, and advocates to help readers deepen their understanding of our past, what needs to change in the present, and what strategies they can use to make progress now.

For many decades, the field has focused educational and professional development predominantely on children's learning and development, creating a gap in our collective understanding about the policies that undergird the complex web of our early childhood system, the political dynamics that shape it, and how we can work together in the field and with other stakeholders to improve it. Many in the field recognize the role of policy and politics in determining our system, but our recognition belies our readiness to participate effectively in the arenas where policies are decided and resources are allocated. Many seasoned veterans, as well as those newer to the cause, are inadequately prepared to navigate and influence the complex policy and political climate in which early childhood services operate today. In addition to the specific areas of expertise we might possess—such as child development, pedagogy, parent relationships, special needs, dual language learning, administration, or advocacy—to be effective agents of change, we are all required to become subject-matter specialists about the field as a whole. Careful reading (and rereading) of *The States of Child Care: Building a Better System* will help us to do so.

Marcy Whitebook

Acknowledgments

The idea for this book came about in 2007, after I attended the National Strategy Session for Early Education and Child Care Workforce Development at UC Berkeley. Throughout the meeting, I was among a group of professionals from all over the country who shared similar ideals for child care in the United States. After the conference, however, we all returned to our home states where these shared ideals were not equally represented in the child care policy landscape. This reality nagged at me. Why was it this way? What would it take to bring about change? This book is my perspective on the problem and my recommendations for incremental progress toward a national, universal system of child care.

Many people made this book possible. The University of Missouri – Columbia, Office of Research, awarded three semesters of research leave and funded the original data collection for several chapters. Bernadette Coley and her staff at Compudex in Passaic, New Jersey, expertly transcribed dialogue from the focus groups and the North Carolina key informant discussions. Alicia Boatwright was my research assistant for categorizing the child care program names, administering the "What's in a Name?" survey to college students, and developing the coding systems. Pam Storey and Jennifer Weedin also helped with data collection. Shannon Cromwell assisted with recruiting the focus group participants, conducting the focus groups, and reviewing the transcripts. With their candor and openness to the process, the women who participated in Chapter 3's focus groups gave me the gift of a new perspective on my ideas. Joanna Lower, my co-author for Chapter 5, was integral to convening the North Carolina key informants, analyzing the transcripts, and identifying relevant background for the chapter. Joanna has wide-ranging experience with child care and early education and is currently the project director for the Winston-Salem State University's Cultural Competence Breakthrough Series Collaborative. Deb Cassidy and Sharon Mims participated in follow-up interviews to keep North Carolina's story current and complete. The other North Carolina key informants (Peggy Ball, Dick Clifford, Sue Creech, Khari Garvin, John Pruette, and Sue Russell) generously gave their time and shared their experiences and insights. Governor James Hunt and his executive assistant Sheila Evans also facilitated bringing the chapter to fruition.

My primary employer, Cooperative Extension, has played a central role in this work. Extension is the arm of land-grant institutions of higher education that reaches out to citizens with research-based knowledge and opportunities. Because of my position as a faculty member and Extension State Specialist, I have been fortunate to work directly with countless child care providers, Head Start staff, and other early educators over the past 15 plus years. Their many and varied voices have informed much of my thinking and writing. I hope that I have represented them well.

Marie-Ellen Larcada at Teachers College Press and Sharon Ryan, the Early Childhood Education Series Editor, have been wonderfully helpful and supportive. Peggy O'Connor, master of the manuscript preparation and proofreading universe, entered my world in the most serendipitous manner. Susan Liddicoat provided valuable editing services, and Aureliano Vazquez Jr. managed the final aesthetic elements. My parents, Barbara and David Gable, have always encouraged me in my professional endeavors. And, I especially thank my husband, Theodore Koditschek, for his good humor and expert advice.

The States of Child Care

A Plea for Real Systems Change

As the United States settles into the 21st century, the lack of a national policy for child care is felt by millions of families every day. Although 64% of women with children under the age of 6 are members of the labor force and 53% of married-couple households with young children have both parents employed (U.S. Department of Labor, Bureau of Labor Statistics [USDL, BLS], 2012b), the United States has yet to establish a cohesive system of child care. American families are thus left on their own to cobble together child care arrangements from uneven and fragmented offerings. (Note that in this book I use the term *child care* to represent all settings attended by infants, toddlers, and preschoolers when parents are working.)

For decades, child care in the United States has struggled under the weight of disparate policy goals. On the one hand, there are programs like Head Start and state-funded prekindergarten that provide the highest-quality compensatory education to children from income-eligible families. Although these programs are often available at no cost, they are not typically full-day (i.e., full parent workday), full-year programs. The other primary sector includes child care programs that are intended to support parental employment. This portion of the system is far more extensive, minimally regulated, and, despite eligibility in many instances to receive public funding sources, mostly privatized. When low-income parents need child care to support their employment, they have no guarantee of access to affordable, high-quality care arrangements. Instead, they are beholden to their state's child care subsidy program and its policy approach. Families that are not income-eligible for high-quality early education or child care subsidies are free to shop for child care and early education opportunities in the local marketplace of services. The likelihood that they can find quality, affordable child care that meets their employment needs and child-rearing ideals is somewhat subject to chance. Despite the different policy goals of the mostly public (e.g., Head Start, state prekindergarten) and mostly private (e.g., child care) sectors, the two approaches overlap in their support of families and attention to children's school readiness.

1

This misalignment of goals means that child care access, affordability, and quality vary by state and, for most families, arrangements differ within years, months, weeks, and even days. Before kindergarten, the average child experiences more than five child care situations (Belsky et al. , 2007), and a notable percentage have more than one regular arrangement per week (U.S. Census Bureau, 2011). Because of child care's notorious "revolving door" of caregivers, dozens of adults are likely to enter and exit most children's lives during the first 5 years. (I use the terms *caregiver, provider, teacher, staff,* and *worker* interchangeably to refer to members of the child care workforce who work directly with children.)

From a developmental perspective, the incoherence of children's early nonparental care experiences is concerning (i.e., "multiplicity of arrangements") (Morrissey, 2008, 2009). Development occurs most readily in stable contexts and relationships. Considering the vital role of quality child care for fostering children's development and school readiness (NICHD Early Child Care Research Network [ECCRN], 2002b; Pianta, Barnett, Burchinal, & Thornburg, 2009), the lack of a more unified policy approach to supporting families is troubling. Although some states have succeeded in creating better-coordinated systems, most U.S. child care remains woefully fragmented.

There is no shortage of evidence that quality child care supports children, families, and employers. However, the United States seems to have lost sight of the ideal of a system with integrated policy goals of family support and children's school readiness. For decades, U.S. child care has suffered from cultural anxiety about maternal employment and nonmaternal care (Scarr, 1998), a lack of common language and purpose (Goffin & Washington, 2007), and a workforce beset by low expectations and low pay (USDL, BLS, 2012c). Even with heroic efforts by states to improve offerings for families, these deep-seated barriers threaten each step of progress.

In this book I discuss these issues in detail and examine how they permeate U.S. child care. With Bronfenbrenner's (1986) ecological systems framework as an organizational rubric, the chapters offer a critical analysis of the complex ecology of U.S. child care from several different, yet interrelated, perspectives. Bronfenbrenner's framework is especially useful here because it depicts child care within a network of other micro- and macrosystems. Child care is traditionally conceptualized as a microsystem; it directly touches (and is touched by) children, families, and schools, and is embedded in several macrosystems such as state and federal policies and societal beliefs about young children and families. Currently, U.S. child care is a complex and fragmented institution in part because it is extolled as a vital public good but treated as a private family responsibility. Careful analysis of all systems that surround the child care ecology is essential for meaningful change at the national level. The book's title is intended to convey the variability in state child care systems and the ever-present ideological and emotional extremes that color policies for working mothers and child care.

This book addresses four major topics. Chapter 1 provides necessary context about U.S. policy for nonparental care, current state-level system-building efforts, recurring sources of funding, and relevant demographic characteristics of children and families.

Chapters 2 through 4 offer an analysis of several persistent forces impeding the emergence of a national child care system. These chapters are ordered by their proximity to children, beginning with Chapter 2's exploration of definitional and functional ambiguity in the child care marketplace. Chapter 3 discusses contemporary ideas about motherhood, employment, and providing child care for pay. Chapter 4 provides an extensive review of research on child care and child development, state quality improvement initiatives, and the chronic misalignment of research and policy.

With a focus on the positive, Chapter 5 reports a case history of North Carolina's early childhood system, a system with great potential for a national approach. Chapter 6 offers a brief set of recommendations for movement toward a more coherent system of child care in the United States. Particular emphasis is placed on incremental steps toward policy integration and workforce development.

The following sections in this Introduction provide overviews of the chapters' focus and content.

CONTEXT: THE OBVIOUS (AND THE NOT-SO-OBVIOUS)

The idea that U.S. child care is a vast nonsystem is not original. Anyone who comes in contact with child care on a regular basis can tell you that it is frighteningly uneven. Extensive public commentary takes place on the subject, and many, many people are committed to improving the system. To fully appreciate the complexity of U.S. child care, Chapter 1 describes and analyzes key policies and funding sources that underlie its day-to-day operation.

Federal involvement in child care frequently conveys political messages about what is best for young children and families. For instance, when child care is needed to support parents', and particularly mothers', employment activities, public investment in child care is justified by linking parental receipt of social welfare with requirements for work. For other mothers who "choose" to work, child care arrangements are a wholly private matter with minimal government intervention or support. Compensatory early education and child development services are often justified with outcomes-oriented attributions. More recently, these investments have been reframed in terms of improved school readiness, closing the achievement gap, and more productive life course trajectories (Pianta et al., 2009). Similar to child care that supports parental employment, families who do not qualify for these no-cost early education services are left on their own in the private market.

From the perspective of working parents, how do these policy approaches appear in children's child care arrangements? Since the 1980s, the majority of U.S. families have relied on nonparental care to support their employment activities. Currently, 61.3% of all U.S. children of prekindergarten age attend at least one child care arrangement for an average of 33 hours per week (Laughlin, 2013). For young children with mothers who work full-time (i.e., 35 or more hours per week), these arrangements take numerous forms. About 10% of children do not have regular child care arrangements when their mothers are working and 29% have multiple child care arrangements in a given week (U.S. Census Bureau, 2011).

Such variability also characterizes state child care licensing rules and regulations, a fundamental component of the child care ecology. Since 1981, states have been fully in charge of setting and enforcing policies about basic public health standards for child care (Michel, 1999).

And then, of course, there is the money. U.S. investment in child care takes two general forms: tax credits to families for child care expenses and federal funding for mostly need-based programs and services. These programs include, for example, Head Start ($7.5 billion for fiscal year 2011) and the Child Care Development Fund (CCDF; $5 billion in fiscal year 2010). States, counties, and local communities also contribute through a variety of mechanisms such as the state CCDF "maintenance of effort" and matching funds, Head Start's "in-kind" requirements, and, more recently, state investments in public prekindergarten.

Some good news is that most states are actively engaged in system-building work centered on child care. The "next step" in state system building was mandated by the Improving Head Start for School Readiness Act of 2007 (Satkowski, 2009; Szekely, 2011). This mandate charged governors with appointing Early Childhood Advisory Councils (ECACs) to create coordinated systems that share as their common goal "to ensure that all children in the state are healthy, thriving, and ready to learn" (Satkowski, 2009, p. 1). The ECACs join several other federal initiatives to coordinate and align state early childhood policies; $100 million of one-time 2009 American Recovery and Reinvestment Act (ARRA) funding was allocated to this particular effort.

While the spirit of this initiative is genuinely optimistic—who can argue with healthy, thriving, and ready-to-learn children?—it remains to be seen how states will achieve such outcomes without significant attention to the key components

of the child care ecology discussed above. With such limited regulatory requirements for the child care workforce, how will states reach the high expectations for
children's outcomes? Furthermore, to achieve the ECACs' stated goals, how will
current financing policies and funding streams be redeployed for "all children"?
Indeed, whereas the 2009 report articulated goals for all children (Satkowski,
2009), a 2011 summary of state activities showed more emphasis on the needs
of low-income, at-risk children and families (Szekely, 2011). Because the original
mandate was embedded in Head Start reauthorization, this targeted approach is
not surprising. Thus, whereas states are being encouraged to better align policies
and programs for young children, their efforts are primarily targeting traditions of
compensatory education for at-risk children and families.

In light of states' ECAC priorities, President Obama's domestic policy plans
for his second administration, which include making "high-quality preschool
available to every child in America," sound familiar (Obama, 2013). This goal will
be achieved with federal–state partnerships to deliver high-quality preschool to
4-year-olds and also to implement Early Head Start–Child Care collaborations
for infants and toddlers prior to preschool entry. Although "early education for all
Americans" is the stated goal, the details of this proposal are firmly embedded in
the language and policy traditions of compensatory education for children from
low-income households. With such stipulations, the question remains, is the intent to meet the needs of all children or those from certain groups?

Considering the ongoing economic challenges faced by U.S. families, it is dis-
appointing to see that the vital role of affordable, quality child care has been overlooked. President Obama's other prominent domestic policy agendas—growing
the middle class, creating job opportunities, increasing access to higher education,
ensuring wage equality for men and women—offered attractive precedents for a
new approach to child care policy that supports parental employment and prepares all children for school. "It's a simple fact the more education you've got,
the more likely you are to have a job and work your way into the middle class"
(Obama, 2013). With the Affordable Care Act of 2010, President Obama distinguished himself as an advocate for universal health care coverage. Time will tell
how the child care needs of all U.S. families are met by his proposals.

CHILD CARE: A DEFINITIONAL CONUNDRUM

For decades, child care in the United States has been plagued by ambiguity of
purpose and a lack of definitional clarity (Michel, 1999). Is child care a custodial
service that supports poor parents' work activities or an educational service that
provides young children with age-appropriate learning opportunities?

Chapter 2 reports on a content analysis of one state's licensed child care center names. The findings show that similar tensions exist today and are apparent in child care's everyday lexicon. Today, what is colloquially known as "day care" is a multibillion-dollar industry that operates under the auspices of various public and private agencies and takes place in homes, free-standing buildings, public schools, strip malls, community centers, churches, synagogues, and, at times, cars and vans. Because child care relies on a blend of private funds and public subsidies, the lack of national standards positions it largely as a private good (Morris & Helburn, 2000). Parents are ultimately responsible for making child care decisions and for monitoring day-to-day quality.

There are pros and cons to this situation. From the perspective of facilitating parental choice, this state of affairs has its advantages. Child care programs are in the unique position to devise a public face of their own choosing. Program operators can use language to convey their philosophy, affiliate with a larger entity, attract a particular clientele, and show creativity. Those who are familiar with child care know that program names and the labels used to describe child care services vary widely. Which program is suitable for a 3-year-old: Puppy Pound, Ms. Deanna's All Day Preschool, Radiant Faith Day Care and Preschool, or St. Charles Community Child Development Center? Chances are, a parent's decision would be based first on pragmatic concerns, such as cost, location, and hours of operation, and only then would desired characteristics of programs and providers be considered.

For many, however, the costs of ambiguity of purpose far outweigh the benefits. Parents and taxpayers are confused about what they are purchasing. And, at the state and federal levels, lobbying efforts are fragmented and weak; too many groups are vying for too few funds. Indeed, as Chapter 2's analysis of college students' reactions to the names reveals, the labels attached to child care programs function primarily as "social addresses" (Bronfenbrenner, 1986). They evoke consumer-like reactions but may or may not be connected with what takes place on a routine basis.

MATERNAL WORKFORCE PARTICIPATION: A LOVE–HATE THING

The diverse private market of U.S. child care characterized in Chapter 2 evolved primarily due to mothers' growing labor force participation. As Chapter 3 recounts, for most women, being a working mom is a mixed bag. Even Michelle Obama, first lady of the United States, recognizes the internal conflicts. She told a group of young women at Howard University, "There isn't a day that goes by that I don't wonder or worry about whether I'm doing the right thing for myself, for my family, for my girls" (Swarns, 2009). Managing multiple roles is hard work, even under the best of circumstances, and the United States has done little to make it easier. Indeed, the United States seems to almost punish working mothers with its hands-off stance toward work, family, and child care. The roots of this position stem in part from contemporary ideologies of motherhood and what it means to be a good mother. Regardless of a mother's daily schedule and never-ending list of things to do, she is deemed singularly responsible for her children's immediate and long-term well-being.

Chapter 3 argues that holding onto contradictory ideas about motherhood has distinct, and detrimental, implications for a national system of quality child care. Focus group dialogue from women with a connection to child care is used to explore why so many mothers with young children work and how societal ambivalence about maternal employment and caregiving for pay is routinely perpetuated.

As illustrated by the diverse focus group participants, the answer to the question, "Why do women work?" is much more dynamic and complex than that reflected in the colloquial language of "choice." Working mothers' wages play an integral role in the household economy, and the proportion of female breadwinners continues to rise (USDL, BLS, 2011b). Furthermore, steady gains in women's educational attainment are also implicated in their reasons for working. "Using one's education" is a powerful motivator to join the labor force.

The focus group participants expressed familiar joys and frustrations in combining work and family. They like using their education and skills, enjoy their jobs, and feel enormous pride from financially supporting their families. They also experience guilt, disappointment, resentment, and sheer exhaustion.

When discussing maternal employment, it is impossible to avoid the topic of child care. Indeed, when contemplating what supports women's work, "finding the right child care" is a common theme. And lest anyone forget, child care workers—an overwhelmingly female group—are members of the same U.S. labor force as their clients. Chapter 3 also examines the complicated relationship that members of the child care workforce have with work. For them, child care is at once a highly rewarding and unrewarding vocation. Long-time child care providers are motivated in part by personal fulfillment and a love of children. Child care employment also means physical and emotional exhaustion, long hours, limited flexibility, and low wages. These conditions, especially the low compensation, have led to alarmingly high rates of turnover; 30% of the child care workforce leave their jobs annually, compared with 16% of K–12 teachers (Kagan, Kauerz, & Tarrant, 2008).

Further, as more women attain higher levels of education, careers in child care have become less attractive (i.e., lucrative) (Bellm & Whitebook, 2006). Female college graduates in other fields earn far more than female college graduates employed in child care (Herzenberg, Price, & Bradley, 2005). Consequently, the child care workforce has an ever-shrinking pool of qualified replacements, while the demand for child care remains. An unfortunate outcome of this situation is a double dose of cultural anxiety for members of the child care workforce. In other words, they are exposed to our nation's unease with maternal employment and with the idea that "care work" has real value (Folbre, 2001). Indeed, a coordinated, national plan for child care would implicitly condone maternal employment as well as place a real value on the caring and educational activities of those who provide child care.

CHILD CARE: RESEARCH TRADITIONS AND POLICY ALIGNMENT

A considerable amount of research has been conducted against the backdrop of child care's fragmented policy goals and the growing presence of mothers in the labor force. As recounted in Chapter 4, this work has informed policy about compensatory education and shaped public sentiment toward child care that "encourages" parental (i.e., maternal) employment. A particularly popular and longstanding line of research concerns the "effects" of day care on young children. Over the years, however, as this research tradition has matured in terms of empirical rigor and study design, the potential harm of routine mother–child separations due to employment has disappeared (NICHD ECCRN, 2006). However, the central role of child care quality as both increasing the likelihood of enhanced child outcomes and mitigating possible ill effects to children has not changed. For all children, child care quality matters, and for economically disadvantaged children, it matters even more.

Another rigorous and informative line of research identified the public health factors and program and workforce characteristics associated with variations in quality. These studies produced practical insights about the structural markers of quality that can be regulated by the state. Common regulations address adult-to-child ratios, group size, and provider preservice and ongoing training requirements. Together, these factors underlie the process and quality of teacher–child interactions and the nature of children's experiences. The findings from this research have a key role in a host of publicly funded quality improvement activities.

Despite this research and longstanding agreement among experts that specially trained and educated caregivers are the focal link between program quality and child outcomes (Pianta et al., 2009; Vandell & Wolfe, 2000), policy has not kept up. Chapter 4 also shows the stunning disparity between what is known about quality child care and state child care regulations for the workforce.

A *New York Times* article in 2009 that forecast changes in the gender composition of the U.S. workforce also included an account of how one family was coping with diminished household income: The former full-time homemaker became a full-time businesswoman; she opened a small day care in her home and "works five days a week, 51 weeks a year, without sick days or health benefits" (Rampell, 2009, p. A1). This is but one example of the ease with which individuals can move into the child care workforce. A recent estimate of the size of the U.S. child care workforce is 2.5 million paid members, or 32% of the instructional workforce that cares for and educates children from birth through college (Brandon & Martinez-Beck, 2006). It's hard to imagine another segment of the labor force of comparable size that is charged with such a vital task and beset by such low standards.

GLIMMERS OF HOPE

What gives child care advocates hope is that some states are actively working to increase access to quality child care for all families. Chapter 5's case history of North Carolina's early childhood system provides a roadmap for other states and a promising model for a national system. NC's system-building efforts began in the 1980s, when several early childhood entities joined forces and decided to try a different approach. This state's story is noteworthy because it illustrates how a shared vision for child development and family support aligns with research-based best practices to produce inclusive, quality services. Also helpful was Governor James Hunt's timely reappearance and extraordinary leadership on behalf of his state's children and families. The early childhood system that NC has established has been remarkably resilient to political winds and flexible in the face of even greater challenges and opportunities. The state's first-round funding from the Obama administration's Race to the Top: Early Learning Challenge suggests that more growth, and more lessons, are yet to come. In Chapter 6, the book concludes with a brief list of recommendations for incremental movement toward a national, universal system of child care.

Throughout Sonya Michel's (1999) history of U.S. child care policy, she mentions the lack of action by working mothers to organize and demand better child care. If only there were more hours in the day, such activity might be possible! Moreover, if working mothers and child care providers joined forces, just think of the possibilities. The vision of a professional and equitably compensated child care workforce is attractive on so many levels, including the legitimization of maternal employment and child care as a profession, the support of working families, and improved school readiness for *all* U.S. prekindergartners.

The States of Child Care provides an up-to-date account of the chronic issues that plague progress in U.S. child care and presents realistic solutions based on a model state child care system. As the U.S. economy continues to falter and states struggle with revenue shortfalls, families are facing ongoing wage stagnation and widening income inequalities. These circumstances constitute a compelling need for a new and better integrated approach to child care in the United States.

CHAPTER 1

The Context of U.S. Child Care

To appreciate the complexity of U.S. child care, it is instructive to consider key contextual factors that underlie its day-to-day operation. This chapter describes several characteristics of today's system. It begins with an overview of how the nation addresses the nonparental care of young children and is followed by an analysis of recurring sources of funding and a description of the families with young children who utilize child care.

TRADITIONS IN U.S. POLICY FOR
NONPARENTAL CARE OF CHILDREN

At no time in U.S. history has there been a single approach to the nonparental care of young children (J. R. Nelson, 1982). Three broad traditions characterize how the United States has addressed these matters. For example, some children need nonparental care because their parents cannot provide for them. This could be due to any number of reasons, including abuse, neglect, and incarceration. Today's child welfare system addresses the needs of these children and families. Although this form of nonparental care is not a topic of this book, children in the care of the state often participate in other types of nonparental care that are considered here. It is not unusual for legal guardians and foster parents to be employed outside of the home and thus to require child care. Moreover, children in the foster care system are categorically eligible for Head Start.

Another tradition of U.S. child care policy is to support parental, primarily maternal, employment (J. R. Nelson, 1982). During the second half of the 20th century, as more mothers entered the workforce, systematic policy approaches were instituted to address this need. Beginning in 1954, the Internal Revenue Service allowed a child care deduction for low-income working parents and for all working mothers who were widowed, divorced, or separated, regardless of income. In the 1960s, "workfare" emerged as a strategy to boost the poor out of poverty. More specifically, the conditions of receiving public welfare began to include a work requirement. For poor individuals who were also parents, this meant that child care would be required. As the 20th century progressed, more women from all socioeconomic backgrounds began to combine motherhood and employment. Several underlying forces, such as the stagnation of men's wages and increases in women's educational attainment, underlie this trend and are discussed in Chapter 3. At present, tax credits for families' child care expenses and subsidies to low-income parents for a portion of their child care expenses remain the federal government's primary investment in this form of nonparental care.

The third tradition of the nonparental care of young children involves compensatory education and comprehensive child development services (J. R. Nelson, 1982). This approach augments the goals of child care to support parental employment since it also focuses on preparing children for school and ensuring their healthy development. In some instances, it involves giving children opportunities that they may not be getting at home. These programs emerged from the nursery schools of the 1920s and the "co-ops" of the 1950s, and were originally intended for preschool-aged children from middle- and upper-middle-class families. More recently, Head Start and state-funded prekindergarten programs have drawn on this tradition, as have some community-based nursery school and child care programs. Unlike the visions of custodial care that tend to be linked with the second tradition of nonparental care, this approach strives to offer children and families more.

Without an overarching approach that integrates these traditions of child care for parental employment and early education to prepare children for school, an oddly diverse and fragmented system has evolved. Furthermore, since the 1970s, several key federal policy decisions have influenced the way that the system looks today. These direct and in some instances peripheral policies have had distinct implications for young children and their families.

The Federal Inter-Agency Day Care Regulations

The Federal Inter-Agency Day Care Regulations (FIDCR) were developed in 1968 to ensure the safety and quality of child care settings for children from low-income families (J. R. Nelson, 1982). During the mid- to late 1960s, the number of individuals accessing social welfare assistance expanded dramatically. Until this time, the regulation of child care settings resided in states' hands and varied widely. Because Head Start was also operational by the late 1960s, the schism between policy for child care and policy for early education was already in place. The FIDCR were thus intended to better align standards for child care with the developmental orientation of Head Start and to improve child care utilized by poor families. They addressed program and staff characteristics such as adult-to-child ratios and staff educational preparation and ongoing training.

Interestingly, even after the FIDCR were initially promulgated, they were not strictly enforced (J. R. Nelson, 1982). Instead, they were presented to states as goals for good practice, not binding rules to be upheld with implications for funding. When actual enforcement via staged implementation looked possible, reorganization of the relevant federal agencies brought such plans to a halt. Specifically, the Nixon administration's reorganization separated the control of funding associated with the FIDCR from the FIDCR enforcement role, thereby stripping the regulations of any real power. The ambivalence that underlies the principles of law versus best practice, mandated versus voluntary, and rule versus recommendation, as these principles apply specifically to "day care," will be a recurrent theme throughout this book.

In 1970, it was decided that the FIDCR needed revision. Edward Zigler, a prominent developmental psychologist, was brought in to oversee the process (J. R. Nelson, 1982). Due to the FIDCR's ambiguous status as far as implementation and enforceability, Zigler sought to create a set of regulations that were enforceable and that established a minimum baseline of care to ensure children's safety and health. Furthermore, Zigler's involvement with Head Start also meant that the proposed revisions were grounded in traditions of compensatory education and child development. This time, the intention was that the FIDCR would be implemented as law, not as goals or recommendations. What made these revisions to the FIDCR notable was that if they had become law, they would have advanced a federal child care policy that integrated the developmental tradition with the support of parental employment. In the end, however, the revised FIDCR, along with the Comprehensive Child Development Act (notable in its own right for extending federal child care assistance to include nonpoor working families), did not survive the Nixon administration.

During the rest of the 1970s, the FIDCR were a source of conflict between states and the federal government (J. R. Nelson, 1982). The regulations remained linked with child care that was associated with social welfare programs. The difficulty lay in the literal cost of complying with the original 1968 FIDCR adult-to-child ratios. For those representing the child development tradition, it was imperative that a solution be found to maintain the ratios. For those from the day care tradition, it was crucial to provide services at the lowest possible cost. The 1968 regulations stipulated a ratio of one adult for every five 3-year-olds and one adult for every seven 4- and 5-year-olds. Although any adult on the premises of a child care program counted toward compliance with these standards, at the time the costs of implementation were prohibitive. Compromise was not achieved and the FIDCR ratio requirements were eventually suspended.

The suspension carried over into the next presidential (Carter) administration, and the ratios continued to generate tension between the ever-growing child care marketplace, child advocacy groups, and federal welfare program administrators (J. R. Nelson, 1982). Although members of the Carter administration tried to revise the regulations, little real change was achieved. It was not until the final report from the Abt Associates National Day Care Study was released (Ruopp, Travers, Glantz, & Coelen, 1979) that the FIDCR were ultimately revised. Interestingly, Abt's research identified maximum group size and not adult-to-child ratios as the most influential factor in determining child care quality. Ratios, they reported, were more critical to differences in cost. The final FIDCR were released in 1980 with notable revisions to the adult-to-child ratios. Specifically, the ratios for children ages 3, 4, and 5 years were one adult to every nine, with 18 children as the recommended maximum group size (Whitebook, Howes, & Phillips, 1989).

However, soon after Ronald Reagan was elected in 1981, the FIDCR became a nonissue because welfare programs (Title XX) were block-granted to states. Child care programs that served children whose parents were participating in workfare programs were required to meet state and local regulations (Michel, 1999). Thus, as rates of maternal employment among all groups were steadily increasing and the private child care market was growing, the fundamental safety, health, and quality of child care were placed in the hands of the states.

Welfare Reform of 1996

In 1996, a massive overhaul of the federal welfare system was enacted by the Clinton administration. The Personal Responsibility and Work Opportunity Reconciliation Act established more stringent work requirements for welfare recipients (U.S. Government Accountability Office [GAO], 1997). Before that time, work requirements for parents receiving welfare began when children were 3 years old. In the new legislation, child-age restrictions were lifted and low-income parents with infants older than 1 year of age were required to work (although states were able to apply for waivers to modify the child-age requirements). Program evaluations of welfare reform pilot projects demonstrated a positive effect of child care assistance on low-income parents' successful transition from welfare to work and eventual self-sufficiency (Raikes, 1998). The increased demand for child care was to be addressed with the new Child Care Development Fund (CCDF)—a block grant that blended several prior funding sources.

A 1997 U.S. Government Accountability Office study of available child care identified several shortcomings with the then-current supply in urban and nonurban areas. A gap was found, for instance, between anticipated need and "known" sources of child care, especially for infants and school-aged children. The availability of child care during nonstandard work hours for parents with low-wage jobs was another concern. It was also shown that child care access varied between poor and nonpoor neighborhoods, with poor areas having the lowest supply of known care. The co-pay burden on household income was another potential problem.

Child care subsidies were intended to cover only a portion of the full cost of child care. Would low-income families be able to afford the required co-pays?

The quality of available child care was a major concern (GAO, 1997). Quality standards associated with child development programs for disadvantaged children, such as Head Start, do not apply to state-licensed and regulated child care programs. Furthermore, it was quickly recognized that the child care needs of poor parents moving from welfare to work would likely be met in both formal settings and informal settings, such as in the care of relatives, friends, or neighbors. Thus, states also received an infusion of funds to improve the quality of both known and unknown care settings. Decisions about how to administer these funds, however, were left to the states. From the very onset, pressures mounted to balance competing agendas. How were states to get parents back to work and off the welfare rolls and guarantee that their children were in safe, reliable, and quality child care?

No Child Left Behind—2001

Although federal education policy is not directly linked with child care per se, it does have implications for U.S. traditions concerning nonparental care via compensatory education during the preschool years. More specifically, early education is intended to increase school readiness, reduce the achievement gap, and set youngsters on a more promising trajectory for academic success. In 2001, the Bush administration enacted major K–12 public education reforms in the package of No Child Left Behind (NCLB). NCLB's broad principles for reform include accountability, flexibility, research-based reforms, and parent choice. How does this reform apply to preschool-aged children? One example involves the principle of accountability and the implementation of standards for children's learning and the programs that they attend. The emerging state Early Learning and Development Standards (Kagan, 2012) and the National Institute for Early Education Research's benchmarks for minimum program quality (Barnett, Robin, Hustedt, & Schulman, 2003) can be used for strategic planning, ongoing quality improvement, and demonstrating accountability. Combined with a renewed interest in teacher quality and child outcomes, policymakers and parents have plenty of data with which to make pivotal decisions. If a school district is unable to reduce gaps in school readiness among different groups of children, funding can be shifted away from that district and toward schools that demonstrate greater teaching effectiveness (Pianta et al., 2009).

The downward shift of K–12 education policy to preschool has several benefits. For example, it builds on the established system and profession of public education. Additionally, monitoring children's academic performance earlier provides more information for tracking achievement over time. This approach also affords greater control when compared with the mostly private and highly diverse market of child care. The challenge, however, is that it adds another sector to an already complex and fragmented system of nonparental care. Gilliam's (2005) findings of discrepant rates of child expulsion from prekindergarten programs located in different child care and early education sectors are relevant here. State prekindergarten programs, as they currently exist, do not readily align with the tradition of supporting parent employment and thus keep a second track of minimally regulated child care barely functioning.

Early Childhood Advisory Councils—2009

As part of the Improving Head Start for School Readiness Act of 2007, states were charged with enhancing coordination of early childhood programs (Satkowski, 2009; Szekely, 2011). Governors were asked to name councils that would advise on matters associated with child care and early education. One-time funding was made available in 2009, and by 2010 $100 million had been awarded to states for 3-year grants. By December 2011, councils had been formally designated in 48 states. Although the grants are time-limited, councils are viewed as having significant potential to inform state legislatures on plans and policies associated with child care and early education.

Overall, the primary goals of the state councils are to better align publicly funded child care and early childhood programs and to improve quality and access (Szekely, 2011). To achieve this outcome, the 2007 act outlined seven priority activities. Several of these activities are being pursued by the great majority of states. For instance, all 48 states that received funding are conducting regular assessments of the availability and quality of child care and early education programs, with particular attention to those programs for children from low-income families. Additionally, 47 states are preparing recommendations for comprehensive data systems to track children, programs, and workforce members over time. Forty-six states are focused on creating statewide professional development systems for "early childhood educators." And, 42 states are identifying the opportunities and challenges associated with the overall task of coordinating such diverse child care and early education programs. Other less common activities include increasing child participation in federal, state, and local programs; assessing the state system of higher education for preparing the workforce; and making recommendations to improve state Early Learning Standards. Several of these priority areas are aligned with the reform principles advanced by No Child Left Behind (2001).

States have also identified unique priority areas for their own councils (Szekely, 2011). A majority of states are developing or revising program quality assessment tools, engaging communities and parents in their planning, and implementing public awareness campaigns. Other state-defined priorities include, for instance, addressing the needs of infants and toddlers, children's physical health and social-emotional development, and children without English as their first language. Twenty-seven states also intend to make stronger linkages between their child care and K–3 public education systems. This particular activity is linked with state system-building recommendations to extend the birth-to-pre-K system to 3rd grade (e.g., Kagan & Kauerz, 2012). State plans are as varied as their own policy climate and the landscape of child care and early education services.

FUNDING SOURCES

Numerous sources provide funding for child care and early education services and programs. Table 1.1 lists the primary recurring sources of large-scale funding and, where possible, the approximate number of children who participate. Dollar

Table 1.1. Recurring Sources of Funding for Child Care and Early Education

	Expenditures	Enrollment Estimates
Child Care		
CCDF (federal government *and* state maintenance of effort and matching funds)	$7.1 billion	1.7 million children per month (as of 2012) (with TANF and other sources, up to 2.5 million)
Temporary Assistance for Needy Families (TANF; transferred to CCDF)	$1.4 billion	——
Parent Fees and Co-pays for Child Care Services		
Child and Dependent Care Tax Credit (IRS)		
Dependent Care Assistance Plan (IRS)		
Compensatory Education and Child Development Programs		
Head Start and Early Head Start (federal government; 20% nonfederal local match required)	$7.5 billion	964,430 children and pregnant women
State Funding of Prekindergarten Programs	$5.5 billion	1.3 million 3- and 4-year-olds

Sources: Barnett, Carolan, Fitzgerald, & Squires, 2011; Blanchette, 2012; GAO, 2012; U.S. Department of Health and Human Services (2012b; 2012c).

amounts for some of these sources are readily obtained and for others are not, such as the total amount of money generated by parent fees and co-pays for child care. Altogether, today's varied sources of funding reflect the traditions of child care to support parental employment and compensatory education services for at-risk young children.

Child Care

Child Care Development Fund and Temporary Assistance to Needy Families. During fiscal year 2010, the CCDF expended about $8.5 billion of federal and state resources (Barnett et al., 2011; GAO, 2012). The CCDF funds subsidized the child care expenses of about 1.7 million children per month and, when combined with TANF transfers and other sources, the total was 2.5 million children on a monthly basis (Blanchette, 2012). Additionally, in fiscal year 2010, states spent an average of 12% of their CCDF funds on child care quality improvement activities.

An analysis of CCDF administrative data from 2009 showed that this funding source subsidized child care for 489,000 infants and toddlers, 440,000 preschoolers (3- and 4-year-olds), and 701,000 children ages 5 years and older (Blanchette, 2012). Children with subsidies were in child care for an average of 144 hours per month. Upward of 78% of this care occurred in state-licensed child care settings, and 21% took place in legal, unregulated child care settings. Sixty-four percent of subsidies purchased care in child care centers, 31% in family child care homes, and 5% in the child's own home (Blanchette, 2012).

States set income eligibility, subsidy rates, and parent co-payment policies using the state median income, child care market rate surveys, and the federal poverty level (Blanchette, 2012). In 2009, the average annual subsidy per child was $4,228, ranging from $1,944 to $7,155. States' co-payment requirements for families, which are based on a sliding fee scale, vary between 1% and 20% of household income. Half of families who receive child care subsidies have incomes below the federal poverty level. One quarter of subsidy-receiving families have incomes between 100% and 150% of the federal poverty level. The large majority (93%) of families who utilize these supports are employed or receiving job training or education. The remaining percentage receive subsidies through child protective services, including legal guardians and foster parents.

Parent Fees. Anywhere from 72% (Cost, Quality, and Child Outcomes Study Team, 1995) to 90% (Child Care Aware of America, formerly the National Association of Child Care Resource and Referral Agencies, 2012) of child care costs are covered by parent fees. These costs range widely by region, setting, and child age. Child Care Aware of America (2012) reported that fees for full-time infant care in centers can range from $4,600 to $20,200 per year and for infant care in home-based programs, from $4,000 to $12,350 per year. For a 4-year-old, costs range from $3,900 to $15,450 annually for full-time center care and from $3,850 to $9,600 for full-time, home-based care.

Data from the U.S. Census Bureau indicate that families with employed mothers of children between birth and age 4 years spend on average $141 to $148 per week on child care expenses (Macartney & Laughlin, 2011). Although poor families spend less for child care, the proportion of household income spent by these families is higher than for nonpoor families. Although estimates vary depending on the original data source, poor families spend, on average, between 20% and 28% of household income on child care, and nonpoor families spend between 6% and 7%.

Child and Dependent Care Tax Credit. All families that earn enough money to owe federal income tax can benefit from the child and dependent care tax credit (Waldfogel, 2006). As mentioned above, this tax credit was enacted in 1954. It applies to families with children ages 12 and younger who pay for child care to support parental employment (U.S. Internal Revenue Service, 2011). The Internal Revenue Service sets upper limits for the expenses that can be applied. For example, to calculate the credit in 2010, families were allowed to report a maximum of $3,000 per qualifying child or $6,000 for two or more qualifying children. Although it is not clear whether this policy directly benefits U.S. child care, it does represent an investment in families by the federal government. Tax credits are revenue for the government that goes uncollected. Twenty-five years ago, in fiscal year 1988, it was estimated that families received $3.4 billion from this tax credit, approximately one-half of all federal spending on child care programs at the time (GAO, 1989). The proportion of families with working mothers who claim this credit increases along with annual household income. However, not all families utilize the option when filing their income taxes (Willer, Hofferth, Kisker, Divine-Hawkins, Farquhar, & Glantz, 1991).

Dependent Care Assistance Plan. The Dependent Care Assistance Plan works through employers (U.S. Internal Revenue Service, 2012). This program allows employees to set aside up to $5,000 of their earnings to pay for anticipated child care expenses. What makes this a benefit is that the monies that are set aside have not been taxed. Thus, parents save on federal income tax that would have been paid on the money that is used instead for child care costs (Waldfogel, 2006). Similar to the child and dependent care tax credit, individuals must earn a high enough salary to take advantage of this benefit. Additionally, it too is revenue that the federal government does not collect.

It is important that these federal tax-credit programs be recognized among the federal government's funding sources for child care. After all, they do put real money associated with child care into someone's purse or pocket. Furthermore, when originally proposed, these tax credits were justified as necessary employment expenses for parents (J. R. Nelson, 1982). Accordingly, they are part of the child care tradition that supports parental employment.

Compensatory Education and Child Development Services

Head Start and Early Head Start. The Head Start program, established in 1965, is the federal government's costliest early education program. As shown in Table 1.1, in fiscal year 2011, Head Start received an appropriation of $7.5 billion dollars to serve 964,430 pregnant women, infants, toddlers, and preschoolers (U.S. Department of Health and Human Services [USDHHS], 2012b). For every dollar of federal funding, programs are required to contribute 20 cents. These additional funds come from a variety of sources, including the state and local communities. Current estimates of annual per-child spending are approximately $8,774 (Barnett et al., 2011).

Eligibility for Head Start and Early Head Start is determined with the federal poverty guidelines. Children ages birth to 5 years from families whose incomes fall below the poverty line are eligible to participate. Additionally, children whose families are homeless, who receive TANF or Supplemental Security Income (SSI), and children in foster care can participate in Head Start. Forty-nine percent of Head Start attendees are 4 or 5 years old, and 34% are 3-year-olds (USDHHS, 2012b). Pregnant women and children younger than 2 years make up about 17% of the total enrollment.

Ninety-six percent of Head Start preschool programs take place in center settings (USDHHS, 2012b). About half of these centers operate 5 days a week for more than 6 hours per day. Twenty percent of center programs run part-day programs (6 or fewer hours) on every weekday. For those Head Start centers that operate 4 days per week, 4% are full day (more than 6 hours) and 26% take place for 6 or fewer hours per day. Early Head Start programs are more variable. Forty-one percent are center-based and operate 5 days per week for more than 6 hours per day. Another 41% take place in the Early Head Start participant's home. The remaining 18% of Early Head Start programs work with pregnant women, take place in family child care settings, are center-based, or have some other design.

State-Funded Prekindergarten Programs. In 2003, the National Institute for Early Education Research published the first annual State of Preschool report for the 2001–02 school year (Barnett et al., 2003). These "preschool yearbooks" compile state-level data concerning publicly funded prekindergarten programs. They are exceptionally useful publications for monitoring trends in funding, access, and state policies associated with preschool quality.

At the time of this writing, the current preschool yearbook described state prekindergarten programs during 2010–11 (Barnett et al., 2011). Fifty-one distinct programs were operating in 39 states. As shown in Table 1.1, states spent approximately $5.5 billion and served approximately 1.3 million 3- and 4-year-olds. Some state expenditures for prekindergarten include federal monies, such as TANF, and 11 programs require a local match, similar to the nonfederal contribution required by Head Start. The per-child average cost for public prekindergarten is $4,847 and varies from a low of $2,422 to a high of $11,669. The reason for such wide variation is that public prekindergarten comes in many different packages.

Unlike Head Start, which has federal rules for program eligibility and performance standards that apply across states and programs, public prekindergarten rules and regulations are set by states. Consequently, program access and quality vary widely. Thirty-one programs set family income eligibility requirements. As a criterion for participation, some states use child eligibility for the U.S. Department of Agriculture's free and reduced-price school lunch program. Others maintain income requirements that mirror Head Start. Twenty programs have no income eligibility guidelines. Depending on the state, public prekindergarten can occur in public schools, Head Start, private child care centers and family child care homes, faith-based facilities, and institutions of higher education. Forty public prekindergarten programs are offered only during the academic year, and hours of operation also vary. Twenty-eight programs determine their hours of operation at the local level, 11 programs run full-day, and 12 are part-day. Twenty-four programs serve at least one meal during a child's attendance. Thus, in the tradition of compensatory education, state prekindergarten does not necessarily support parental employment.

There is no doubt that public prekindergarten is good news for children and families. It upholds what is best about the tradition of compensatory education. Children are prepared to start school, learn age-appropriate academic skills, and socialize with peers. Moreover, in some states it brings high-quality early education to children and families who otherwise would not have access because of income ineligibility or other issues. The challenge to its ongoing growth and potential for success rests in the careful balancing of greater access, more high-quality programs, and sustainable, institutionalized funding streams. Indeed, how all of the various funding sources blend together to support children's child care and early education experiences is a puzzle that has yet to be solved.

CHARACTERISTICS OF FAMILIES WITH
CHILDREN IN NONPARENTAL CARE

Who utilizes child care and early education programs? This section provides an overview of the employment and income characteristics of today's families with young children. It also describes the child care and early education arrangements of children under age 5 years who live with their mothers.

Parental Employment

The most recent employment statistics about families with young children indicate that most young children have parents who work (USDL, BLS, 2012b). In 96% of married-couple families with children under 6 years of age, at least one parent is employed, and in 59% of these families mothers are employed. For families with children 6 years and younger that are financially headed by an unmarried woman, 59% of mothers are employed; for similar households that are headed by an unmarried man, 79% of fathers are employed. Employment rates for mothers hold steady even for mothers of younger children. For women with children under age 3 years, 61% of mothers are employed, ranging from 56% of mothers with babies under 1 year of age to 64% of mothers with children age 2 years.

Independent of marital status, 94% of employed fathers with children under age 6 are employed full-time (i.e., 35 or more hours/week) and 71% of employed mothers with children of the same age work full-time (USDL, BLS, 2012b). About 30% of working fathers and 32% of working mothers with young children have flexible schedules (McMenamin, 2007). This type of work arrangement allows for varying start and end times. In the past 20 years, the proportion of workers with such schedules has more than doubled. For both men and women, the likelihood of having a flexible work arrangement increases with educational attainment. For men, 44% of college graduates have flexible schedules compared with 20% of men with a high school diploma. For women, the trends are similar. Thirty-four percent of female college graduates have flexible work schedules compared with 26% of women with a high school diploma. Upward of 70% of working fathers and 71% of working mothers with children ages 18 years and younger typically work on weekdays. Twelve percent of fathers and 16% of mothers have employment schedules that vary by day, from week to week.

Family Income

How are families faring economically at the start of the 21st century? The income data to be presented are for households with children who are 18 years of age and younger (U.S. Census Bureau, 2012). The figures reveal several worrisome trends. For married-couple households with children 18 and younger, 2011 inflation-adjusted median household income was $82,446 in 2001 and, 10 years later in 2011, was $78,699. For female-headed households with children under 18, comparable trends emerged. For this group, similarly adjusted median income in 2001 was $28,622 and, in 2011, was $25,353. For male-headed households with children of the same age, 2011 inflation-adjusted median income in 2001 was $42,424 and, in 2011, was $38,167. These findings show significant income stagnation and decline for all families with children ages 18 years and younger. For single-mother-headed households, the trends are particularly distressing.

In 2012, the federal poverty level for a family of three was $19,090 and for a family of four was $23,050 (USDHHS, 2012a). These are the official guidelines used to determine whether a person or a household is eligible for needs-based programs such as the child care subsidy program, Head Start, and some state prekindergarten programs. In 2010, 26% of children ages newborn through 5 years were poor (Chaudry, 2012). Between 1980 and 2010, this percentage is a record high, up from a low of 18% in 1998. Fifty percent of young children with an unmarried mother are poor compared with 13% of children from married-parent households.

The trends in parental employment and family earnings indicate that the demands on the U.S. system of nonparental care will likely continue to increase. Furthermore, if household income and child poverty rates worsen, child care and early education programs for low-income families will be under mounting pressure to serve more children and families. With funding for state prekindergarten diminishing over the past few years (Barnett et al., 2011), will access to these early education opportunities be tightened, or erased, as recently took place in Arizona? The time for effective policy alignment and real system building is now.

Children's Nonparental Care Arrangements

Table 1.2 presents recent data about the child care arrangements for children age 5 years and younger who live with their mothers. The information was gathered between January and April 2010 by the U.S. Census Bureau's Survey of Income and Program Participation (U.S. Census Bureau, 2011). Mothers were asked, "During a typical week last month, please tell me if you used any of the following arrangements to look after [child's name] on a regular basis. By regular basis, I mean at least once a week during the past month." All arrangements for all children are displayed by monthly household income, and the primary arrangement types for children with employed mothers also are shown. Primary arrangements are those settings where children spend the most hours per week.

Table 1.2. Child Care Arrangements for Children Under 5 Years Old Living with Their Mothers

Arrangement Type	All Children and All Arrangements (n = 19,978,000)				Children with Employed Mothers: Primary Child Care Arrangement (n = 10,879,000; 54%)					
	By Monthly Family Income*				By Maternal Employment Status			By Child Age		
	Under $1,500	$1,500–$2,999	$3,000–$4,499	Above $4,500	Full-Time	Part-Time	Self-Employed	< 1 Year	1 to 2 Years	3 to 4 Years
Number of Children (in thousands)	3,173	3,748	3,071	9,171	7,275	2,841	763	1,901	4,548	4,430
Parent (mother or father), Sibling, Grandparent, or Other Relative	49.2%	58.2%	58.2%	57.0%	48.6%	60.9%	52.1%	57.8%	55.2%	46.3%
Day Care Center	9.3%	10.0%	9.1%	18.0%	23.2%	12.2%	6.8%	15.6%	20.7%	19.3%
Nursery or Preschool	3.3%	4.9%	4.9%	9.3%	6.3%	5.2%	9.6%	0.9%	3.4%	11.4%
Head Start	1.7%	1.2%	1.7%	0.5%	0.8%	0.8%	0.5%	NA	0.1%	1.5%
School (kindergarten)	4.5%	5.1%	5.1%	4.6%	3.6%	4.5%	4.6%	NA	NA	9.6%
Family Day Care or Other Nonrelative Arrangement	9.0%	8.6%	12.2%	14.6%	15.4%	12.4%	16.4%	16.9%	16.3%	12.1%
No Regular Arrangement	49.1%	43.3%	40.0%	30.7%	10.0%	11.9%	21.9%	16.9%	11.2%	9.3%
Multiple Arrangements	16.6%	18.4%	18.9%	21.4%	28.7%	29.0%	27.5%	NA	NA	NA

Source: U.S. Census Bureau, 2011.

Note. Percentages may not add up to 100% because of multiple arrangements and ties in number of hours among primary arrangements.

*n = 816,000 households with missing income data.

Among all children, those whose families earn more than $4,500 per month, or approximately $54,000 annually, are more likely to attend centers, preschools, or home-based programs than children from the other three income categories. Those children in the lowest income category (under $1,500 monthly) are the most likely to have no regular child care arrangements (49%) compared with the other income groups. And those children whose families earn between $1,500 to $2,999 and $3,000 to $4,499 per month have child care arrangements that are quite similar, with the exception of the percentages who attend family day care programs or who do not have regular arrangements. Regardless of child age or maternal employment status, over half of all U.S. children ages 5 years and younger regularly spend time outside of their mothers' immediate care.

Of those children with full-time employed mothers, 48.6% have primary care arrangements with a parent, such as the child's father, a grandparent, or another relative. The others have a variety of primary arrangement types. Close to one-quarter attend child care centers, almost 10% go to preschool or kindergarten, just under 1% attend Head Start, 15.4% attend a home-based child care program, and 10% have no single regular child care arrangement. Of these children with mothers who are working full-time, 28.7% have multiple child care arrangements in a given week. For children whose mothers are employed part-time, the primary difference is seen in the higher percentage of children in the care of a parent or relative, which is balanced by fewer children attending child care centers.

For children 5 years and younger with employed mothers, primary child care arrangements vary by child age. For infants under 1 year, most are cared for in a home setting, such as at home with another parent or grandparent (57.8%) or in a family day care program (16.9%). Sixteen percent have no regular arrangement, 15.6% attend child care centers, and less than 1% go to a nursery or preschool. For toddlers, similar to infants, the majority are cared for in home settings by other parents or relatives (55.2%) or in a family child care program (16.3%). About 20% go to child care centers, a little over 3% attend preschool, and fewer than 1% are in Head Start. Just over 11% of toddlers with mothers who work do not have a regular child care arrangement. For children ages 3 and 4 years, 46.3% are cared for by another parent or relative, 19% attend a child care center, 12.1% go to a home-based child care program, 11.4% are in preschool, a little over 1% are Head Start participants, 9.6% go to kindergarten, and 9.3% do not have a regular child care arrangement.

Since the 1960s, child care in the United States has become extraordinarily diverse. Furthermore, with the exception of Head Start, without careful analysis of individual states' child care policies and regulations, virtually nothing is known about the safety or quality of the other child care settings. Despite all of the effort that has gone into maintaining separate funding streams, creating tax credits for families' child care expenses, and establishing programs to set children on promising academic trajectories, these recent accounts of children's nonparental care arrangements reveal a directionless system. Even the "per-child" costs associated with publicly funded programs are incomplete. Among those children whose mothers are employed, almost 30% have multiple child care arrangements in a given week (U.S. Census Bureau, 2011).

CHAPTER 2

The Public Face of Child Care

What's in a Name?

> Zaire Hines is standing in front of a pint-size table, building a castle out
> of red and blue plastic cups. He stacks them into a tower and then, in
> his excitement ("Look what I did!"), accidently knocks them to the floor.
> If he were at day care or in his bedroom, Zaire, 4, might have shrugged
> and moved onto another set of toys. But he's at Project Enlightenment,
> a publicly funded preschool, where his teacher, Kim Jackson, is using
> the cups to help Zaire work on counting and other premath skills as
> well as underlying ones like being patient and listening to directions.
> Together they start the castle again.
>
> —Webley, 2011, p. 47

This anecdote unknowingly illustrates the challenges of creating a unified system
of child care. In particular, it builds from an explicit assumption that the academic and social-emotional opportunities available at Project Enlightenment do
not exist at day care. Indeed, day care is placed on par with being at home in
one's bedroom. Furthermore, at Project Enlightenment, children have teachers,
not caregivers, day care providers, or babysitters. This all sounds very admirable
and progressive but system-building efforts are undermined when programs like
Project Enlightenment are publicly pitted against "day care." How do we know
that Project Enlightenment is really more educational and enlightened than what
goes on in day care or Zaire's bedroom? As anecdotal accounts of programs like
Project Enlightenment gain in prominence and divert attention away from child
care, the vision of a unified system of child care and early education does not stand
a chance. Indeed, the most recent federal mandate to states for early childhood system building was bundled in Head Start reauthorization (Satkowski, 2009; Szekely,
2011), subtly implying that the needs of all young children and families are not
relevant, despite wording to suggest otherwise.

Child care in the United States has long been plagued by a lack of common language and consensus concerning its purpose (Goffin & Washington, 2007; Kagan et al., 2008; Michel, 1999). On the one hand, this free-for-all creates a colorful marketplace. Is there another public good that comes in such diverse packaging? Children's World Learning Center, Growing Gardens for Little Bloomers, Kidz Kabana (misspelling intended), Head Start, and Buchanan County R-IV Tiger Cubs Preschool are all members of the current system of child care and early education. On the other hand, such diversity in labeling conveys an underlying ambiguity of purpose. What is child care and what function does it serve for children and families? Such uncertainty compromises the vital role of child care as a collective good, weakens lobbying efforts, and keeps the public in the dark about how tax dollars are spent (Goffin & Washington, 2007). The implications of this ambiguity are far-reaching. With little agreement on child care's fundamental purpose, how can a coherent system be established and a skilled workforce be developed? How can local, state, and federal investments be meaningfully monitored? Moreover, how can families be assured access to quality services that support them as parents and meet their children's developmental needs? Practically speaking, enhancing school readiness and reducing the achievement gap alone would require consensus on the core function of child care programs. Although research indicates that child care programs with a stronger education focus are linked with better outcomes for children (Pianta et al., 2009), how are parents to determine which programs have a "strong education focus"?

This chapter focuses on the amorphous nature of our current system. It begins with background about the emergence of different forms of child care over the past century and how federal policies have facilitated continued growth and diversification. Next, it reviews the child care "market" as it currently exists, with attention to supply- and demand-side characteristics. The chapter then presents a content analysis of one state's child care program names. The study is presented in two parts: The first shows how child care services are defined and how programs distinguish themselves with their names. The second part surveys the reactions of future child care consumers (i.e., college students) to lists of representative child care center names.

This undertaking is illuminating because it offers a means of probing into the child care marketplace, where those most affected by the field's uncertainty of purpose meet on a daily basis. As long as a common language for child care eludes policymakers and advocates, most child care programs are in a position to create a public face of their own choosing. This has some advantages, but movement toward a unified system will require a shared sense of purpose and agreement on a common vernacular to describe the system's intended function. This chapter tracks one important measure of the ambiguity in language and purpose that the field needs to surmount.

HISTORICAL ROOTS OF DEFINITIONAL
AMBIGUITY AND SYSTEM DIVERSIFICATION

The history of U.S. child care policy illustrates how the labels attached to programs became associated with different philosophies, different clientele, and different expectations of workers (Michel, 1999; J. R. Nelson, 1982). The philanthropic *day nurseries* of the 19th century, for example, were driven by social welfare for indigent mothers who had to work because of family crises, such as the death of a spouse or abandonment. This form of custodial day care kept children safe and families together, and employment in day nurseries was viewed on par with domestic service. From the public's perspective, this was acceptable, but only for those in the lower classes. Near the turn of the 20th century, educators who were members of the newly emerging discipline of early childhood education actively worked to create settings that would be different from day nurseries and appeal to the middle classes. Their *nursery schools* were designed for middle-class families that sought early socialization and educational experiences for their young children, not child care to support maternal employment.

During the Great Depression, the *emergency nursery schools* (ENS) were established originally as part-time educational programs for children from needy families and employment opportunities for out-of-work teachers (Michel, 1999). Then at the beginning of World War II, through the Lanham Act of 1941, the ENS provided early social and educational opportunities for poor children whose mothers were called to employment to support the war effort. These programs represented a blending of the earlier, separate philosophies of day nurseries and nursery schools. However, the ENS were planned as a temporary fix for child care needs. When the war ended and factory jobs were given to returning soldiers, the large majority of ENS programs were closed.

Thus, despite the federal government's involvement during World War II in programs that provided both day care for working mothers and preschool education, this integration of functions at the highest levels of government was not to appear again. As described in Chapter 1, the policy traditions toward the nonparental care of young children have operated on separate tracks since the 1960s (J. R. Nelson, 1982). Reagan-era legislation of the 1980s can be considered the starting point for today's highly diverse market of child care. Public funds to support low-income, employed parents' child care needs were block-granted to states with few strings attached, and middle-income employed parents continued to receive tax credits for their child care expenses (Michel, 1999). These expenditures and investments did little to build needed infrastructure and made possible what is now an extraordinarily fragmented system of services. Thus, as federal child care policy became decentralized, deregulated, and privatized (M. K. Nelson, 1990), child care became necessary for most U.S. families and the marketplace responded wholeheartedly.

The tensions permeating the above account originated in ideological differences concerning the purpose or function of nonparental care. These conflicts continue to suffuse policy struggles today. Is child care simply a custodial arrangement that supports poor parents' work activities, such as the original day nurseries and some states' child care subsidy programs? Or is child care a service that can provide at-risk young children with nurturing and age-appropriate learning opportunities, such as Head Start and state-funded prekindergarten? What national goals exist for community-based child care centers and home-based child care programs that are used by more affluent families and that, in many states, also serve low-income families? The state-level variation in child care regulations, child care subsidy administration, and public prekindergarten programs renders identifying a common purpose across these settings virtually impossible.

TODAY'S CHILD CARE MARKET

Because of the lack of consensus on child care's purpose, the private market has evolved to provide a vast range of services that individual consumers navigate and select from. Parents can take their pick from Mary Margaret Day Care and Learning Center, Sweet Springs Preschool, Tabernacle of Love Daycare, Future Geniuses Child Care Center, or Caterpillar Crossing. Whereas some families will find a single child care program to meet their needs, others will cobble together multiple arrangements because no single one meets their needs (Morrissey, 2008). With increases in the prevalence of shift work, some children attend day care for the evening and overnight hours (e.g., Ropers Round the Clock Child Care and Learning Center). Today's child care market is as diverse as the families who rely on its existence and the employment that they can secure.

Supply-Side Characteristics

A Mixed Market. Several characteristics of the child care market contribute to its underlying fragmentation, beginning with its public–private, mixed-market designation (Morris & Helburn, 2000). As described in Chapter 1, child care programs operate under different governmental and financial auspices. Some programs are directly attached to public entities, such as school districts or community action agencies. Additionally, some programs are officially designated as not-for-profit (i.e., 501[c][3]) whereas others are officially "for-profit" (a label that provides considerable amusement among child care program directors). To keep the lights on, the staff paid, and the children fed, the large majority of child care programs rely on a blend of public and private income sources (Helburn & Howes, 1996). Although some programs do not collect fees, the majority of U.S. families use child care programs that are best conceptualized as independently owned and operated small businesses that rely on parent fees to keep their doors open. Furthermore, in many states, public and private child care programs alike can apply for and receive public funding as part of their operating budget, such as monies from the child care subsidy program and state accreditation facilitation efforts.

Information Asymmetry. The child care market is also distinguished by asymmetric information (Morris & Helburn, 2000). In this case, it means that the seller knows a lot more about the product than the buyer. Child care quality, in particular, is not easy to discern without considerable background knowledge. With the exception of states' reports of child care facilities' licensing history and efforts to implement quality rating and improvement systems (QRIS) (Tout, Starr, Soli, Moodie, Kirby, & Boller, 2010), public information about the quality of child care programs is not easily obtained. Moreover, because the U.S. embraces a program-level approach to licensing and regulation, unless a parent knows to ask, staff qualifications and rates of turnover remain a mystery.

Quality as a Trait and Quality as a State. Estimating child care quality at the market level is challenging, even for state-level regulators. Child care quality is determined by a combination of structural factors and process characteristics. The structural indicators most readily measured include, for example, public health assurances, adult-to-child ratios, group size, and staff preservice education and ongoing professional development requirements (Payne, 2011). Because child care regulations associated with these structural indicators vary across states, national estimates of the "state" of child care quality are difficult to ascertain.

The process characteristics of quality—that is, how things happen, primarily how caregivers interact with children—can also fluctuate in a given child care program from room to room, from one day to the next, and over the course of a day. Furthermore, the quality of a child's personal child care history varies from infancy through kindergarten entry (Hynes & Habasevich-Brooks, 2008). These fluid dynamics of the complex child care ecology are referred to as "known elasticity" of quality.

Making sense of fluctuations in process and tracking structural indicators of quality is an expensive and labor-intensive task. At present, 26 states conduct routine inspections of child care centers one time per year; 14 states implement more frequent visits, and the other 10 states visit less frequently. Of the 44 states that license home-based child care programs, 15 states visit homes annually, 10 states visit more often and the remaining 19 states visit less frequently (National Child Care Information and Technical Assistance Center [NCCITAC] & National Association for Regulatory Administration [NARA], 2010). Quality rating and improvement systems (QRIS), the most recent approach to comprehensive quality assessment, combine measures of structural and process indicators, and are intended to convey quality-relevant information to the public. However, with the exception of three QRIS, the remaining 23 are partially mandatory or voluntary (Tout et al., 2010). Accordingly, they do not provide accurate assessments of a state's full child care market. In other words, voluntary QRIS systems yield quality ratings only for those programs that elect to participate. Thus, without publicly available information about the quality of the marketplace as a whole, parents are left on their own to compare and contrast the available options. Consequently, monitoring day-to-day program quality becomes an informal process taken up by child care staff and parents.

Relationship of Cost to Quality. The relationship between what it costs to provide child care and the quality of the services rendered is not well understood. Research on the subject shows modest associations between operating costs and quality in both center- and home-based child care settings (Helburn & Howes, 1996). The characteristics of the child care market described above, combined with several additional factors—the most salient being labor costs—make this a tangled relationship in the current, highly diversified system of child care. For consumers, the relationship is virtually impossible to assess. How are parents to gauge what they are getting for their money? How is the general public to know? Head Start and state-funded prekindergarten are funded with public dollars, and other programs, such as Fun Time Day Care, Peter Rabbit Learning and Development Center, and Cuddle Bugs, most likely provide services with a mix of public and private sources. Combined with the inherent difficulties of evaluating child care quality in the current system, estimating the true cost of quality services is a difficult undertaking.

The Myth of Parent Choice: Somewhere Between Supply and Demand

It has been argued that in the mostly private marketplace of child care, parents are unwilling to pay for quality (Blau, 2011). This argument implies that the problems associated with the current system of child care in the United States are not on the supply side but instead are on the demand side. Such a position enables policymakers to call on "parent choice" when setting parameters for child care policy. Indeed, parent choice is often used to justify the decision that child care subsidy dollars can be spent in the informal, unregulated, and unmonitored child care market. From a free-market perspective, one might conclude that parent choice is unproblematic and that the current nonsystem works perfectly well. Yet, because of the problems associated with the current supply of child care, the way that "choice" actually works is somewhat mythological (Kagan & Neville, 1992).

If true choice were available, the supply of child care would resemble, for instance, the ice cream freezer in a local supermarket. Consumers would have a vast array of feasible options to select from, and the quality-related characteristics of said options would be clearly communicated. Measures of quality would be meaningful to consumers and linked to social norms. In reality, parent choice in child care decisions is actually quite limited and depends on many factors, including household income (Kagan & Neville, 1992). When child care policy decisions are rationalized with the ideal of parent choice (e.g., spending subsidy dollars in the informal child care market), they allow for ongoing ambiguity concerning the purpose of the nation's child care investments (Raikes, 1998) and further impede system-building efforts. Does the nation really want public monies flowing into child care settings about which virtually nothing is known? This is not to say that informal care arrangements, such as family, friend, and neighbor care, cannot provide quality services; it is to say that the quality of the services provided is *unknown*. Furthermore, invoking "parent choice" in such matters can have an inestimable impact on the formal child care market, since licensed and regulated providers can themselves exercise choice when deciding which families to enroll.

Because of the imperfections of the child care supply, it is a mistake to assume that parents really have a fully free choice in securing quality services. There is not enough affordable, convenient, quality child care to go around. If there were, system-building efforts would not be such a priority and federal child care subsidy dollars would not be spent in the informal marketplace. Additionally, families would not be spending from 7% to over 28% of their household income on child care expenses (Macartney & Laughlin, 2011), and children would not have upward of five different arrangements before school entry (Belsky et al., 2007). When parents approach the child care market, what are they looking for and how do they make child care decisions?

Demand-Side Ideals and Realities

Parents' child care decisions involve balancing practical concerns and preferences with personal beliefs about what is best for infants, toddlers, and preschoolers. A long line of research indicates that children's child care arrangements are not random. Demographic characteristics of children and families, such as child age and household socioeconomic status, are systematically associated with child care type and quality (Gable & Cole, 2000; Meyers & Jordan, 2006). In today's child care market, household income is the primary factor that accounts for variation in families' child care arrangements.

Pragmatic Considerations and Preferences. When parents approach the child care selection process, they have preconceived ideas about their own needs and preferences and the desired characteristics of programs and providers (Rose & Elicker, 2008). For example, parents typically consider a constellation of factors, with pragmatic considerations taking priority, such as cost, location, and hours of operation (Johansen, Leibowitz, & Waite, 1996). Because of the limited supply of affordable, high-quality programs and the varied needs of working parents, the relationship among these factors can force parents to make trade-offs among preferred qualities of child care (Meyers & Jordan, 2006). For example, although most low-income families have the same preferences and ideals as higher income parents concerning child care, the nature of low-wage jobs (e.g., irregular work schedules, evening shifts) and state variation in administering child care subsidies means that these families make child care decisions under significantly different conditions (Chaudry, 2004; Holloway, Fuller, Rambaud, & Eggers-Pierola, 1997). The same could be said about working poor families who are just outside of their state's subsidy program income eligibility guidelines and about more affluent families who have limited access to convenient, preferred program types in their local communities.

Child age also plays a role in parents' preferences for child care program type. Home-based settings are typically preferred for infants and toddlers, and center-based arrangements for preschoolers (Galinsky, 1992). Although most mothers would prefer to have their baby cared for by a spouse, partner, relative, or friend, the majority of women are unable to achieve a match with their preferences because of employment characteristics, such as the number and shift of hours worked (Riley & Glass, 2002). An obvious shortcoming of the current system is that it does not guarantee reliable, affordable, and quality child care for all families.

Child-Rearing Ideals and Program Preferences. Child-rearing values also weigh in parents' child care decision making. For instance, parents who seek to expose their children to early literacy and learning opportunities are more likely to enroll their children in center programs than in home-based child care (Fuller, Holloway, & Liang, 1996; Johansen et al., 1996). Parents who place more emphasis on nurturing and loving relationships with caring adults tend to seek home-based programs (Johansen et al., 1996; Kontos, Howes, Shinn, & Galinsky., 1995).

Numerous features of child care programs also contribute to parents' decisions. Parents value safe, clean, and healthy child care environments (Cryer & Burchinal, 1997). They also attend to program philosophy. Some parents prefer programs that utilize teacher-centered approaches to instructing young children, some value educational and learning opportunities that are more child-oriented, and other parents seek programs that provide a balance between the two (Stipek, Milburn, Clements, & Daniels, 1992). Curriculum type is also noted by parents. Rose and Elicker (2008) reported that parents highly value play-based curriculum. Staff and caregiver attributes are another important consideration for parents. Parents want teachers and child care providers who exude warmth and who have specialized training and education in child-related topics (Barbarin et al., 2006; Early & Burchinal, 2001; Rose & Elicker, 2008). Furthermore, the value that parents place on staff who are educated, sensitive, and caring toward children is the same across different levels of household income (Barbarin et al., 2006; Early & Burchinal, 2001).

Reality of Parents' Child Care Decisions. Meyers and Jordan's (2006) careful and extensive review illustrates the trade-offs that parents make with their child care choices. Equating parents' actual child care arrangements with their child care preferences and ideals discounts the difficult decisions that families make when securing care for their young children (Early & Burchinal, 2001). Indeed, while socioeconomic status is associated with what parents can purchase in the marketplace and the quality of those selections (e.g., Capizzano, Adams, & Sonenstein, 2000), income is not systematically associated with what parents value for their children's child care and early education experiences (Barbarin et al., 2006; Early & Burchinal, 2001).

EXAMINATION OF CHILD CARE PROGRAM NAMES

To gain a full appreciation for how ambiguity of purpose appears to the public, in 2006 I initiated a study to systematically analyze the licensed and license-exempt child care program names of one state, Missouri. (See Appendix A for study methodology, including how the list of names was obtained, reduced, and subsequently coded.) The names of these child care programs function as "social addresses" (Bronfenbrenner, 1986) and evoke consumer-like reactions. Although they may not convey much about what occurs behind closed doors, they do show where the supply side and the demand side meet. The names reveal how program operators express themselves, strive to meet consumer demands, and work to maintain full enrollments. Furthermore, these names embody the aspirations that will have to be coordinated if the United States is to ever get serious about creating a coherent child care system. After all, the names of Missouri's licensed and license-exempt child care programs are public information.

The names were first analyzed for evidence of intended function and consumer appeal. Representative lists of program names were then presented to future child care consumers (i.e., college students). The students rank-ordered the lists of names and explained their most and least preferred options. The study's findings provide a means for concretizing the above discussion on supply- and demand-side characteristics of child care. They reveal the challenges of definitional confusion (and opportunities for definitional clarity) that will be confronted by any effort to create a more coherent system of child care.

Missouri's child care regulations make it an ideal candidate for the task at hand. Although several center-based programs, such as Head Start, public-school-affiliated preschool programs, and religiously affiliated facilities, are exempt from licensure (NCCITAC & NARA, 2010), they are required to meet minimum public health and safety requirements. The state also monitors and licenses home-based child care programs with more than four unrelated children enrolled. Thus, the universe of Missouri names examined yields a fairly accurate rendering of the formal child care marketplace as it exists nationally.

Intended Program Function and Consumer Appeal

By analyzing our final list of 1,778 Missouri child care centers, Head Start programs, religiously affiliated centers, and public-school-operated preschools, we found that eight categories captured how child care programs describe their services (see Table 2.1). The most commonly used terms (24%) were *academically oriented* and include, for example, preschool, learning center, school house, institute, academy, school, and early learning (e.g., Mary's Little Lambs Early Learning Center). Fifteen percent of program names referred specifically to *care*, such as child care center or day care (e.g., J and J Day Care Center). The *unclear* category (14%) contains program names that did not include a description of their services (e.g., Our Little Sidekicks, The Rugrats Resort). *Child-centered* services (10%) were characterized by phrases such as child development center, early childhood center, and children's center (e.g., Willow Woods Child Development Center). The *combination* category (10%) includes those center names that combined at least two of the previously described categories (e.g., Carol Jones Daycare Preschool). The least frequent service descriptor emphasized *play/fun* (6%) and was denoted by use of the word *play* or euphemisms that convey play and fun (e.g., Noah's Ark Playhouse). *Head Start* (15%) and *nationally recognized chains* (6%) or philosophies (e.g., Kinder Care Learning Center, Sullivan Montessori Preschool) were placed in separate categories. This decision followed a perception that these names represent something unique in the current private market of child care.

Table 2.1. How Child Care Centers
Describe Their Services

	Number	Capacity*
Total Centers	1,778	106,663
Categories		
Academically Oriented	431 (24%)	24,657 (23%)
Care	272 (15%)	15,349 (14%)
Head Start	260 (15%)	11,269 (11%)
Unclear	244 (14%)	10,950 (10%)
Child-Centered	186 (10%)	14,442 (14%)
Combination	173 (10%)	11,217 (11%)
National Brands/Chain	105 (6%)	12,385 (12%)
Play/Fun	107 (6%)	6,394 (6%)

*The percentages do not add up to 100%
    because of rounding.

Themes Present in Child Care Center Names

Seven broad themes comprising 27 specific subthemes emerged from the analysis of child care center names. Table 2.2 displays the frequency and prevalence of the broad themes that emerged.

Child-Friendly. The largest number of Missouri's licensed child care center names were categorized as child-friendly (n = 397; 22%). These program names are "cute," have a "kid" focus, or emphasize play and fun. They were considered child-friendly because of their light-hearted, playful, and sometimes silly nature.

Table 2.2. How Child Care Centers
Appeal to Consumers

	Number	Capacity
Total Centers	1,778	106,663
Consumer-Oriented Themes		
Child-Friendly	397 (22%)	21,652 (20%)
Brands	386 (22%)	25,223 (24%)
Parent-Oriented	360 (20%)	22,647 (21%)
Formal Names	321 (18%)	18,385 (17%)
Religious	151 (8%)	10,019 (9%)
Co-Located Ed. Institution	117 (7%)	4,772 ((5%)
Other	46 (3%)	3,965 (4%)

The cute subcategory includes names that reference familiar nursery rhymes and characters from children's literature, nonsensical and alliterative phrases, baby animals, and other child-friendly expressions (e.g., Humpty Dumpty Daycare, Twittily Dittily Doo Child Care Center, Little Pirates Learning Center, Bunnies Burrow Daycare and Preschool). The "kid" focus explicitly references child care's intended participants—children—with words such as *kid, little, child,* and *tot.* (e.g., Lil Tots Daycare, Kids Korner Preschool, Kids World Child Development Center). The play-oriented names idealize childhood through an emphasis on play (e.g., Susie's Stay N Play Daycare, Happy Go Lucky Child Care Center, Toyland Day Nursery), fun (e.g., Fun Time Day Care), and fantasy (e.g., Magic Kingdom).

Brands. Twenty-two percent (*n* = 386) of Missouri's child care center names were categorized as brands. The names included here are child care programs or philosophies such as national chains (e.g., Kinder Care Learning Center, La Petite

Academy), Head Start (e.g., West Plains Head Start II), Montessori programs (e.g., Casa Dia Montessori), and names that are explicitly affiliated with a not-for-profit agency (e.g., Easter Seals Child Development Center, Salvation Army Westport Day Care). The majority of programs in this category are Head Start (260 of 386; 67%).

Parent-Oriented. The 20% of child care center names categorized as appealing to parents touch on a wide variety of topics. Parent-oriented names were perceived as more serious than the child-friendly names and reflect relevant constructs from the research on parent ideals and preferences for child care. They contain words and expressions that emphasize education and learning (e.g., ABC and One Two Three Daycare and Preschool, Learning Connection Child Development Center), creativity and discovery (e.g., Creative Learning Day School LLC, Curious Kids Growth & Development Center), relationships and nurturing (e.g., Warm Hearts Child Care Center, Apple of Your Eye Learning Center, Best Friends Child Care Center), prestige and affluence (e.g., Elite Child Care Center LLC, Little Einsteins), and child growth and development (Ages and Stages Learning Center, Watch Me Grow Day Care and Preschool).

Formal Names. The 18% of Missouri's child care centers that identified themselves with a proper name were categorized as formal names. This category includes employers (e.g., UAW-Ford Child Development Center, 601 Federal Complex Child Care Center), individuals after whom the program is named or dedicated (e.g., Mel Carnahan Learning Center of Phelps County), the program owner/operator (e.g., Walkers Day Care), or the facility's geographic location (e.g., Miniola Day Care Center, Walnut Street Dayschool).

Religious. There were 151 child care centers (8%) that were deemed religious because they are either affiliated with a religious institution (e.g., Grant Avenue Baptist Daycare, St. Paul's Learning Center) or expressed a religious connotation in their name (e.g., Blessings from Above Day Care, Chapel of Praise Rich and Little Preschool). What makes this latter subcategory distinctive is that the theme hints at something that does not appear in any of the other themes or service descriptors—a connection with religion that is not due to program affiliation.

Co-Located in an Educational Institution. The 117 Missouri child care names included in this category (7%) are distinguished by their affiliation with an educational institution, such as a college or university (e.g., Washington University Nursery School, MSSU Child Development Center), or a K–12 school district (e.g., Growing Place PS Washington West Elementary, Eugene Field Elementary Preschool).

Other. Three percent ($n = 46$) of the state's child care center names are categorized as *other*. This category includes names that are nonspecific (e.g., Community Child Care Center), that identify programs as international (e.g., Los Niños Bilingual Preschool) or intergenerational (e.g., Learning Tree Intergenerational Center), or that explicitly convey serving children and families with special needs (e.g., Children's Center for the Visually Impaired).

Analyzing the Findings

Several notable findings emerged from this effort to describe and summarize one state's supply of child care centers. First, the ambiguity of purpose that plagues policymakers and the field was present in the way child care programs described their services. The range of expressions used illustrates the challenges associated with identifying a single phrase that captures the essence of child care's purpose, appeals to consumers, and satisfies advocates. Moreover, the variety of consumer-oriented themes that were revealed in the program names also illustrates several general characteristics of the supply side of child care. For example, the mixed-market designation of U.S. child care and the broad diversity of program auspices emerged from the universe of this state's child care center names. Additionally, what was described as information asymmetry (i.e., the seller knows more about the product than the buyer) was apparent from the first phase's overall findings. All things considered, from the consumer side of Missouri's child care marketplace, little is known about the services under consideration without prior knowledge of specific facilities or some amount of personal inquiry. Because of the mostly private nature of the child care market, those who name child care programs can describe their services and devise consumer-oriented themes so as to attract (or repel) a certain type of consumer. Consequently, the way that child care centers distinguish themselves can be construed to reflect parents' child-rearing values in their child care decision making and, consequently, support the ideology of parent choice.

What the names do not convey, however, is the single quality-related thread that connects all of the programs. Specifically, the one element that the program names share is the thread of state regulation (i.e., licensed and license-exempt) and minimum public health standards. In the absence of standardized program quality information (e.g., QRIS), there is no mechanism in place for parents to distinguish level of quality among the child care options whose names vary so dramatically. Thus, while families may be grateful that they can exercise "choice" and select what they believe is best for their children, unless they are income-eligible for Head Start or public prekindergarten, the absolute floor of quality is the same across all licensed child care centers within a given state, regardless of what the program name conveys. Furthermore, in Missouri, license-exempt programs, while complying with basic public health requirements, do not meet the same minimum standards of quality as licensed child care centers. Welcome to the private marketplace of U.S. child care, where "competitive pressures can have perverse effects" (Folbre, 2001, p. 64).

Potential Consumers' Responses to Program Names

The second part of the study investigated future child care consumers' reactions to program names and evaluated the way names convey practical and quality-related information. We surveyed 123 undergraduate students enrolled in a lifespan human development course as to their future, hypothetical child care preferences. Representative lists of child care center names were compiled using the broad consumer-oriented themes derived from the first part of the study. The primary goal was to learn which program names were and were not preferred, and why. Because the students were not yet child care consumers and had not learned about child care in class, they would presumably be free of bias, except possibly for their own childhood recollections.

The survey was administered during weekly small-group discussion sections. Students were presented with the following scenario:

> Your family just moved to a new community and you need to find full-time child care for your child. A local agency sent you a list of child care programs. Because of time constraints, you need to make a decision based on name alone. Rank-order the list of five child care names below, with *1* being the most desirable program and *5* being the least desirable program. Briefly describe why you selected the program ranked as number 1; describe why you selected the program ranked as number 5.

The lists included exemplars of the most common types of child care names as identified during the first phase and those program types that were accessible to most if not all families. For this reason, Head Start and public school–affiliated programs, which have income eligibility requirements, were not included.

Parents' child care preferences for children of different ages (e.g., Galinsky, 1992; Riley & Glass, 2002) were accounted for by creating three separate lists of program names—one for a 9-month-old, one for a 3-year-old, and one for a 5-year-old. Each list included at least one brand, one parent-oriented, one child-friendly, and one religious child care program name.

Students' top and bottom preferences were tallied and appear in Table 2.3. Their narrative explanations for the most and least desirable options were coded and summarized using an inductive process similar to that originally applied to the child care center names. This process revealed that students explained their preferences with one or more of the following rationales: interpersonal warmth and fun, familiarity, safety, literal interpretation, "gut feeling" (i.e., subjective reaction), credibility and staff characteristics, education, balance and age-appropriateness, religion, pragmatic considerations such as cost and location, and prestige. Each rationale could explain why a program was, or was not, preferred. For example, for 3-year-olds, Abundant Blessings Christian Child Care and Preschool was equally preferred and not preferred for the religious nature of its name.

Reactions by Theme

Child-Friendly Names. The names originally categorized as child-friendly elicited a mix of student reactions. Whereas Alphabet Soup Learning Center and Little Learner were primarily preferred, Play House Child Development Center and Babies, Bottles, and Books were more often least preferred, and Child's Play was uniformly disliked.

Both Alphabet Soup Learning Center and Little Learner evoked subjective appeal (e.g., "a catchy name"; "just went with instinct") and feelings of warmth and fun (e.g., "a fun learning environment and warm atmosphere"). The emphasis on learning and education (e.g., "implies that it will teach my child the alphabet") and balance/age-appropriateness was also appealing (e.g., "education is a primary focus but realizes that they are still little kids"). One student inferred credibility and staff characteristics from the subjective appeal of Little Learner: "Little Learner's alliteration is undeniably attractive. My 3-year-old deserves the care of an institution with such wit and ability to strike me so strongly. The people running it must be qualified."

On balance, Play House Child Development Center and Babies, Bottles, and Books were more often ranked as least desirable than as most desirable. Students explained their unfavorable rankings with subjective reactions (e.g., "I just don't like the name") and problems of credibility and staff quality (e.g., "too informal"; "doesn't sound like the caregivers know what they are doing"). For Play House in particular, the primary reason for the poor ranking was the lack of focus on education (e.g., "unsure about the quality of the education"; "all play and no education").

For the few who preferred these programs, staff qualifications were favorably inferred from the names. Specifically, for Babies, Bottles, and Books, one student commented: "Is catchy. So anyone that can think of that name must be creative and have a good personality and be caring." For Play House Child Development Center, explanations included, "because the name suggests that they have people who are knowledgeable about a child's development."

Table 2.3. Students' Top and Bottom Preferences

Most Desirable	Center Names	Least Desirable
for a 9-month-old		
51%	Kinder Care Learning Center (brand)	2%
10%	Grandma Jane's (parent-oriented)	49%
22%	Alphabet Soup Learning Center (child-friendly)	0%
5%	Babies, Bottles, and Books (child-friendly)	20%
12%	Eternity Child Care (religious)	29%
for a 3-year-old		
21%	Little Learner (child-friendly)	0%
23%	Abundant Blessings Christian Child Care and Preschool (religious)	26%
23%	Greenbrier Montessori Academy (brand)	19%
0%	Child's Play (child-friendly)	53%
33%	Circle of Friends Learning Center (parent-oriented)	2%
for a 5-year-old		
38%	Ready Set Grow Child Care Center (parent-oriented)	5%
10%	La Petite Academy (brand)	18%
8%	Play House Child Development Center (child-friendly)	28%
13%	Ozarks Technical Community College Early Childhood Education Center (co-located)	33%
31%	Radiant Faith Day Care and Preschool (religious)	15%

These names also elicited a mixed response concerning age-appropriateness. For example, of Babies, Bottles, and Books, one unimpressed student wrote, "The center will simply hand my child a bottle and a book (babies can't read anyway!) and not provide much interaction, attention, or education relevant to my child." Whereas another, more impressed student remarked, "A place pertaining to the needs of a 9-month-old baby."

Child's Play, as pointed out by several students, has the unfortunate distinction of being the same name as a horror movie. "Child's Play is a movie about a possessed doll. There will be no possessed dolls in my child's future. Thanks but no thanks." Other comments highlighted the absence of education (e.g., "just for play and your child doesn't learn anything"), limited credibility (e.g., "seemed very unprofessional"), and questionable staff quality (e.g., "[the] name is not very creative so . . . child care workers would not be either").

Parent-Oriented Names. Circle of Friends Learning Center and Ready Set Grow Child Care Center elicited mostly favorable responses from students, although for different reasons. For instance, students remarked on the education-oriented "service descriptor" associated with Circle of Friends (e.g., "learning center shows they will have opportunities to expand minds"), whereas Ready Set Grow elicited subjective appeal because of its "catchy" and "creative" name (e.g., "quick and simple . . . playful name"). One student, however, ranked Ready Set Grow as least preferred "because the name seemed a little unprofessional."

Both program names, however, evoked a sense of warmth, balance, and age-appropriateness. Circle of Friends Learning Center was preferred because it "seems like a friendly learning environment where my child can feel like an individual, discover themselves, and make friends." Ready, Set, Grow Child Care Center elicited similar explanations that centered on a well-rounded approach: "Seems like a fun place to be for a child but also seems like it intends to help children grow and develop at the same time."

Grandma Jane's, originally coded as parent-oriented/nurturing, was ranked least desirable by half of the students. Because of past research about parents' child care preferences for infants (Galinsky, 1992; Riley & Glass, 2002), this was surprising. Nonetheless, for most students, the name evoked a lack of credibility (e.g., "sounds more like dropping your child off with your mother who has no formal education on how to care for children"). Concerns with safety were also mentioned: "Although it may be safe, it doesn't sound like it." Additionally, several students reacted to the lack of clarity in services provided (e.g., "Grandma Jane's could be a restaurant or a child care facility").

For the few who ranked Grandma Jane's as most desirable for their infant, the name evoked feelings of interpersonal warmth, familiarity, and safety. "When

I think of the name 'grandma,' I think of a loving, caring, and safe environment. Grandma would take care of my child the way that I would." For this student, the function of child care for an infant is a mother replacement.

Brands. Kinder Care Learning Center elicited a range of favorable responses, and student reactions were more mixed for Greenbrier Montessori Academy and La Petite Academy. As a brand, Kinder Care Learning Center was familiar to some respondents: "It is the name of a child care facility where I live . . . never heard anything negative." However, the balanced and age-appropriate approach to learning and care was cited most frequently. "It sounded like an educational program where my baby would be cared for and stimulated in a learning environment. 'Kinder' seems like it is either referring to kind, sensitive care or preparation for kindergarten." The name also conveyed a sense of credibility and staff quality: "Sounds more professional and well-organized. . . . My child would be under experienced caregivers." The academically oriented service descriptor was also acknowledged: "'Learning Center' shows that the center will provide a learning environment for my child, rather than simply keeping him/her busy."

Greenbrier Montessori Academy and La Petite Academy were equally preferred and not preferred. Brands, or curriculum approaches, like these benefit from familiarity, such as when students referred to their own (e.g., "I am a graduate of the Montessori method . . . [and] intend to send my children to a Montessori school") or others' experiences (e.g., "my friend went there as a child . . . [and] talked about how great it was"). However, a lack of familiarity with the somewhat unique names might also dissuade a potential consumer. One student commented, "[I] don't know if Montessori school provides different education. . . . [It] might not appeal to what I want for my child," and, about La Petite, another wrote, "[It] may be focused on foreign language . . . not what the child needs." Familiarity with program philosophy can also evoke favorable (e.g., "Montessori schools focus on learning in a way that is very child-friendly") and unfavorable reactions (e.g., "Montessori schools generally don't have a strict learning structure and are more 'hands-on' and I prefer a more traditional learning environment").

These names also conveyed a sense of prestige and credibility that was simultaneously attractive (e.g., "sounds very elite and I would feel like my child would be learning something as well as be in good, well-experienced hands") and off-putting (e.g., "it sounds too fancy with the French name"). The word *academy* in both names was enough to elicit favorable reactions (e.g., "academy sounds more prestigious. . . . [My] child will not only be cared for but . . . get some educational play"). Conversely, the lack of specificity in the names was problematic to others (e.g., "[it's a] very general name and doesn't tell a lot about the establishment"). Finally, some students experienced the names as lacking in warmth (e.g., "seems very strict. . . . School and learning should be exciting for the child and a strict environment would discourage them *[sic]* from liking those things"), age-in-appropriate (e.g., "looks very academic and not very nurturing . . . maybe for a 5-year-old but not a 3-year-old"), and impractical (e.g., "might be expensive").

Religious Names. As with certain brands or philosophies, child care program names containing references to religion were both desirable and not desirable. Eternity Child Care, for example, elicited primarily negative reactions because of the word *eternity*. One student wrote, "Eternity child care makes me think of the afterlife and that is unsettling when talking about child care." Others similarly indicated that "eternity is not a good adjective for taking care of a child." What was perceived as a subtle reference to religion was mentioned by one student: "It sounds to be too religious or spiritually centered." The few students who selected this program as most desirable explained their choice with interpersonal warmth and literal meaning (e.g., "sounds very warm and loving, as if they will care for your child for an eternity"), credibility (e.g., "sounds professional"), and age-ap-propriate (e.g., "since my child is only 9 months, he/she doesn't need the learning center aspect").

Abundant Blessings Christian Child Care and Preschool and Radiant Faith Day Care and Preschool more frequently garnered an explicit mention of religion as weighing in student rankings. For those who preferred these programs as their top choice, references to religion were common (e.g., "my faith is important to me"; "feel that children should be exposed to faith early in life"). Those students who ranked these programs as least desirable on the basis of religion explained, "because of 'Christian' in the name . . . [it] could be a place where adults try to persuade children one way or the other," and, "I am not particularly religious."

Other students coupled religion favorably with safety (e.g., "church-based . . . means pretty safe"; "sounds the most trusting") and staff quality (e.g., "with peo-ple whom *[sic]* believe in God come caring and sensitivity"). Others reacted to the religious character of the name as "cold" and age-inappropriate (e.g., "sounds too controlling and forcing of religious beliefs at a young age. Not fun for a child"). A more literal approach to explaining preferences was used by students who focused on the service descriptors (e.g., "includes child care and preschool in the name, revealing just exactly what you are enrolling your child in").

Co-Located in an Educational Institution. Ozarks Technical Community College Early Childhood Education Center was more frequently endorsed as least desir-able, but a few students ranked it as their top preference. For those who ranked this program last, the name elicited a variety of reactions. The most frequent source of dissatisfaction addressed balance and age-related needs of 5-year-olds (e.g., "seems way too advanced for a 5-year-old . . . very strict and un-enjoyable"; "not really sure that sending my child to a day care run by a technical school would help them grow"). An absence of warmth and subjective appeal (e.g., "doesn't appeal to a parent or child as a fun place to go every day") and prestige (e.g., "doesn't sound very prestigious") were also cited as reasons for poor rankings. Pragmatic reasons, such as lack of affiliation (e.g., "associated with a college that I have no affiliation with") and inconvenient location, also were mentioned (e.g., "it is also not close").

Coincidentally, the factors that were off-putting to some students were appealing to others. For example, the Ozarks Technical Community College name evoked concerns with credibility and staff quality (e.g., "sounds like it will have students that are learning about working at a day care"). Other students, however, interpreted the community college affiliation as a boost to credibility (e.g., "it's for people who are going into that field and they have to do their best for their class grades") and a benefit to children (e.g., "sounded the most professional and could be the best learning facility my child could go to").

Analyzing the Responses

Students attributed a range of characteristics to the program names and expressed clear ideas about what they want, and don't want, from child care. Regardless of the type of name or service provided, students' likes and dislikes revealed several common themes. For example, students often explained their top choice with statements that conveyed the importance of an age-appropriate balance of education and fun. When justifying their least preferred programs, education alone was too strict and play alone was not credible enough. Students also linked the appeal (or lack thereof) of program names with credibility and staff quality. Although these findings indicate that students recognize the importance of caregivers in children's child care experiences, they also reveal considerable naïveté about the relationship between program names and workforce qualifications. Student inferences about staff quality are further evidence of information asymmetry. In the current market of U.S. child care, the seller clearly knows more than the buyer about the product.

OVERALL CONCLUSIONS

In the end, "you cannot judge a book by its cover," or a child care program by its name. This descriptive analysis of one state's child care center names illustrates the ambiguity of purpose that plagues the field and the uneven and diverse services available to families. What is troublesome about this ambiguity is that it is perpetuated by current U.S. child care policy. Although the demand side is fairly clear about what families want—a blend of care, education, and fun that is age-appropriate and provided by credible staff—policy continues to enable a highly diverse and fragmented supply of services. The diversity in offerings poses a great challenge to system building (Goffin & Washington, 2007). Indeed, the program names analyzed for this chapter give a good sense of the matter that is to be organized into a coherent system! Problems of definition and purpose provide fertile ground for division among constituencies and permit scornful intergroup comparisons, such as the simmering tensions between early education and child care. Furthermore, such ambiguity of purpose—and ambivalence on behalf of the field to agree on something and move forward with it—shortchanges our commitment to all young children and families.

CHAPTER 3

The Private Face

Dialogues About Women and Work

Creating a national system of child care in the United States has long been stymied by cultural anxiety about maternal employment and discomfort with nonmaternal child care (Scarr, 1998). This discomfort stems, in part, from different prescriptions of what it means to be a good mother. Women are bombarded with contradictory messages about how to conduct themselves, especially after they become mothers. On the one hand, mothers are told they need to stay home if they want to do right by their children. They need to put aside any desire for self-fulfillment outside of the domestic realm and be fully and unselfishly devoted to their children.

On the other hand, girls and young women are encouraged to set the stage so that one day they can "do it all": go to college, pursue a career, make money, buy nice things, get married, become a mother, provide for a family, and ultimately earn the title of "Supermom." Such rule books for how women are to live their lives uphold the fiction that mothers *choose* between staying at home *or* going to work. According to this rule, being a good mother is not a choice, but being a working mother is (Dillaway & Paré, 2008; Hays, 1996). Furthermore, although these strategies may appear at odds, they do share a common belief: regardless of whether mothers are employed, they are solely responsible for their children's burgeoning character and ultimate destiny; no one else matters quite so much as mothers do. This chapter makes the argument that it is detrimental to hold onto the belief that mothers singularly determine their children's development. It shows how such beliefs have adverse implications for creating a national system of child care.

For mothers who work, the ideology that emphasizes their singular primacy in children's lives is challenged every day. For, along with maternal employment comes the reality of nonmaternal child care. As discussed in Chapter 1, the majority of children age 5 and younger experience some form of regular nonmaternal care on a weekly basis. This reality of contemporary family life highlights the awkward intersection of several social imperatives, including the ideal mother, the ideal worker, and the need for care work (Drago, 2007; Feree, 2010). Interestingly, the people—primarily women—who provide child care for pay are also subject to certain societal beliefs about what makes a good mother. Care work, whether for a child or an elderly adult, is seen as a natural skill, bestowed primarily on women, and one that comes from the heart (Folbre, 2001). Thus, there is no need to place a real value on the provision of child care or to expect workers to come to the job prepared with special training and education. Moreover, to some, the idea that care can be purchased is distasteful. The "invisible heart" of caring relationships is not to be subject to the "invisible hand" of the competitive market (Dillaway & Paré, 2008; Folbre, 2001; Uttal, 2002). Combined with the prevailing cultural beliefs that mothers alone are responsible for their children's upbringing and ultimate well-being, there is great pressure to devalue child care and to keep hidden those who are paid to provide this service. These massively contradictory beliefs have resulted in the emergence and perpetuation of a deeply fragmented system of child care in the United States.

A national system of child care will become possible only if the United States disconnects maternal employment and child care from social constructions of "the good mother." To begin, the prevailing rhetoric of choice, as in mothers "choose" to work, must be dismantled and reconceptualized in contemporary and practical terms. Maintaining beliefs concerning the role of mother, such as those described above, can be construed as one possible explanation for why the United States has settled on such a vast and diverse (non)system of child care, as analyzed in Chapter 2. If a mother's love and devotion are the end-all and be-all for children, why invest in a national system of child care? Indeed, a national plan for child care would implicitly condone maternal employment and place a real value on nonmaternal caregiving activities.

This chapter begins with a continuation of the historical narrative presented in Chapter 2. Then, to bring discourse about mothers, employment, and child care into the 21st century, I explore the thoughts, feelings, and experiences of employed women who have a direct relationship with child care.

HISTORICAL CONTEXT FOR
PUBLIC DISCOURSE ON MATERNAL EMPLOYMENT

The U.S. history of maternal employment and nonmaternal care during the late 19th and the first half of the 20th centuries took a new turn after World War II. Working mothers didn't return home as expected and their presence in the workforce steadily increased. One result was the emergence of more sophisticated public discourse on maternal employment.

In arguing for more child care funding, for instance, in 1959, Alice Leopold at the Women's Bureau and Katherine Oettinger at the Children's Bureau conducted descriptive studies that documented women's labor force participation and the vast landscape of available child care that varied in safety and quality (Michel, 1999). Others put maternal employment into a broader economic context. At the 1960 National Conference on Day Care of Children, Ewan Clague from the Department of Labor forecasted the constant increase of mothers in the workforce. He deemed women's workforce participation as necessary if the nation was to succeed in the postwar economy. Feminists of the era put forth a "self-fulfillment" agenda and argued that child care provisions were necessary in order for women to pursue motherhood and employment if they so desired. And debates ensued among developmental psychologists and other child development scholars.

The range of opinions about maternal employment and children's adjustment was effectively captured in a feature article in *McCall's* magazine titled, "Is a Working Mother a Threat to the Home?" (Pope, 1955). According to this article, motherhood, at least until children are age 6, is a 24/7 job that cannot be done by anyone else. Maternal employment was deemed to be motivated by "sick, competitive feelings toward men, or some other personality problem" (p. 29). It came with grave consequences for children and should be taken up only by "unloving" mothers so as to not harm children. On the other hand, the article indicated that what mattered most was the quality, and not the quantity, of time that mothers spent with their children. Moreover, under conditions of quality day care and a positive mother–child relationship, some believed that maternal employment could be good for children. Among those interviewed, only one point of consensus was reached: that children under the age of 3 years fared best when mothers were at home. All combined, these conversations brought the complexity of maternal employment and the pressing need for a system of child care into the public eye. They also underscored the fact that maternal employment, especially among those with young children, was here to stay. By the end of the 1950s, however, despite the efforts of many to normalize maternal employment, the "center mostly held," and mothers were told that they belonged in the home, with their children (Michel, 1999, p. 154).

The 1950s have also been identified as the era when present-day ideals of "the good mother" and the primacy of the maternal role for children's well-being took hold (Arendell, 2000). How the prevailing culture defines what it means to be a good mother is, like other ideologies, subject to change. That is, the role of mother and its enactment can be shaped on the basis of what the larger culture believes is important, particularly when it concerns children's well-being. Indeed, parenting ideals from other eras have discouraged breastfeeding, encouraged mothers to leave crying babies alone, and advised parents to avoid hugging, kissing, or being affectionate with their children (Hays, 1996). After World War II, when mothers were told to return home and engage their entire being in the job of child rearing, they became the singular edifying force behind shaping a child's burgeoning character and destiny. "Mother" was (and still is) cast as a powerful role, even if the power is confined to the sanctuary (and the privacy) of the home.

There is considerable danger in conceiving of mothers, or any single person or entity, in this all-powerful manner. Such conceptualizations create an easy scapegoat for when things go wrong and, when applied specifically to mothers, provide powerful groups with more than enough reason to limit universal supports, such as child care, to working families (Jong, 2010). Indeed, when politics enters the picture, the contradictory messages that women receive about how motherhood is to be enacted begin to make a great deal of sense. Recall the fragmentation of U.S. child care (and compensatory education) policy (J. R. Nelson, 1982) and the image of "the good mother" as one who is all-powerful in determining the shape and course of her children's lives. This image does not apply uniformly to mothers from all socioeconomic and racial groups.

As predicted, the period from 1960 to 1990 saw the labor market open up with more female-oriented occupations. Rates of maternal employment climbed and options for child care expanded dramatically (Michel, 1999). Although there were federal initiatives during the 1970s to establish a system of universal child care that would support poor families and promote *all* children's development, the rise of the New Right, which was founded in part on the belief that [some] mothers should not work, effectively stopped any such developments. Indeed, the New Right was strongly opposed to universal child care and was more committed to child care as a way to move poor mothers from welfare into employment. This was supposed to halt the intergenerational cycle of poverty (Hayes, 1982). As described in Chapter 1, social welfare–related federal legislation that linked child care with "workfare" was popular with conservatives and seemed to foreshadow the eventual block-granting of funds to states, complex child care financing schemes, and parent "choice." In the 1980s, child care became routine for the majority of U.S. families; in 1985, 53.5% of married mothers with children ages 6 and under were members of the civilian workforce (USDL, BLS, 2011b), and since then rates of maternal employment have remained above 50%.

As the 21st century gets under way, most women experience paid employment, childbearing, and child rearing with little interruption (Laughlin, 2011). Whereas during earlier decades there were differences in rates of maternal employment based on child age, with fewer mothers of infants and toddlers in the workforce, such differences are not as pronounced today. For all women who gave birth to their first child between 2005 and 2007, 64% were in the labor force within 12 months of delivery, up from 52% who gave birth between 1981 and 1984, and 28% between 1971 and 1975. For women who were employed during their first pregnancy, the percentages of mothers who went back to work before their child's first birthday are even higher. Maternal workforce participation creates a huge challenge for enacting contemporary ideals of motherhood. Mothers cannot do it all by themselves. Others must assist with caring for their children. However, as child care currently exists in the United States, this form of nonmaternal care is equal to maternal employment in the depth of societal ambivalence that it elicits.

THE VOICES OF EMPLOYED MOTHERS
AND CHILD CARE WORKERS

For discussions in the following sections of this chapter, I draw on the experiences of participants in three focus groups I conducted, two during the fall of 2008 and one in the spring of 2009. Details of the focus group methodology appear in Appendix B. One group comprised 11 home-based (HB) child care providers, and another group included seven individuals (six women and, unexpectedly, one man, with a gender-neutral name) who worked in community child care centers (CC). The third group included 14 working mothers (WM) who worked at least 30 hours per week, 12 months per year, and who had at least one child of preschool age in full-time child care. Demographic characteristics of the participants appear in Appendix C.

The original goal for this project was to explore how the sometimes tense relationship between working mothers and their child care providers can impede progress in U.S. child care policy. During the discussions, however, an alternative and much more meaningful reality emerged. These are not really distinct groups of women who have a fraught relationship. Rather, they combine to form a single group of women, primarily mothers, who have a complicated relationship with work, defined throughout the chapter as "paid employment activity."

The focus groups took place during an unprecedented time in U.S. history. The election of our nation's first African American president, a man married to a career-oriented woman and devoted mother of two school-aged daughters, brought renewed hope for addressing the needs of U.S. families. However, that hope was tempered by ongoing and expensive wars in Afghanistan and Iraq, a sagging national infrastructure, record job losses, and chronic financial uncertainty in the U.S. economy. Since that time, the U.S. and global economic situation has remained in flux, making the messages anticipated in this chapter even more demonstrative of the plight of working mothers, their families, and members of the child care workforce. During the final preparations of this chapter, President Barak Obama was re-elected to a second term (2012–2016).

In the subsequent section I begin with a multilayered, contextual description of the economic, personal, and social conditions that surround maternal employment. The discussion draws from focus group comments and contemporary scholarship on maternal employment, and argues that applying a framework of "choice," such as one that follows from current ideals of motherhood, is overly simplistic. Next is a lengthy discussion of how 21st-century societal ambivalence toward working mothers and nonmaternal care is subtly, and not so subtly, expressed throughout routine experiences associated with employment, child care, and daily life. Three topics are presented as particularly illustrative, including progress from the women's movement for gender equality, contributions from the media, and several structural and process characteristics associated with present-day child care. This portion of the chapter is intended to reveal how ambivalence toward maternal employment perpetuates ideals of motherhood and hinders movement toward a national system of child care.

CONDITIONS THAT SURROUND
WOMEN'S AND MOTHERS' EMPLOYMENT

A myriad of factors underlie maternal labor force participation. Maternal employment is linked with the stagnation (and fall) of men's wages and the need for two-earner households, the women's movement, gains in women's educational attainment, and the rise of single-mother-headed households (Cotter, England, & Hermsen, 2007). Whether cause or consequence of employment, the idea that employment decisions are a simple matter of "choice" is painfully out of touch with the reality of most working mothers' lives.

Several strategies were used to elicit participants' thoughts about why women work. Each participant was given the opportunity to share a reason, without discussion, and a list was subsequently generated that included all ideas that were offered. Participants then used the group-generated lists to identify the top three reasons why women work. Specifically, they were asked to "look over the list that we have made on the easel and write down the most important reasons women have for working. Please write down the top three reasons in order from the most important to the least important." This was followed by a brief discussion of what individuals listed and why. As shown in Table 3.1, four broad topics emerged from the participants' individual lists and capture the multiple conditions, or reasons, associated with maternal employment: basic financial needs, personal reasons, others' expectations and family obligations, and intergenerational considerations.

Basic Financial Needs

At the start of the 21st century, basic needs and economic pressures are "givens" when talking about maternal employment. The money earned by mothers is crucial to keeping families financially afloat. The average contribution of wives'

Table 3.1. Reasons Women and Mothers Have for Working:
By Focus Group

Reason	Participants Selecting Reason as #1			All 3 Reasons (including #1)		
	HB	WM	CC	HB	WM	CC
Basic Financial Needs	5	10	4	7	16	8
Personal Reasons	1	4	1	10	16	6
Others' Exp. and Family Obligations	1	0	1	10	8	3
Intergenerational Considerations	4	0	1	6	2	4

HB = home-based child care provider group ($n = 11$).
WM = working mothers group ($n = 14$).
CC = child care center provider group ($n = 7$)

earnings to household income was at a record high of 37.1% in 2009 compared with 26.6% in 1970 (USDL, BLS, 2011b). Thus, although rates of employment for women with children ages 18 years and younger have declined modestly across the first decade of the 21st century, from about 68% in 2000 to 65% in 2010 for married-couple families and from about 75% in 2000 to 67% for single-mother-headed households (USDL, BLS, 2011a), the percentage contribution of women's earnings to the household economy steadily increased across the same period.

When listing the three most important reasons why women work, 19 of the 32 focus group participants listed basic financial needs as the number-one reason. Whether to pay the bills, obtain health insurance, and/or to put food on the table, contributing to the household economy is a major factor underlying maternal employment. Participants from all focus groups matter-of-factly acknowledged the economic pressures faced by today's families, including their own, as central to maternal employment. Some explained it as the "cost of living" (e.g., "I think cost of living is mainly a reason why many women are in the workforce" [HB]), and others referred to "paying the bills" (e.g., "mine was make money to pay bills" [CC]). For one working mother, access to health insurance was critical: "I have a son with a rare medical condition and if we didn't have insurance and we had to take him to [a local hospital], it would be bad." The "normalcy" of maternal employment in light of today's economy also was expressed: "To me, I don't even think of it being women in the workforce. It is just, especially in today's world now, there's going to be two incomes that it takes to survive" (HB).

Several participants referred to themselves as sole providers, and the need to support their families as their top priority. "When I think about work, I think about [how] I have to get up every day because of my kids because it's just me, pretty much" (CC). One home-based provider spoke passionately about the struggles of her primarily low-income families:

> I work with a lot of single parents, and I have some couples, and so forth. They are all lower-income people, and they really don't have any choice but both need to work to provide for the little one. The mothers that are single, they work so hard, not even [getting] much pay for their jobs and ... people forget [that] they don't like leaving their baby either. They hate it. They don't have a choice.

The fiction of choice doesn't apply only to single-parent, "low-income" families. A member of the working mother group, wife and mother, employed as a nurse full-time and with a household income of $40,000–$45,000 per year, articulated it this way:

> I do love my job but being a mother of four, ages 13 to 3, I work because I have to, not because I want to. I would much rather stay at home and have more time to take care of my kids. I [feel] I could fulfill all their needs better if I had more time to focus on them.

The reality is that most families are confronted with hard decisions concerning trade-offs associated with employment. A 28-year-old lead teacher in a child care center, mother of a 2-year-old and 8-month-old twins, who earns between $20,000 and $25,000 annually, shared the following:

> My husband actually stays home with our three kids now because I have more steady work and I just can make more than he can. I have to go to work every day and leave my kids because I have to provide for my kids.

Personal Reasons

Table 3.1 shows that personal reasons were listed by six participants as the top reason for women's employment; however, when all of the reasons were tallied, they were listed as frequently as basic financial needs (32 times versus 31 times, respectively). The topics in this category include financial independence, self-fulfillment, and use of education and pursuit of a career.

Financial Independence. Several participants mentioned financial security and independence as a reason for women's employment. These reasons were categorized separately from basic financial needs because they were expressed in terms of personal needs and desires. For example, with divorce rates among couples with children at approximately 40 to 50%, (Bramlett & Mosher, 2002), it was no surprise to see financial independence listed among participants' reasons why women work (e.g., "independence: knowing I can support myself and my family on my own if needed" [WM]). A different perspective on financial independence also was mentioned and concerned how independently earning money allows women to make independent choices about how they spend their money ("I put financial independence, which I think is distinct from need. I like to make my own choices" [WM]). The oldest participant among the focus groups, a 68-year-old woman who worked as a staff assistant, similarly noted "freedom to make your own choices too, without depending on your husband for everything and your spending money."

Self-Fulfillment. A myriad of items from the participants' lists addressed the ways in which employment is associated with self-fulfillment. Several touched on linkages between working and enhanced self-esteem and feelings of independence ("self-worth/personal fulfillment" [HB]; "independence—having own life" [WM]). Others listed social opportunities outside of the home ("develop friends/support/adult conversation" [HB]; "to stay in the game, get ready, get out of the house, communicate with others" [CC]) and to "have worth and identity beyond family" (HB) as reasons why women work. The sheer enjoyment of going to work was also mentioned (e.g., "just the enjoyment of working. My husband thinks I'm insane but I actually enjoy going to my job" [WM]). For women with jobs that permit independence and flexibility (i.e., *not* positions in child care!), work time can offer opportunities for essential self-care. A 30-year-old married mother of one who works full-time in a technical field said:

> I almost feel in some ways it is indulgent. For one thing, it is intellectual and social; but also I find on the weekends, I don't ever drink water, I don't go to the bathroom, I don't eat a meal. So during the week I drink my 64 ounces of water, I go to the restroom on a regular basis. When I eat lunch it's like silence. . . . It's in normal bite-sized, grown-up pieces. I just sort of indulge in that in some ways.

Child care providers, perhaps by virtue of their shared vocation, spoke more specifically to the nature of their work and the intrinsic satisfaction that it brings ("I always look forward to seeing a new baby that comes in" [CC]). Another child care center staff member listed, "To teach children and help them to feel good about themselves" as a reason for her employment. The following was mentioned by a 42-year-old woman, wife and mother, who had been operating her home-based child care program for 19 years:

> In my job, well in the job we all do, it is rewarding to watch the children grow. Just to be a part of their lives as they learn new things. . . . To love them and be able to comfort them is very rewarding.

Use of Education. "Use of education" and career advancement ("career advancement based on education [AA, BS, MBA]" [WM]) were listed by several of the working mothers and one of the center workers ("freedom to work in a career we love") as reasons why women are employed. Gains in women's educational attainment are indeed linked with several trends in maternal employment and child care. Between 1969–70 and 2000–01, the proportion of all bachelor's degrees conferred to females climbed from 43% to 57% (Freeman, 2004). Furthermore, of the young women who graduated from high school in 2010, 74% were enrolled in higher education for the fall (USDL, BLS, 2011b). Consequently, mothers are also more highly educated. In 2007, 24% of mothers had at least a bachelor's degree, whereas in 1970, 9% of mothers had attained this level of education (Laughlin, 2011). As a woman's level of education increases, she is also more likely to work during pregnancy and to work later into pregnancy; 72% of women with a bachelor's degree or more worked until less than 1 month before their child's birth compared with 56% of women with a high school diploma (Laughlin, 2011). The percentage of women who receive a paid leave after their child's birth similarly increases with educational attainment (Laughlin, 2011). As mothers' educational attainment increases—and, presumably the demands of their jobs—so, too, do their earnings and the number of hours that children spend in child care (Bub & McCartney, 2004). Moreover, as household income increases, mothers' emotional well-being is stronger and parents are better able to create a stimulating home environment for their children (Yeung, Linver, & Brooks-Gunn, 2002).

For participants in the working mothers group, the concept of "career advancement" appeared to have more salience. This was not surprising; most state child care systems do not require post–high school education for workers in licensed child care facilities (NCCITAC, 2011), nor do many states implement career ladders that reward individuals with higher salaries and wages for attaining more education (e.g., Austin, Whitebook, Connors, & Darrah, 2011). Nonetheless, similar to M. K. Nelson's (1990) "professional" home-based providers, two members of the home-based child care group spoke with great pride about furthering their education ("I did it, after 30 years, honey, I went and got a CDA" [HB]). In particular, one 43-year-old married wife and mother spoke enthusiastically about her recent return to school:

> I'm back in school. I just turned 43 but 11 years ago, that is when I stopped. I cut my career and decided I was pregnant and that was it. So 10–11 years, I'm back again. I told my husband this is my turn. He has been back to school twice, thanks to the day care. I said, "Now, it's my turn before you change your mind to a different career." (HB)

As educational attainment increases, however, the jobs it commands are more difficult to perform when also raising a family. Indeed, the entire world of paid employment is becoming more difficult to smoothly integrate with family life. Further, as occupational complexity (and presumably educational requirements) increase, there are fewer options for part-time careers and employment. In 1995, 20% of professional, technical, and managerial positions were held by mothers with preschoolers, and 76% of these jobs were full-time (Edwards, 2005). These are demanding, most likely salaried positions that are difficult to balance with the needs of young families. Indeed, in 1995, 32% of the same positions were held by childless women, with 91% of them working full-time. The costs of scaling back or stopping one's career when children are young were mentioned by the working mothers. As conveyed by a single mother of one:

> I have a bachelor's degree and I was out of the workforce for 2 years and I had to start at an entry-level job just to get back in. I'm still not satisfied with where I am. It has been 2 years. (WM)

Another working mother similarly expressed: "If there was a mechanism to get off the track and get back on . . . . I'm in the technical field. If I'm out, I'm done" (WM).

The ongoing increases in women's educational attainment raise countless questions concerning future employment trends and work/family balance. Moreover, as will be discussed later in the chapter, these trends also have distinct implications for a national system of child care and members of the child care workforce.

Others' Expectations and Family Obligations

Being in a committed relationship, having a family, and being a member of society were also mentioned by participants as playing a role in women's employment. As presented in Table 3.1, these factors were listed twice as the top reason for working and 21 times among the complete lists of the top three reasons. For example, several participants listed, "doing your share in marriage" (HB), "equality and contributions" (WM), and "equal to partner or anyone living with" (CC) as reasons for maternal employment. "Contribute to family" (HB) and "money to provide extras for family" (HB) were among reasons categorized as family obligations. One of the working mothers shared the sentiment: "Knowing you are supporting your family. These people can rely on you." Such comments recall the hard numbers about women's financial contributions to the household economy and also speak to the importance for many working mothers of providing for their families. Indeed, for employed mothers, embracing the role of provider has positive implications for family harmony and personal well-being (Helms-Erikson, Tanner, Crouter, & McHale, 2000).

Societal expectations for women's employment were mentioned at least once during each discussion. These are pressures from outside of oneself and one's family to either give to society or respond to social pressures to better oneself. For example, a working mother wrote, "contributing to society, having a purpose," as one of her top reasons why women work. A home-based provider similarly explained: "[It is] expected of you—if you are healthy and capable—you should be doing some type of work that contributes to our society." For some, social expectations can mean improving upon one's economic status; in the United States, this is still a valued pursuit. One participant commented, "How about social expectations? Meaning if all my friends work then I should probably work too or [even] my neighbors. I want to be equal or better than my neighbors" (WM).

In addition to fulfilling a spouse's or partner's expectations, financially supporting one's family, and meeting societal expectations, creating a comfortable existence for children and securing better opportunities for their future were also mentioned as a reason why women work.

Intergenerational Considerations

Any time that a focus group participant made explicit reference to bettering the next generation's lives, it was included in this category. Table 3.1 shows that this was listed five times as a top reason for women's employment and 12 times as one of the top three reasons. Participants remarked that many women (including themselves) work to improve their children's immediate material comfort ("from my experience, the better life for children sums up a lot of what I hear" [HB]), future opportunities ("to make sure their children can attend college" [HB]), and, more broadly, to improve children's lives beyond parents' own early lives ("a better life for their children than maybe they had" [HB]).

During the discussions, someone from each group put her current lifestyle into the context of being a role model for the next generation. Some women presented this in a positive light:

For us as women working in the workforce, to be able to show our children that you can make a life in the world. We will show our children that you can contribute to the family or show our children no matter what happens in life, you can accomplish things. (HB).

One child care center teacher who was the sole provider for her family expressed pride in explaining her employment by writing: "My girls see me work every day and still spend time with them and [they are] proud and they know they can do it." Some participants, however, were less confident about what they were modeling. As one working mother put it:

I struggle with that. I have a daughter and I think I want to encourage her just like my parents did to get a career and to get an education. But then I think, well, if things don't change, are you going to be right back in the same situation? Obviously I want to encourage her to do that, but that was kind of my issue. I have this opportunity, I've been trained. I've been given this gift of education from my parents and do I just get out of the workforce? What kind of model does that set for her? I hope that something changes in the next 20 years or so, so when she is in this position, she can have both. Which I think we have so much more than people did 20 years ago, but we are still not there yet.

Summary

Maternal workforce participation is far more complex than the rhetoric of choice versus necessity. Mothers' employment is embedded in numerous economic, personal, social, and intergenerational considerations. Many women and mothers do work because their household economy depends on them to do so. Employment brings a sense of self-fulfillment, connection to other social worlds, and the knowledge that financial independence is possible. For many women, employment allows them to use their education and to pursue a career. Meeting spousal and societal expectations and financially supporting one's family also underlie women's employment. Showing children what it means to be a worker and providing for children's need and wants, today and in the future, are also important reasons for employment. Nonetheless, participants' accounts about women and work were not uniformly rosy. Indeed, when the focus groups discussed the challenges and costs of employment, participants expressed considerable ambivalence and frustration about just how hard it is to perform this balancing act.

SOCIETAL AMBIVALENCE TOWARD
MATERNAL EMPLOYMENT AND CHILD CARE

Few adult roles are more aptly characterized in ambivalent terms than that of working mother (Hays, 1996). *Merriam-Webster* (2010) defines ambivalence as "a state of having simultaneous, conflicting feelings toward a person or thing." While the fulfilling aspects of employment were acknowledged by the focus group participants, the "downsides" were also discussed in great detail. Economic gain and self-fulfillment are not guaranteed by employment; indeed, not all women want to be working mothers ("I never really wanted to go out to work" [HB]), and even for those who do, the personal and familial costs can be pronounced. Extensive discussion took place about the downsides of being a working mother: missing out on children's milestones and school activities; longing for more time with babies ("I remember just hoping, just stay awake long enough. I'd say, 'Please stay awake so I can spend more than an hour and a half with you'" [WM]); sleep deprivation; and the challenges of enacting meaningful family routines ("you can't really do the meal thing" [CC]).

For some working mothers, ambivalence colors even the news of a pregnancy. Consider the following quote from a 39-year-old married nurse clinician, mother of two with one on the way:

> I feel like I'm in a complete vicious cycle. Because, I have a 9-year-old and when he was getting ready to go to kindergarten I had another baby. Now that [daughter] is going to start kindergarten in the fall, and oops, I'm pregnant. I wish I could say that I'm so thrilled about this because I want to be thrilled about it; but at the same time, I'm going, oh, my god. I've got to do this all over again. . . . I continually improve my career and go back to school and get the credentials behind my name so I can make more money. But why am I making more money? Because I've got to pay to put my kid in day care. I still have student loans because I had to put myself through college. And, I just keep thinking I don't know how financially I'm going to do it.

The issues raised—education, opportunity, money, child care—and the simultaneous, conflicting feelings and actions are not limited to working mothers. Scholars and other experts are also agonized by the cultural anxieties that accompany maternal employment and nonmaternal care (Hays, 1996). Indeed, the literature about maternal employment abounds with competing perspectives on the social acceptance of mothers with young children in the workforce. The situation is viewed by some as having "shifted dramatically" for working mothers (Uttal, 2002, p. 107), whereas others write that working mothers with young children still experience a lukewarm reception in the workplace (Edwards, 2001). Some research shows marked negative bias against mothers as employees before they are even interviewed or hired (Correll, Benard, & Paik, 2007)! Arendell's (2000) review of scholarship on mothering during the decade of the 1990s concluded, "Although most mothers are employed, social attitudes remain critical of women's work-related absences from their children" (p. 1199).

These contradictory perspectives on society's acceptance of maternal employment have allowed U.S. child care policy to be equally ambivalent. Although child care is an essential source of support for working mothers (and fathers!) and for some women represents an ideal vocation, our current system is terribly fragmented and provides uneven services depending in large part on household income. Furthermore, research on maternal employment and on child care, despite their uniquely interdependent nature, has proceeded on parallel tracks and thus the two subjects remain mostly separate fields of inquiry (Perry-Jenkins, Repetti, & Crouter, 2000). When that research dichotomy is combined with the prevailing societal belief that mothers are responsible for children's developmental outcomes, the net result is a rationale for avoiding creation of a national child care system and for devaluing nonmaternal caregiving activities and those who perform them (Drago, 2007).

Thus, while young women are encouraged to "have it all" (i.e., educational attainment, family, motherhood, earnings, self-fulfillment), those who decide to go for it find that their goals are pursued under virtually impossible conditions. As a 31-year-old working mother of one put it, "I don't understand how the society expects us to multiply and have children but then the whole government and everyone doesn't offer you any support." With no standard parental leave policies or national system of affordable, quality child care, it doesn't take long for a working mother with young children to feel ambivalent about "doing it all." Even in this age of "choice and opportunity," working mothers recognize that it is time to reframe the issue. A 35-year-old, center-based child care provider and married mother of two school-aged children expressed the point as follows:

> Women out in the workforce, society is adapting to that. It's also a negative because so much [is expected] out of women in general. We have the children. We take care of the children. We clean the house. We feed them. That's women's work. I think society looks at it that way still. If they looked at it a little differently maybe it wouldn't be as rough on us women that do work and do the things that we do.

Although the focus groups were not planned to elicit illustrations of societal ambivalence toward maternal employment and child care, numerous examples emerged from the participants' discussions. Their accounts addressed the women's

movement for gender equality, encounters with the media, and several characteristics of child care, including financing and economics, education requirements
for the workforce, and demand-side expectations.

The Women's Movement and Efforts for Gender Equality

The 1970s are viewed by some as the decisive decade for the rise of the two-worker
household (e.g., Edwards, 2001). Several cultural and economic conditions con-
verged, including changing ideas about women's roles, rising divorce rates, and
the stagnation of men's wages. Together, these circumstances created a feeling of
"economic uncertainty" that was serious enough to prompt families to adopt previously unfavorable arrangements. Families wanted to maintain, and better, their
economic standing, and to do so at a time when real wage rates for many men
were declining meant that more than one income was needed for the household.
Thus, rates of maternal employment, particularly for married women, "accelerated"
beyond the slow and steady growth of the 1950s and 1960s. In 1970, 29% of mothers with children younger than 6 years were employed; by 1980, this figure was
43% (Hofferth & Phillips, 1987). One 48-year-old married mother and long-term,
home-based child care provider shared this retrospective account of her and her
husband's decision-making processes:

> Twenty-five years ago, when I first started, I was a teacher, I became pregnant
> [and] I wanted to stay home with my children but I felt the expectation to
> bring in a salary. So at that point, I could have lived on my husband's salary,
> all those years ago, and I started Home Sweet Home Child Care and I just
> loved it. Anyway, today we couldn't. We need two incomes more, but my day
> care started because of a love of children but the biggest reason, because I
> could have chosen at that time to just stay home with my children, but that
> expectation . . . I thought, "I'm going to do my part." As a young woman of
> the late 1970s, that was just the way of thinking then. . . . That is what I said,
> and he said okay. Then we did it.

At the same time, women were being encouraged to strive for equality with
men, and this status was to be achieved primarily by joining the workforce. Several
focus group participants cited achieving equality with men as a perfectly acceptable reason for maternal employment; indeed, for one woman, not working is
associated with looking like a failure. "Some may feel like equals if they're in a
relationship with a man who works or [who] live with a man who works. Then
you want to be equals. . . . Even if it was like your mom, equal with your mom or
anybody. You don't want to look like a loser" (CC). As of 1990, 25% of married

women earned more than their spouses, regardless of men's employment status, and for married women with employed husbands, 19% earned more. By 2010, the percentages were 38% and 29%, respectively, showing an increase in the percentage of married female bread winners (USDL, BLS, 2011b).

Motherhood Wage Penalties. Not all focus group dialogue, however, embraced the opportunities afforded by the efforts of past generations. Just because a woman is employed is not a guarantee of workplace equality with men ("even though women are earning more and more, branching out into many fields, there is still a discrepancy in the income" [HB]). Other participants expressed skepticism about advances in gender equality and the ideals of the women's movement. "My friend says that women who were fighting for equality ruined it for us today. We are still not equal to men and all work paid or unpaid is not appreciated and acknowledged the same" (WM). Although the wage gap between women and men is currently about 83 cents for every dollar (USDL, BLS, 2012d), the wage gap between mothers and nonmothers receives much less attention. When women start having children, they experience a wage penalty that more than doubles when a second baby comes along (i.e., the "family penalty") (Waldfogel, 1997). What this means is that women with children earn lower wages than women without children.

Even more troubling is how mothers are perceived during the interview and hiring process. Because the social institutions of the "ideal mother" and the "ideal worker" (e.g., Drago, 2007) call for undivided attention and devotion, how could a woman raising children possibly be a good hire? Indeed, when holding all employment credentials equal in job application materials, female job applicants who were identified as mothers, when compared with nonmothers, were rated as less competent and committed to the job, and were permitted fewer late days, held to higher standards on a job entrance exam, and recommended to earn lower starting salaries (Correll et al., 2007). Similar comparisons of fathers and nonfathers actually showed a positive bias toward fathers for perceived level of job commitment and recommended base salary.

The Second Shift. At least once per focus group, the work that awaits employed mothers when they return home was mentioned. The "second shift," originally identified by Arlie Hochschild (1989) and revisited by Hays (1996), has not been fully resolved.

> The thing about women and work is that somehow, when women
> go to work either in or out of the home, they are often expected to
> do all of the housework, or a majority of the housework as well. It is
> two full-time jobs. (HB)

Nonetheless, several participants mentioned that their husbands are quite helpful with domestic chores and child-rearing activities.

From cooking meals to transporting children and managing children's out-of-home activities and appointments, husbands can play a major role in achieving an effective balance between the demands of work and family (e.g., "Who has a husband that cooks? He does all the cooking, just makes the afternoon and evening run so much better because he cooks" [WM]). Another working mother reported: "He does the dropping off of her [at child care] and the picking up and that type of thing. I do the stuff here in town" (WM). For home-based child care providers, whose jobs offer very little flexibility during work hours, supportive and helpful husbands are essential: "As my kids were growing up, my husband was the room parent, ran them to doctor's appointments, and now even as they are older he still helps with housework." Thus, although there is evidence that fathers are increasing their share of particular household duties, such as child care (U.S. Census Bureau, 2011), in most households, housework and child-rearing responsibilities still fall primarily on women (USDL, BLS, 2012a). When husband and partner contributions to domestic life are considered, the shortcomings of upholding the societal ideals that mothers are solely responsible for children's immediate and future well-being become even more apparent.

Isolation. Although one might think that this time of "choice and opportunity" encourages working mothers to draw support from one another, the isolating nature of "doing it all" was raised more than once. As both Michel (1999) and Crittenden (2001) have noted, working mothers are reluctant to speak out for themselves. As a working mother reported: "Many of my friends are working moms. We've not had extensive conversations about it. I think we're afraid to open up the can of worms. There is much judgment when it comes to this topic." Indeed, after the focus group concluded, another working mom remarked: "I feel relieved that there are other working mothers that feel and think the same things I do. . . . It makes me feel so [much] less alone!"

As discussed earlier, the rhetoric of choice purports that women don't choose to be mothers but they do choose to be mothers who work (Dillaway & Paré, 2008; Hays, 1996). Such messages dissuade working mothers from publicly exposing their exhaustion and possible disappointment with the "choices" they've made. There's a form of social pressure that tells them to keep these matters to themselves, squarely in the private realm. Society is thus safe to assume that women and mothers accept these conditions without question and, in fact, that they recognize their good fortune now that they can make such choices. Working mothers convince themselves to feel "lucky" when the reality is more along the lines of "bad options and difficult decisions" (Crittenden, 2001, p. 237). Perhaps this explains why support groups for different forms of motherhood are commonplace (e.g., moms of multiples, single moms by choice), but support groups for working mothers are not. Such opportunities might open the can of worms referred to above by a member of the WM group. Or perhaps working mothers would organize and begin to advocate on behalf of themselves and their families. As one home-based child care provider observed, "I think the workforce realizes if all women stayed home [for] a day, the entire country would shut down" (HB). Situating our societal ambivalence toward maternal employment in ideals about motherhood has deeply privatized what is in essence a public issue.

When bringing discussions about working mothers and nonmaternal care into the 21st century, the women's movement for gender equality inevitably comes up. While producing benefits for women in the workplace, the feminist movement has not produced comparable gains for mothers, employed and otherwise! (Crittenden, 2001). Indeed, contemporary ideologies about mothers, established during the 1950s, have withstood any external or internal pressures; employed mothers are still subject to societal discomfort about work-related separations from their children (Arendell, 2000). Finger-pointing at feminism, however, is unfair since the problem is that the women's movement achieved only half of its goals—large-scale integration of women into paid employment. It has proven much more difficult to enlist men into domestic work at home. Although there is evidence of positive change emerging in the household division of labor, men have been slow to take up their share of domestic and parenting duties.

The Media

The media is a powerful purveyor of cultural expectations and ideals and is a complex force in shaping contemporary societal norms about the good mother, maternal employment, and nonmaternal care. The media is a pressing issue, in part because of the sheer volume of content available and the ease with which the public can engage with it. Devices providing access to media of all forms literally fit in one's purse or pocket. For youth in particular, time spent per day with the media equals time spent in school (Rideout, Foehr, & Roberts, 2010). During every focus group discussion, participants mentioned encounters with the media. For instance, someone repeated matter-of-fact reporting about the benefits of employment outside of the home: "On the news it said it's good for people to work because they have a chance to communicate with other people instead of just children. It prevents them from Alzheimer's" (CC). Another participant mentioned a radio debate that captured her attention:

> I heard a report on NPR [National Public Radio] the other day on whether or not people would consider day care being like a public school, to have public day cares. . . . Working parents wouldn't have to pay so much money to have

day cares. Because the majority of the workforce is made up of both parents now, it was kind of a debate on the radio, it was very interesting. (WM)

Another reason why the media has such relevance for the subject at hand is that it tailors its messages to different audiences and, in the process, upholds different societal ideals for women's lives, depending on who is paying attention.

Judging. Some media encounters left participants feeling judged and unworthy. One working mom worried ". . . that we are all going to be Carol Brady and Betty Crocker and everybody else. If you can't, you are a failure." During each group, someone mentioned experiencing unrelenting pressure from media messages of "doing it all": "Everything in the media makes women feel like they have to accomplish everything. It's so overwhelming sometimes" (CC). The visual imagery embedded in media messages can be very powerful. In *The Second Shift,* Hochschild (1989) wrote about idealized images of working mothers. These women were portrayed as high-level, career-minded individuals who were always in forward motion and pushing ahead. Fashion and entertainment magazines and websites capitalize on these visual images by publishing photo spreads depicting supermodels and celebrities as "super-working-mom." When Hochschild showed her interviewees such photos, she was met with laughter and incredulity. Not much has changed; when working mothers talk about themselves, they don't convey glamorous images:

> I find that [when] my daughter goes to gymnastics . . . it is a split down the center of the gym. You can see who the working moms are and who the stay-at-home moms are. The working moms all look very exhausted. The stay-at-home moms . . . [did not complete thought]. I'm sure it's just a stereotype and they are thinking how lucky are you that you get to go to work.

Misleading. The media's unreliable depictions of mothers, whether employed or not, were also mentioned ("remember, Carol Brady was a stay-at-home mom who had Alice" [WM]). For working mothers, the messages that surround them, in magazines and on TV and the Internet, simply do not correspond to the day-to-day realities of balancing home, family, and work. As shared by one of the home-based child care providers:

> I've never believed in the existence of a supermom. To me it is an impossibility to do it all yourself. You look at the magazines, or the shows, E Entertainment: "Oh, she's a great mom, great actress." I'm going, excuse me, she has a hairdresser, she has a personal secretary, she has a nanny, she has a cook, she has this, she has that. It is not all her. She is not the superman or superwoman or supermom that she is being portrayed [as].

This observation highlights a strategy used to depict working mothers' achievement of supermom status—all on their own. One working mother shared her own internalization of these ideals:

> A lot of it has to do with . . . . the time when we grew up. For example, if I look at my mom, she did everything, so I just kind of internalize it. It is on me to do everything, to run the whole household, to say okay we are doing this. . . . I think as women, we just think, "If I don't do it, it's not going to get done."

What this memory does not convey is whether this woman's mother also worked outside of the home. Portraying employed mothers as single-handedly balancing work and family sends the message that working moms should be able to do it all by themselves. And the media, while hawking all forms of consumer goods that necessitate work, presents itself as upholding the ideals of "supermom" and, furthermore, as devaluing the contributions of the child care workforce. When considering the vital role of the child care workforce in supporting families—their own families and those of their clients—these storylines are particularly misleading.

Perpetuating. On Labor Day 2009, *The New York Times* ran a front-page story about the current-day struggles of four unemployed adults who had stopped looking for employment (Luo, 2009, pp. A1, A11). One of the interviewees, a woman, spoke about how becoming unemployed shifted her perspective on "what's important." "From a nonstop career to focus on the home," ran the subtitle, supporting the mother or worker conundrum attributed to employed mothers. In particular, she could now spend more time with her 5-year-old daughter, who, starting at 3 months of age, attended child care every day from 7 a.m. to 6 p.m.

> Mrs. Salinas had been a manager of corporate marketing and media relations at an oil and gas company in Houston, where she lives. She was so focused on her career, she said, that she never noticed her daughter had a lazy eye. Mrs. Salinas's mother mentioned something to her, but only after Mrs. Salinas was laid off did she realize that her daughter needed to see an ophthalmologist. (Luo, 2009, p. A11)

This account exemplifies how one woman's experiences can be portrayed to enable an entire nation to embrace the rhetoric of choice and its accompanying ambivalence toward maternal employment and nonmaternal care. As reported, it was only when the mother stopped working that she was able to attend to her child's needs. Is this to suggest that all children's needs will be attended to only when all mothers are not working outside of the home? Or that mothers who are not employed are the only good mothers? What about the individuals who staffed the child's 11-hour days in child care? There was no mention of them or their employment conditions on that Labor Day 2009, or of their vital role in sustaining the U.S. economy. This story is painfully representative of how the mainstream press reports on issues associated with maternal employment and work/family balance (Graff, 2007; Williams, Manvell, & Bornstein, 2006). The stories tend to focus on women who leave high-prestige careers with little attention to the realities of trying to re-enter the workforce at a similar level or to the potential consequences for a woman's personal financial security and the economic stability of her family.

The media's perpetuation of the either/or nature of employed mothers' lives is problematic for several reasons. From a purely practical perspective, it is far off-base from the reality of most working mothers' lives. But perhaps more important, these narratives present mothers' employment-related decisions as private matters, which gives the United States a free pass to avoid addressing its retrograde family policies (Graff, 2007; Williams et al., 2006).

Child Care

Nowhere is societal discomfort with maternal employment as palpable as in the current system of child care in the United States. Most aspects of the system, from policy to financing, and regulation to workforce development, are colored by contradiction. As one working mother said when addressing supports for women's employment: "Good-quality day care. It makes such a difference. Whether you feel like you are running home to rescue your baby or you feel like she's in good hands all day. It makes a huge difference." This simple remark about child care illustrates what working parents have learned to expect: Finding and keeping affordable, convenient, and "good-quality" child care is a roll of the dice. During the focus group discussions, several pathways emerged by which child care perpetuates societal ambivalence about maternal employment and for-pay nonmaternal care.

Money Matters

Paying for Child Care. Because U.S. child care is financed primarily through parent fees, on balance, economic motivation for employment is not a simple calculation of "gain" for working mothers. Employment also costs money, most notably for child care, and these expenses can have numerous consequences for families. Although little is known about how families balance child care costs against employment decisions, assessing the impact of child care fees on the household budget could result in a mother needing to stay home with her young children. One working mother remarked:

We talked about the financial need to go to work. But when you have your children, then you start thinking about the financial barriers. Are you going to make enough to pay for the day care? If you don't make enough to pay for the day care and the commuting and if you go and nurse [i.e., travel to breastfeed and possibly expend personal time off from work] . . . there are a lot of expenses that you incur for all the care. You have to weigh that out. Sometimes it is better to not have your income.

Furthermore, when household income stagnates or declines, and other costs of living increase (e.g., utilities, gasoline, food), families may need to find more affordable child care. Two center providers from different programs mentioned decreases in their enrollments: "We just had a dry spell. For a while, infant care is so hard to find. We used to get so full. It's like, where's the babies?" Infant care, particularly in center settings, is notoriously expensive to provide and to purchase. When parents have to modify their child care arrangements, a ripple effect can occur, with implications for children's adjustment to new settings, programs that rely on parent fees for day-to-day operations, and workers who rely on their wages.

Anticipated child care expenses may also play a role in family planning. The following example, from a 31-year-old married, working mother of one, illustrates how macro forces, in this case the lack of affordable child care for two-worker families, can creep into private decisions:

I got this new job and a promotion for more money so I told my husband, I said, maybe we can think about baby number 2. He said that shouldn't be a deciding factor, but it is if you have one in a day care and have another one. We would barely be covering both of them.

As the end of their child care consumer days draw near, parents speak with great joy and relief. Said one married, working mother of four: "We have been paying for day care for 13 years. My son started half-a-day preschool this school year and we like danced outside because we are only paying for a half a day of day care now." Although this enthusiasm suggests a positive turn in families' finances, it overlooks several broader issues concerning how child care is currently financed in the United States. Child care expenses can have significant implications for families' lifespan economic health and stability. At the very least, when parents are paying for child care, they are less able to save for a "rainy day" and for the future. Recall the quote from earlier in the chapter, when a focus group participant described how she currently combines child care payments for her children with repayment of her own college loans. When families begin planning for their children's future, they also need to consider the ever-increasing costs of attaining post–high school education and the potential for their child(ren) to accumulate student loan debt. The way that U.S. child care is currently financed is punitive to working families at just the time when they are establishing themselves in jobs and careers, working toward financial stability, and planning for their families' future.

Earning from Child Care. Devaluation of care work in the United States appears loud and clear in the meager wages earned by most members of the child care workforce. Said one child care center staff person, "Our wage is a disadvantage. Even though we need to be working that wage is barely enough to cover things." Among all occupations, child care workers have among the lowest hourly wages. In 2010, child care workers earned a median hourly wage of $9.28 compared with a median hourly wage of $16.27 for all other occupations (USDL, BLS, 2012c). With 48% of child care workers having a high school diploma or less, these low wages are not entirely surprising (GAO, 2012). However, the other 52% of child care workers have at least some college, a 4-year degree, or graduate education, and earn less than comparably educated women working in other occupations (Herzenberg et al., 2005).

The following exchange about the reality of child care wages took place during the child care center participants' discussion of "what supports maternal employment?" It began when one provider mentioned the importance of quality child care for working mothers' peace of mind:

CC(a): It's worth it to a mother to have a really good day care or school or something. You feel more at ease that you can do your job knowing your child is well cared for.

CC(b): You know what, though? I don't see why because they don't know how much we make. Once we had a price increase, one of the moms was asking me, "Where in the world is all this money going?" She figured out all the bills [i.e., child care program expenses] at home and she estimated that I made over $13 an hour, which is almost twice what I make. They think they're getting really good care. Really they're getting a lot of minimum wage employees who don't care. Even no matter what they're paying. That's sad. Parents should know that— how much we're making.

From a workforce development perspective, child care providers' low wages are inextricably linked to the lax, state-level expectations for preservice education and training prior to employment. Together, these structural factors perpetuate the devaluation of child care providers and impede movement toward professionalizing the work and improving the current system. There is an unstated belief that care work comes naturally to women (Folbre, 2001) and, when it involves caring for children, does not require any type of specialized training or education. As Chapter 4 discusses in detail, this highly gendered and idealized notion of caring for children is far from the reality of what decades of sound research indicates is necessary to provide quality services to young children and families.

Educational Requirements for Workers

Earlier in the chapter, women's gains in educational attainment were discussed as a motivating force for employment. Coincidentally, because most states do not require any formal education or preservice for workers in licensed facilities, child care, as a vocation, has not benefited from these trends. In fact, as more women have attained higher levels of education, careers in child care and early childhood education have become less attractive (i.e., lucrative) (Bellm & Whitebook, 2006), and the number of workers with a college education has steadily declined (Herzenberg et al., 2005). For women without post–high school education, however, who need gainful employment, child care is a viable source of work, with above-average anticipated job growth (USDL, BLS, 2012c). Thus, despite considerable agreement among child development experts that teachers and caregivers with specialized training and education are the primary link between program quality and children's experiences (Pianta et al., 2009; Vandell & Wolfe, 2000), state educational requirements for child care providers are minimal at best, making it easy to enter the vocation.

Coupled with ambiguity of purpose among policymakers and advocates, this disparity between best practices and reality sends contradictory messages to members of the child care workforce about what is required to succeed at the job. On the one hand, if child care is viewed as a mother replacement (i.e., day care, babysitting), then being educated to perform the job does not make sense. "Good mothers" do not require education or training; in fact, proponents of attachment parenting warn mothers to beware of "baby trainers" (Sears & Sears, 2001). Motherhood experience is a far better credential for the job (Ridgeway & Correll, 2004). Yet, when child care programs pay higher hourly wages to staff with formal education (and no "mom" credentials), staff with mother experience and no formal education beyond high school graduation can feel resentful. As related by a member of the child care center group:

I would say sometimes there's . . . you work at a place, everybody works good, they work hard. Sometimes there's somebody who may have the education, a degree to back them up, but they really have no clue what they're doing. They're totally inexperienced with kids. Then you have a person who has kids, who's had kids for years, but financially they don't get the same respect as the person who doesn't know what they're doing.

Although preservice and formal education are rarely mandated for center- and home-based child care providers, most states require center directors to have preservice, college credits, or a specialized credential (e.g., child development associate [CDA]) prior to employment (NCCITAC, 2011). Because of their own educational attainment, center directors may recognize the benefits of employing college-educated or credentialed staff. In comparison to child care workforce members with no formal education beyond high school, those with an associate's, bachelor's, or graduate degree are more likely to endorse specialized training and education as necessary for the job (Gable & Hansen, 2001). However, as illustrated by the following exchange, being the only staff member with a bachelor's degree can lead to higher expectations and feelings of exploitation, especially when remuneration is not offered in exchange for expertise:

> CC(a): I'm the only one at the center that has a bachelor's degree. I think there's more expectations on me. There's one other lady that's getting an associate's degree right now. I think there's so much more that they look to us for. Like we're trying to get accredited and our director's asking me to help mentor some of the other ladies that are trying to get degrees. They haven't even started it yet, but they want to get accredited in a year. They've got me to actually help them whenever they do start the process. It's going to be even more expectations on me.
> CC(b): Are they paying you more for that?
> CC(a): They haven't said anything about that.
> CC(c): You should tell 'em. For your knowledge you need to be paid.

Having a college education can also lead to holding higher expectations for one's *own* job performance. Knowing how to create a fun and engaging learning environment for young children and experiencing the benefits of doing so, especially in terms of child guidance and supervision, are not easy to set aside. Preparing lesson plans and locating new resources and materials take time, however, and most child care programs are not able to provide paid time outside of the classroom for planning.

> I do that a lot [i.e., take work home]. I take all my stuff home, like lesson plans. It's easier to do. I've got 20 kids and I only get an hour during their nap time to do lesson plans if I'm able to do that. We have kids up jumping around. I'm the only one in the room. It's just, I have to take it home. I

have to do stuff on weekends. The way that things are now you have to make stuff [on] your own. I just made all kinds of stuff over spring break for our classroom. I'm finding different stuff that's either free or cheap to go into our classroom because the director's not really providing what we need to do activities. (CC)

How long can an employee be expected to give unpaid time to a job that provides limited tangible return? For those who pursue child care as a vocation, the good feelings and satisfaction associated with the work play a big role in entering and staying in the field. But when workers feel little appreciation and receive limited tangible rewards for their efforts, burnout is common (Folbre, 2001) and explains the challenges associated with retaining workers and building a workforce. Indeed, most state QRIS systems do not include indicators reflecting intentional strategies to financially reward workers (e.g., wage enhancements, salary schedules) or to create a professional workplace (e.g., paid planning time) (Austin et al., 2011). As long as mothers are judged unfavorably for working, child care will not be viewed seriously and will not be considered a bona fide profession. It is care work after all, performed by women, and because of its tight linkages with maternal employment, is provided for women.

Most of the focus group discussion about education and workplace conditions occurred during the child care center group, perhaps because variation in educational attainment is more apparent when people work together. Nonetheless, home-based child care providers are also afflicted with low expectations for their educational credentials, but they have more control in some ways over their work environment because, all things considered, they own and operate small businesses. This arrangement, however, creates its own unique set of expectations, especially from the demand side of the market.

Demand-Side Expectations

Home-Based Providers: Pseudo Mothers. Women who work in their own (or others') homes as paid child care providers can be subject to market expectations that are akin to those prescribed by contemporary ideals of motherhood (Wrigley, 1995). A key principle underlying how some child care providers view themselves, especially those who operate home-based programs, is that care should be provided out of feelings of love rather than a need for money (e.g., Folbre, 2001). As one home-based provider related, "I don't look at my day care as my job because it is something fun that I love doing." Coincidentally, when the HB focus group discussion began, and participants were asked to freely state what comes to mind when they think about "women and work," this group, unlike the other two, referred mostly to their clients and not to themselves. However, by the end of the focus group, their perspective had shifted and the participants acknowledged themselves as women who work. As M. K. Nelson (1990) noted, "Women who transform caregiving into a paid activity located in the domestic domain both challenge and reconfirm traditional definitions of womanhood" (p. 5). Indeed, caring for love and caring for money can be compatible pursuits (Folbre, 2001).

Nonetheless, much like the good mother who is beholden to her children, home-based child care providers are beholden to others' work schedules, needs, and expectations (M. K. Nelson, 1990). As shown in Appendix C, the women in the home-based child care group worked far more than 40 hours per week. Such conditions of employment leave virtually no flexibility for running errands, getting a haircut, or scheduling health care appointments ("I'm still trying to get a mammogram since last summer. I'm going to get it this week, though" [HB]). When talking about the downsides of employment, one home-based provider mentioned her vocation specifically:

> If you don't have the resource of a good student or even a good backup it is difficult to make even a dentist's appointment, a doctor's appointment, to have any time to get out to do the things you have to do that are only open between 9:00 to 5:00. . . . You are a mom, you are a wife, you have all those things you have to accomplish; and I know for myself many days it is 11:30 before my day ends, and my day starts at 5:00 [a.m.].

Compared with the participants in the working mother group and the child care center group, who mostly worked 40-hour weeks, participants from the home-based child care provider group reported much less flexibility. "It is a little bit harder for us to take a day off, especially if you do it around the year. If I'm sick last minute, I have to call 10 people." And who do those 10 people have to call? Without a national system of child care that provides its workforce with employment benefits (e.g., paid sick and personal days) and supports (e.g., substitute pools), expectations, particularly for home-based providers, will remain along the lines of mother and household support.

Parent–Provider Conspiracies. Societal discomfort with maternal employment and nonmaternal care also infiltrates routine parent–provider interactions. Although it has long been recognized that active, two-way communication between child care programs and parents is a marker of quality (Frede, 1995), some parents and providers conspire to limit the content of child-related conversation. Indeed, some parents want to keep a lid on discussing their children's developmental accomplishments that appear for the first time in child care. One working mother talked about it this way:

I had to tell them, "If they do anything don't tell me. I don't want to know if they have done anything. Don't tell me that they rolled over or that they walked. Wait until I tell you, 'Oh, my gosh, he is walking.' And just go, 'Yeah.'"

Not sharing a child's accomplishments is seen as a desirable quality in nonmaternal caregivers (M. K. Nelson, 1990; Wrigley, 1995). As Wrigley (1995, p. 141) wrote about her sample of in-home, privately employed nannies: "The most sophisticated and thoughtful caregivers do not try to outshine their employers. They say that if they see a child take his first steps, for example, they remain silent. They let the parents see it for themselves." Treading on maternal turf with such disclosures is viewed as unsympathetic and insensitive; working moms already feel guilty enough about the time away from their children. Thus, working mothers are protected, and child care providers feel "sophisticated" (while earning paltry wages!). Although intended to counteract the feelings of dual powerlessness experienced by working mothers and child care providers (Uttal, 2002), this delicate process of avoidance leads nowhere. Mothers still feel guilty about working and being away from their children, and child care providers experience a discounted sense of purpose about their place in young children's lives. And U.S. ambivalence about maternal employment and nonmaternal care freely lives on.

CONCLUSIONS

Much has been written about the dance between working mothers, child care providers, and children. The script goes like this: Child care providers are told to keep their affection for another's child in check so as to not make a parent jealous, and working mothers are to keep an arm's-length distance between themselves and their child care provider so as to not appear insecure about working (M. K. Nelson, 1990; Uttal, 2002; Wrigley, 1995). Indeed, bringing this dance into the 21st century was the original goal for this chapter. It wasn't until I was conducting the focus groups and really listening to the participants that it became clear that framing the discussion in such terms was missing the point. The United States needs to reconsider the way that it conceptualizes maternal employment and child care, and find a common point of consensus that clarifies the function of child care and moves toward the more realistic (and helpful!) goal of supporting parents and families.

In M. K. Nelson's (1990, p. 185) study, the home-based child care providers that she categorized as "professional" viewed their role in children's lives as teachers and as something different from an "attachment figure." They recognized that "mother means something different." As described in Chapter 2, when the college students were explaining their hypothetical child care preferences, the sentiment "mother substitute" rarely appeared. For the most part, our future child care consumers wanted age-appropriate care and learning opportunities for their imagined children. Good child care reflects a form of "educare," the term coined and put into practice by Bettye Caldwell (1990) to describe the ideal pairing of early care and education. Indeed, when child care works for a family, it is one of the unexpected, and positive, surprises of working outside of the home. As shared by a member of the working mother focus group:

> Something that I got that I never expected from having to go to day care was an education from my infant teacher, priceless. I learned things from her that I didn't think . . . I'm an intelligent person and I'm having a baby, but it is like, What is that? Where did that come from? And how do I handle that or take care of that? The expectations and the things that infants can do and toddlers can do that I would never have [had my child do] had I stayed at home. So I think it was an advantage for the child to be able to learn at an advanced rate when I would have probably cuddled him and spoiled him even more. So I learned way more than I think I ever would have if I had stayed at home. Sure you learn from *Sesame Street* and you learn from all these things too, but the education that I got from the teachers at the day care was absolutely priceless. Being in a workforce with other moms, you can share those things. "What do I do in this situation? How do I handle this?" Those are some positives you get from having the interaction rather than being home all the time.

If the United States could move toward a system, or a state, of child care with a professionalized workforce, society's concerns about other "maternal" and "non-maternal" figures in children's lives might be alleviated and child care providers' vital work and contributions to society could be taken seriously. Both groups—working mothers and child care providers—may well experience greater self-fulfillment and reward from their "worker" roles and lead more balanced lives.

CHAPTER 4

How Precious Are the Early Years?

The Quest for Child Outcomes

The relationship between child care–related research and U.S. policy traditions about nonparental care is somewhat disjointed. Programs associated with compensatory education emerged from studies showing that early development is not fixed and that well-planned, high-quality interventions hold promise for particular groups of children. Research on child care to support parental, primarily mothers', employment has followed a far windier and more emotionally charged path, as briefly mentioned in Chapter 3. In these studies, the pendulum has swung wildly to both dispute and confirm day care's "badness" for children. Both bodies of research, however, have been ultimately concerned with the immediate and long-term well-being of children who participate in these different forms of nonparental care. More recently, the nation's increasing reliance on learning standards, quality benchmarks for programs, and calls for accountability requires public investments in child care and early education to be evaluated. Indeed, current system-building initiatives are being driven by efforts to improve school readiness and to reduce the achievement gap. Although these are noble goals for the nation's children, they are somewhat unrealistic because one tradition of nonparental care is far better positioned than the other for this particular burden of proof.

A 2001 report from the Board on Children, Youth, and Families (National Research Council & Institute of Medicine [NRC & IOM], 2001) presents the challenge that persists to this day. How best to evaluate current system performance? This is a fundamental question for justifying the use of public funds for child care. Some phrase it as the "so what?" question. What difference does it make if a child attends South Side Head Start, End of the Rainbow Child Development Center, or Bright Beginnings Day Care Inc.? In the 2001 report, two approaches to performance measurement were discussed and debated: (1) assess child outcomes, and (2) monitor the inputs associated with quality services. These strategies, while not mutually exclusive, are motivated by fundamentally different goals.

Assessment of child outcomes is grounded in the belief that causal relations exist between program participation and child development outcomes. Monitoring and continually improving the elements needed to produce quality programs are supported by evidence that better child outcomes are more likely with a particular combination of quality-related factors. Both approaches have implications for the allocation of funds. For example, if no measurable improvements are evident in children's school readiness, child care and early education programs that receive public funds could suffer funding cuts. Conversely, tracking quality inputs could result in enhanced resources to low-quality programs for improvement efforts and/or maintenance funds to high-quality programs to be utilized for discretionary purposes. Reaching consensus on how (and why) to monitor and evaluate system quality and performance is fundamental to a more coherent vision for U.S. child care (Zaslow, Tout, & Halle, 2011).

This chapter tells the story of what is known about both parts of the performance assessment debate. It begins with an overview of the scientific approaches used to produce a certain kind of proof, or guarantee, that public investments in programs for children and families have promise. Next, I critically review several decades of relevant research and advocacy efforts and argue that the recurring interest in evaluating child outcomes as an accountability tool overlooks more pressing needs. If the goal is to create a system of child care that supports families and fosters children's development, a stronger commitment is needed to better align the markers of quality across sectors.

BACKGROUND: WAYS OF KNOWING

Different epistemological traditions brought about the evolution of research on nonparental care and child development. How do we know what outcomes can be expected from children's child care experiences? What is necessary to produce quality child care services? Although it is natural to interpret results from studies of child care as applying to all children, from all families, who attend any form of child care, not all research is designed with such goals of generalizability in mind (e.g., McCall, 1977). For example, some investigations are motivated by questions of *what is possible* under theoretically driven, highly controlled conditions. These studies use experimental designs that randomly assign individuals to treatment or control groups. Participants are matched on important background characteristics and undergo pre- and post-intervention assessments. The goal of these designs is to isolate the treatment effect (such as Head Start or prekindergarten participation) on outcomes, while holding constant all other possible sources of influence. Although their results are generalizable only to the conditions under which they were obtained, these designs can ascertain causal relationships.

Other methods of inquiry, especially those from developmental science (McCall, 1977), are intended to describe and evaluate *what is*. These studies investigate phenomena at a single moment, or over time, as they occur and unfold naturalistically, and their results are more generalizable to the broader population. Findings from naturalistic studies typically estimate associations and probabilities between and among variables under study. This kind of research generates knowledge about complex phenomena, such as child care quality, parent employment, and child development. For example:

- What characteristics are associated with differences in program quality?
- What processes link program quality with measures of child functioning?
- How are household factors related to children's child care arrangements?

A chronic challenge to these research designs is identifying and measuring all of the relevant and naturally occurring factors that could possibly explain significant associations that are discovered.

With the advent of more complex statistical models, a body of quasi-experimental research is emerging. These studies manipulate naturalistic, descriptive data to simulate randomized controlled experiments so that discrete conditions can be evaluated. For example, evaluations of child outcomes associated with publicly funded prekindergarten have become more prevalent during the first decade of the 21st century, due in part to state investments and trends in federal education policy (e.g., Magnuson, Ruhm, & Waldfogel, 2007; Wong, Cook, Barnett, & Jung, 2008). The value of such approaches is that they come closer to determining causality than naturalistic research, but they are less informative concerning how positive effects are produced. Furthermore, by extensively controlling for child and family background factors, such as household income or parent mental health, they create artificial situations that do not exist in nature (Newcombe, 2003). Despite their sophistication and best intentions, these studies oversimplify what are in reality highly complicated, multivariate phenomena, such as those encapsulated within Bronfenbrenner's (1986) ecological framework.

Since the 1970s, a vast amount of child care research has been conducted. However, because of the inherent shortcomings in both experimental and naturalistic approaches, translating the resultant knowledge about families, children, and child care into a coherent system has been stymied. Indeed, the real challenge in applying this research to policy is mostly a matter of ideology. Said differently, facts are hard to come by and decisions become a matter of what is believed to be right. Consequently, child care and early education policy is akin to a leap of faith—albeit an evidence-based leap—based on what is believed best for children, for families, and for society overall. Because current quality initiatives and assessments are entangled with mandates to increase school readiness, reduce the achievement gap, and enhance academic outcomes, many system-building efforts are centered on these goals. This chapter argues that if such goals are to be met, both traditions of U.S. policy for child care need careful attention to better align quality indicators. Only then will a spotlight on child outcomes be sensible.

NONMATERNAL CARE AND CHILD DEVELOPMENT

Research about nonmaternal care and child development is as diverse as the policies that underlie our fragmented system. The review that follows discusses the studies that are often cited in contemporary policy discussions. These studies are exemplars of the epistemological traditions discussed above. In all instances, each one is theoretically intriguing and highly realistic about the fundamental nature of human development. How their findings translate to wise and inclusive policy decisions is the thorny point.

Early Origins: What Is Possible?

During the 1960s and early 1970s, several studies were conducted to determine whether experimental interventions could alter the developmental trajectory of children born into poverty. These efforts were pursued not because of concerns about the effects of maternal employment and nonmaternal care on children's development, but rather because of interest in the malleability of early development. Was a child's developmental potential fixed at birth or could it be manipulated, and presumably improved, with carefully planned and highly controlled interventions?

Prominent Intervention Studies. The HighScope/Perry Preschool Project (1962–1967) sought to prevent at-risk children's future problems with school (Schweinhart, 2010) and to halt the intergenerational transmission of poverty. The intervention was conducted with 123 African American 3- and 4-year-olds who exhibited "low intellectual performance," had parents with low levels of education, and lived in poverty. Children were matched on relevant demographic characteristics and randomly assigned to the intervention or to the no-program control group. For 30 weeks, children in the intervention group attended 2.5 hours of daily center-based preschool and had a weekly 90-minute home visit. Four bachelor's-degreed teachers implemented the HighScope curriculum with groups of 20 to 25 children. Select child outcomes were attributed to preschool participation, including higher IQ at kindergarten entry, better academic achievement across the school years, and greater likelihood of high school graduation than children from the control group.

The Carolina Abecedarian Project, conducted during the 1970s, was designed to "prevent progressive developmental retardation among children born into poverty" (Campbell & Ramey, 2010, p. 76). Participants included 112 children (98% African American; 24% from two-parent households) who were born to poor, young mothers who had completed on average 10 years of schooling. Children were randomly assigned to the experimental or the control group. The primarily education-oriented intervention started at approximately 4 months of age and continued until formal schooling began. The program was delivered full-day and full-year by college-educated staff. Health care professionals were also on-site. Both groups of children received infant formula until 15 months of age, and the control group also received disposable diapers until children were toilet trained. The results were impressive. Compared with children in the control group, the children from the intervention group scored higher on IQ, reading, and math until age 15 years. Furthermore, at age 24, intervention group members had attained higher levels of education and were pursuing more skilled vocations.

Chicago Child–Parent Centers. The Chicago Child–Parent Centers (CPC) began in 1967 with federal Title I education funding and are still in operation today. The CPC combines an educational, school-readiness focus with complementary services to strengthen school–family relationships (Reynolds, Temple, & Ou, 2010). Families eligible for the CPC have low incomes and live in school districts with high concentrations of disadvantaged students. The program is initiated with half-day preschool for 3- and 4-year-olds, followed by part- or full-day kindergarten. Some programming for grades 1 to 3 and over the summer is available. During preschool and kindergarten, children are in groups of 17 with two bachelor's-degreed teachers. Ancillary, on-site staff include lead teachers, principals, parent-resource teachers, school-community representatives, and nurses. A rigorous, quasi-experimental evaluation was begun between 1983 and 1985 and assessed CPC families and matched control families not attending the program. Long-term outcomes from age 24 indicate that CPC participation was associated with higher rates of high school graduation and occupational attainment; lower rates of criminal behavior, such as felony arrests and incarceration; and fewer out-of-home placements via the child welfare system (Reynolds, Temple, Ou, Arteaga, & White, 2011).

Utilization of Findings. These studies have produced valuable knowledge about what is possible under conditions of exceptionally high-quality, no-fee early childhood intervention programs for children at risk for problematic academic and social trajectories. As short-term findings were released, they informed larger-scale efforts, such as Head Start. Moreover, they laid the foundation for current policy focused on compensatory education and the interest in child outcomes. Indeed, these findings continue to influence prominent economists who are committed to cost-effective strategies for human capital formation (Heckman, 2011; Rolnick & Grunewald, 2011).

Scaling Up "What Is Possible": Head Start

Head Start began in 1965 as part of President Lyndon Johnson's War on Poverty. It was designed to be a two-generation family support program. For children, Head Start's goals were to provide compensatory education and to improve children's well-being in all areas of development, including nutrition and health. Parents were included in the children's program and also had access to social services, parenting education, and support with personal educational goals and learning English as a second language. Although Head Start has experienced "pendulum-like shifts in philosophy" over the years (Resnick, 2010, p. 123), its mission to give disadvantaged children a boost early in life has not wavered. Head Start's federal performance standards, first published in 1974 (Advisory Committee on Head Start Research and Evaluation, 2012), position it as a national laboratory in which to implement and evaluate new policies and practices. There is no other publically funded early childhood program like it.

Evaluations of Head Start's impact on children's development have produced mixed results (Resnick, 2010). Begun in 1997, the Family and Child Experiences Survey (FACES) was the first national, longitudinal evaluation of Head Start and included a large, representative sample of programs, classrooms, and children. Although it was a naturalistic study, certain features of the research permitted the results, especially for child outcomes, to be compared with population norms on standardized assessments. This was important for estimating Head Start's role in narrowing the achievement gap. Select findings indicated that over the course of a year in Head Start, children showed gains in vocabulary, early math and writing, and letter and word identification. When compared with population norms, however, children who attended Head Start were still lagging behind their more advantaged peers. Upon children's transition from Head Start into kindergarten, family factors, especially parent educational attainment, proved to be stronger predictors of children's academic skills than did measures of previous experience in Head Start classrooms.

The Head Start Impact Study (HSIS), conducted between 2002 and 2006, implemented higher standards of experimental control (Resnick, 2010). Head Start–eligible 3- and 4-year-olds were randomly assigned to participate or not participate in Head Start. The goal here was to compare Head Start–eligible children who attended Head Start with Head Start–eligible children who experienced other forms of care, including exclusive parent care, community-based child care, or public school preschool. After 1 year, the Head Start group scored higher on measures of literacy, other pre-academic skills, and receptive language when compared with the Head Start–eligible control group. Head Start effects on social-emotional development were limited to those children who attended when they were 3 years old, and included fewer behavior problems and lower levels of hyperactivity. The two groups were followed into kindergarten and 1st grade; by the end of 1st grade, any beneficial effects of Head Start participation had faded away. In other words, the two groups were scoring similarly.

An enormous challenge to conducting evaluation studies such as the HSIS concerns identifying an appropriate control group. Against what "control condition" are Head Start effects to be compared? Indeed, it is quite likely that the HSIS control group, especially the 4-year-olds, attended child care and preschool programs that rivaled the quality available at Head Start (Resnick, 2010)! Such realities of children's child care and early education participation make it a challenge to isolate discrete treatment effects. Furthermore, they indicate that a focus on child outcomes in the current fragmented system of U.S. child care may not yield reliable findings.

There are several lessons from the studies reviewed above. They show that exceptionally high-quality, compensatory preschool education programs can have beneficial effects on disadvantaged children's developmental trajectories. As the Head Start evaluations reveal, however, scaling up such interventions means that some control is bound to be lost when trying to isolate program effects. Furthermore, in light of changes to federal welfare policy during the 1990s, these programs' goals of education, socialization, and family strengthening may not be sufficiently aligned with low-income families' child care needs (e.g., GAO, 1997).

Maternal Employment, Child Care, and Children's Development: What Is?

Around the same time as the Perry Preschool Project and the Carolina Abecedarian study, other research was asking more explicit questions about the effects of maternal employment and day care on children's well-being. Unlike the highly controlled interventions, these studies assessed children's development under naturalistically occurring conditions. Over time, this line of research has evolved considerably. It began with simple comparisons of children who attended child care and those who did not, and moved to more nuanced investigations. These studies systematically disentangled characteristics of child care participation such as child care quality, type, and exposure. Furthermore, they delved into the parent and household factors that are associated with children's child care arrangements (Belsky, 1990).

Review of Pertinent Research. An influential review published in 1978 by Belsky and Steinberg summarized the results from a select group of well-designed, quasi-experimental studies that compared infants, toddlers, and preschoolers with and without nonmaternal care experiences. The authors' general conclusion was that there were no immediate effects, beneficial or detrimental, of day care on children's cognitive development or the mother–child affective bond. Several study-specific differences emerged in measures of social development, with children who attended child care exhibiting more aggressive and less cooperative behaviors. However, because of methodological limitations in study design, attributing those specific differences, or the general lack of differences, to maternal employment and/or to child care participation was beyond the scope of the studies reviewed.

The authors noted several shortcomings of the research reviewed (Belsky & Steinberg, 1978). For example, the studies were conducted primarily in high-quality university laboratories and assessed concurrent child behaviors or short-term child outcomes. Furthermore, they did not randomly assign children and families to different conditions or match children on key demographic features when making comparisons. Although the review concluded that there seemed to be no developmental consequences from attending child care, the authors cautioned that the research design limitations were concerning. Especially problematic was the uniformly high quality of the child care programs under study and the lack of attention to family characteristics that preceded child care enrollment. For example, measures of parenting, child-rearing beliefs, and household income were not examined. Recall from Chapter 2 that children's child care arrangements are meaningfully associated with demographic characteristics of their families.

Is Day Care Bad for Babies? During the 1980s, as the landscape of maternal employment changed notably to include more mothers with infants, a new child care research agenda took hold. The questions came, in part, from the ascendancy of attachment theory (Bowlby, 1969) in developmental research and the growing acceptance of the "strange situation" (Ainsworth, Blehar, Waters, & Wall, 1978). The strange situation is a highly original laboratory procedure that measures variation in the nature of the mother–infant bond. It was devised with basic tenets of evolutionary theory and child development at its core. Infants are exposed to incremental levels of stress brought about by a careful sequence of mother and/or female stranger entrances, exits, and re-entrances. How infants respond, particularly to the reappearance of the mother at a period of potentially heightened stress, is key to assigning attachment classifications. Because of theoretical concern with repeated mother–infant separations due to maternal employment, nonmaternal care was being cast as a causal factor in the development of insecure mother–infant attachment relationships. Indeed, it was reported that infants who experienced regular nonmaternal care, in comparison with those who did not, were at elevated risk for insecure attachment relationships with their mothers (Barglow, Vaughn, & Molitor, 1987), and that when hours in child care exceeded 20 per week during the first year of life, risk for insecurity was similarly increased (Belsky & Rovine, 1988).

These findings fit squarely with cultural conceptualizations of the good (and the bad!) mother and made their way into the public consciousness (e.g., Wallis, 1987). Combined with well-publicized hysteria about child abuse at the hands of nonparental caregivers (Rabinowitz, 1990), including the McMartin Preschool abuse trial in Southern California, social anxiety about maternal employment and day care was heightened. That the child care research was beset with conceptual and design problems did not seem to matter. For example, neither Barglow et al (1987) nor Belsky and Rovine (1988) evaluated the quality of nonmaternal care. Not surprisingly, this research and media involvement reignited opinion-driven controversies from the 1950s when working mothers were blamed for their children's poor emotional health (Pope, 1955). Furthermore, a new angle on the child outcomes question was introduced. It was okay for some, but not all, children to be separated from their mothers for compensatory education or because of social welfare program mandates. This class-based stratification of children further complicated child care policy alignment.

Coincidentally, other research was under way to explore variations in child care quality and to determine family factors associated with selection into different types of care. The quality-oriented research, which will be discussed shortly, sought to identify the characteristics that distinguished different levels of quality. However, to once and for all answer the question, "Is day care bad for babies?," it became clear that a different empirical strategy was needed. Because of obvious ethical issues associated with randomly assigning families and children to differing levels of quality, causality could never be fully ascribed. Nonetheless, a rigorous, naturalistic, longitudinal study with a sample recruited from different parts of the country would be a start. Such a research design would allow for estimating family and child care effects on child outcomes and would bring the nation closer to an answer.

A National Study of Parenting, Child Care, and Child Development

In 1989, the National Institute of Child Health and Human Development (NICHD) awarded a cooperative agreement to a consortium of researchers from universities across the nation (for more information, visit www.nichd.nih.gov/research/supported/Pages/seccyd.aspx). The group undertook the Study of Early Child Care (SECC), which was designed as a large-scale prospective study of how child care type, amount, and quality, in combination with family factors, were linked with children's early development. During 1991, a sample of 1,364 mothers and their newborns were recruited into the project from ten sites across the country. At enrollment, the sample included about one quarter minority children, and one in ten women had not completed high school and 14% were single parents. Extensive data were gathered about children's lives and observations were conducted in the home and in child care and school settings. Parents, caregivers, and teachers were interviewed, and state-of-the-art assessments of child cognitive, language, and social-emotional development and measures of child health were administered. Children's child care experiences, defined as any nonmaternal care arrangement above 5 hours per week, were carefully chronicled. The study set out to answer two primary questions:

1. Does development differ for children with and without nonmaternal care experience?
2. How are child care type, amount, and quality associated with a) short- and b) long-term developmental outcomes? (NICHD ECCRN, 2006)

A major contribution of the NICHD SECC is its ecological perspective on children's development and equal attention to children's home and child care experiences. With this approach, the researchers were able to account for relationships between measures of parenting and child outcomes prior to estimating relationships between child care characteristics and child development. What follows is a mere brushstroke of the breadth and depth of analysis the study has afforded. At the time this chapter was in the final stages, 84 network and 155 named-author publications had been written from data gathered as part of the NICHD SECC.

Question 1: Group Differences. To evaluate the first question, children with and without child care experience were compared. Specifically, the research examined measures of children's cognitive and language development, social-emotional well-being, and peer relations at 15, 24, 36, and 54 months. With the exception of child care–attending children's better performance on the Bayley Scales of Mental Development at 24 months, no other significant differences were detected between the two groups. For the most part, after accounting for child and family demographic characteristics, the developmental outcomes of children in exclusive maternal care and children who attended child care were not significantly different (NICHD ECCRN, 2006). The same trend was also revealed in the quality of the mother–infant attachment relationship (NICHD ECCRN, 1997). No significant differences emerged in mother–child attachment security at 15 months between children who had child care experience and those who did not. Further, there were no differences in attachment classifications based on child care quality, age when child care began, hours spent in child care, or the number of changes in care arrangements. The security of mother–child attachment relationships was predicted primarily by measures of maternal behavior, such as sensitivity and responsiveness during semistructured play, independent of employment status and child care experiences.

Question 2a: Short-Term Follow-Ups. This research question called for an analytic approach that examined child care type, amount, and quality after first accounting for measures of parenting and household demographics (NICHD ECCRN, 2006). In all findings to be discussed, parenting and family demographic effects on child outcomes were statistically controlled. In other words, the unique contribution of child care characteristics on child development has been isolated. For example, above and beyond family factors, only nonmaternal care experiences in child care centers were significantly associated with child development outcomes, when compared with home-based relative and non–relative care arrangements (NICHD ECCRN, 2002b). Similarly, as the hours that children spent in any form of child care increased, independent of quality, so too did caregiver ratings of child behavior problems at 36 and 54 months, and conflict with the caregiver and negativity toward peers at 54 months (NICHD ECCRN, 2006). Thus, the research team addressed child care type and exposure with a variable that represented the proportion of time children spent in centers prior to kindergarten entry.

To assess child care quality, the NICHD SECC developed the Observational Record of the Caregiving Environment (ORCE), which evaluated caregivers' attitude, emotional expressions, and interactions with the study child. Observers made qualitative ratings and compiled behavior frequencies that reflected caregiver sensitivity, responsiveness, and age-appropriate efforts to foster child social and cognitive development (NICHD ECCRN, 2002b). After accounting for family characteristics, as child care quality improved, so too did child cognitive development, language, and school readiness at 24, 36, and 54 months. Several measures of children's social skills were also positively associated with child care quality. Children who experienced higher-quality care were rated as more socially skilled and less likely to have conflict with caregivers. When child care type, hours, and quality were examined concurrently, at school entry (54 months), higher-quality care and more hours in centers were associated with better cognitive, language, and memory skills, and more skilled peer interactions during free play (NICHD ECCRN, 2006).

Question 2b: Long-Term Follow-Ups. After kindergarten entry, child assessments and teacher reports were gathered at 1st, 3rd, 5th, and 6th grades and at age 15 years (Belsky et al., 2007; Vandell et al., 2010). The assessments targeted children's reading, math, and vocabulary. Teachers rated children's social skills, peer relations, behavior problems, relationships with teachers, and classroom work habits. After accounting for numerous child and family factors, these outcomes were then predicted with child care type, hours, and quality. As reported by Belsky et al. (2007), child care quality at 54 months, regardless of type, predicted better child vocabulary at 5th grade. Additionally, the proportion of time that children spent in center care from birth through 54 months was associated with teacher reports of more child externalizing behaviors in sixth grade.

At age 15, the quality of children's early child care experiences, after accounting for parent and family effects, predicted a composite measure of child cognitive development (Vandell et al., 2010). Children who experienced higher-quality care before school entry performed better on assessments of vocabulary, tests of verbal analogies, reading, and math. Of note, the positive effects of quality were strongest for those youth who experienced moderately high- and high-quality child care. A modest relationship emerged between hours spent in child care centers (versus all other forms) and youth self-reports of problem behaviors. Specifically, as hours increased so too did youths' risky behaviors and impulsivity. This was the first time in the course of the study that child participants self-reported on measures of social-emotional development, and thus the results must be interpreted with caution. Indeed, no significant relationships were found between exposure to center care and teacher reports of youth problem behaviors, as previously reported by Belsky et al. (2007). Similar to the studies of short-term child outcomes, parent and household effects remained consistently significant and were statistically stronger than child care effects on measures of youth development.

In summary, the NICHD SECC provides a complete, naturalistic account of relationships among parenting, child care, and child development. Early findings allayed public concern about generalized, harmful effects of maternal employment and nonmaternal care. Furthermore, the short- and long-term follow-ups underscored the significance of quality caregiving early in life for academic abilities and social skills at school entry and later academic achievement. Perhaps the most notable contribution of the NICHD SECC is its ample evidence of the enduring role of parents and the home environment for children's ongoing development and well-being (Belsky et al., 2007; NICHD ECCRN, 2006; Vandell et al., 2010).

QUALITY IN CHILD CARE

During the 1970s and 1980s, as mothers' labor force participation continued to increase across all socioeconomic groups, reliable assessment of child care quality became more urgent. Early studies indicated that as long as child care was of "high quality," child development would not be compromised and, at especially high levels of quality, child outcomes could be enhanced. However, outside of experimental interventions and the university setting, questions were being asked about what was necessary to produce quality care. It was during this period that a body of knowledge began to form about dimensions of child care that, when combined, produced quality services for children and families (e.g., Ruopp et al., 1979).

Evaluation of Child Care Quality

The most common approach to evaluating child care quality combines measures of *structure* and *process*. Structural factors are objective and easily measured, and consequently are often included in state child care regulations. For example, adult-to-child ratio, maximum group size, and staff education and ongoing training requirements are typical structural considerations when assessing program quality.

Process is about how things happen. It is not as easy to reliably measure or to regulate. Process primarily addresses how adults get along with the infants, toddlers, and preschoolers in their care. Are they kind and do they pay attention to children? Are they able to manage and lead groups of children? Can they inspire children to learn about themselves, their peers, and the world around them? Additional process factors include how daily schedules are organized and implemented, how transitions are facilitated, and how routines such as diapering or toileting, meals and snacks, and nap time are managed. Other equally important processes that are linked with quality include center directors' leadership and management style (Jorde-Bloom & Sheerer, 1992) and active program–parent communication (Frede, 1995).

At the time (i.e., the late 1970s and early 1980s), although much was known about what quality child care looked like, little was known about the individual and program-level characteristics needed to produce it. The experimental interventions and government-funded programs were well-resourced and able to provide exceptional quality. Furthermore, parents did not have to pay for these programs. In the ever-growing private market of child care, where resources were constrained and parent fees essential, it was necessary to balance safety, quality, and affordability. Thus, knowing how to produce and measure quality in a vastly different context was a pressing matter.

Study Inclusion Criteria. To effectively present the research on the predictors and correlates of child care quality, I have made decisions about which studies to include. Discussing everything could be potentially counterproductive to making recommendations for a national system of child care. For example, research conducted in a single locale does not adequately account for state-to-state variation in child care regulations. Thus, the studies to be presented were selected because of their large, multistate samples. This strategy permits analysis of variation in structural features of child care quality, such as baseline child care licensing regulations across states. The studies included also implemented the same assessments of child care quality. The child care environment was evaluated with the original Early Childhood Environment Rating Scale (ECERS) (Harms & Clifford, 1980), Infant/Toddler Environment Rating Scale (ITERS) (Harms, Cryer, & Clifford, 1990), or the Family Day Care Rating Scale (FDCRS) (Harms, & Clifford, 1989). This suite of environmental rating scales observes and rates both structural and process indicators of program and classroom quality.

These tools are widely used for several reasons. They function as self-assessments for individual programs seeking to understand their strengths and areas needing improvement. Additionally, for research purposes, they yield sufficient variation in quality for meaningful comparisons and prediction. Each rating scale assesses multiple facets of program operation. The child care center scales comprise seven subscales: space and furnishings, personal care routines, language-reasoning (ECERS) or listening and talking (ITERS), activities, interaction, program structure, and parents and staff. The home-based environmental rating scale (FDCRS) includes subscales for space and furnishings, basic care, language and reasoning, learning activities, social development, and adult needs. For both centers and homes, each subscale comprises a set of observable items that can be examined separately or summed into an overall program quality score.

How caregivers interact with infants, toddlers, and preschoolers was measured with the Arnett Caregiver Interaction Scale (CIS) (Arnett, 1989). The CIS captures interpersonal qualities of the caregiving environment with measures of caregiver positive interaction, punitiveness, permissiveness, and detachment. Although the CIS is a valid and widely used tool, with more emphasis on improving school readiness and decreasing the achievement gap, it is common to see the CIS paired with other observational measures of adult behavior that target age-appropriate instruction and teaching (e.g., La Paro, Pianta, & Stuhlman, 2004). Together, the environment rating scales and the CIS capture meaningful variation in structural and process elements of child care quality.

The National Child Care Staffing Study. Knowing that child care quality originates primarily with caregivers gave rise to a large-scale study of the conditions associated with sensitive, responsive caregiving and overall program quality. The National Child Care Staffing Study (NCCSS) (Whitebook et al., 1989) assessed the role of center staff and the conditions of employment associated with quality care. It also examined relationships between child care market diversity and program quality. The investigators carefully sampled and recruited 1,309 teachers,

444 assistants, and 227 directors from nationally representative programs in five metropolitan areas. The participants were observed using the CIS and interviewed about their employment experiences, educational attainment, and child-related, specialized training. Additionally, the ECERS and the ITERS were implemented to evaluate the quality of the child care environment. The sample was followed over time, by telephone, in 1992 and again in 1997.

The NCCSS also called attention to a newly emerging crisis in the child care workforce. Every bit of evidence about the vital role of child care providers in producing quality services was needed to raise professionalism and bring new resources to the workforce. In 1988, when the NCCSS data were gathered, the average hourly wage for the child care teaching staff was $5.35, or approximately $9,363 annually for full-time employment. At the time, the poverty threshold for a family of three was $9,431 per year (Whitebook et al., 1989). Demographic data indicated that the NCCSS teaching staff and directors were, on average, better educated than the overall female civilian labor force and earning considerably less.

Findings described the multiple factors associated with the production of quality child care (Whitebook et al., 1989). Specifically, measures of the child care environment indicated that higher-quality centers paid better wages and provided better work environments. Higher-quality programs also employed more formally educated staff, experienced lower staff turnover, and implemented better adult-to-child ratios. Additionally, adult-to-child ratios and appropriate activities for children were meaningfully associated with caregiver behaviors. Specifically, as the quality of ratios and activities improved, so too did teacher sensitivity, while ratings of detachment and harshness diminished. Teachers who were more skilled caregivers were also better educated, with college degrees. For staff working with infants and toddlers, specialized, child-relevant, college-level training was similarly associated with better caregiving behaviors (Howes, Whitebook, & Phillips, 1992).

More positive adult–child interactions were also linked with higher wages, a better benefits package, and employment in programs that allocated more resources toward staff salaries. The highest-quality programs and caregivers were located in states with child care regulations for adult-to-child ratios, allowable group size, and provider training requirements that met the 1980 Federal Interagency Day Care Requirements. The FIDCR ratios and allowable group size appear in Table 4.1. The training requirements specify, "All caregivers without a nationally recognized child development credential regularly participate in specialized training" (Whitebook et al., 1989, p. 30). Thus, although caregivers are the key factor in quality, the NCCSS also shed light on how the work environment and employment conditions set the stage for quality caregiving.

Table 4.1. Child Care Centers: Adult-to-Child Ratios and Maximum Group Size (by Child Age)

Child Age	FIDCR (1980)[a]		State Child Care Licensing Regulations (1989)[b] States' Median		Best Practices: Caring for Our Children (2011)[c]		State Child Care Licensing Regulations (NARA, 2011)[d]					
							Ratios (n = 50 states)			Group Size (n = 40 states)		
	Ratios	Group Size	Ratios	Group Size	Ratios	Group Size	Most Common	Low	High	Most Common	Low	High
6 weeks	1:3	6	1:4	8	1:3	6	1:4 (33 states)	1:3 (3)	1:6 (4)	8 (20)	6 (1)	20 (1)
9 months	1:3	6	1:4	8	1:3	6	1:4 (32)	1:3 (3)	1:6 (5)	8 (20)	6 (1)	20 (1)
18 months	1:3	6	1:4	8	1:4	8	1:6 (14)	1:3 (1)	1:9 (3)	12 (12)	8 (8)	20 (2)
27 months	1:4	12	1:7	14	1:4	8	1:8 (10)	1:4 (4)	1:12 (2)	12/14 (8, 8)	8 (2)	22 (1)
3 years	1:9	18	1:10	20	1:7	14	1:10 (23)	1:7 (2)	1:15 (4)	20 (18)	14 (2)	30 (2)
4 years	1:9	18	1:12	20	1:8	16	1:10 (17)	1:8 (1)	1:20 (2)	20 (18)	20 (18)	36 (1)
5 years	1:9	18	n.a.	n.a.	1:8	16	1:15 (14)	1:9 (1)	1:25 (2)	30 (11)	20 (9)	40 (2)

a. Whitebook et al. (1989).
b. Phillips, Lande, & Goldberg (1990).
c. American Academy of Pediatrics, American Public Health Association, & National Resource Center for Health and Safety in Child Care and Early Education (2011) .
d. National Center on Child Care Quality Improvement (NCCCQI) & NARA (2011).

Because the follow-ups were conducted by phone, the findings focused on employment-related characteristics of the workforce. The first follow-up (Whitebook, Phillips, & Howes, 1992) indicated that staff wages remained far below those earned by other comparably educated workers and that health care benefits were rare, at best. Because of the study's longitudinal design, it was possible to estimate staff retention and turnover. By 1992, 70% of those interviewed in 1988 had left their original positions. Wages contributed significantly to these findings, with turnover rates highest among the lowest-paid workers. The second follow-up (Whitebook, Howes, & Phillips, 1998) reported still-dismal earnings among those who were interviewed. It also determined that about one-third of the participating child care programs employed individuals who were receiving Temporary Assistance to Needy Families, with the percentage of recipients ranging widely by program auspices. For instance, 80% of for-profit child care chains employed low-income individuals compared with 20% of independent, for-profit centers.

Staff retention also remained a significant problem, with 20% of programs reporting that at least half of their staff had left in the past 12 months. Over the course of the decade-long study, 14% of teachers were employed in the same program and 32% had been in the same center for 5 years or more. The NCCSS provided solid evidence for the multiple factors that could be used for performance assessment purposes as indicators of ongoing quality maintenance and improvement. Furthermore, it forecast a troublesome trend in the composition of the child care workforce by highlighting the chronic abysmal conditions of employment. The message was clear: Regardless of educational attainment, wages were low, career opportunities were limited, and very few incentives existed to remain in the field.

The Study of Children in Family Child Care and Relative Care. Centers were not the only setting for nonparental care. The National Child Care Survey showed that in 1990, 33% of children under age 5 with employed mothers were cared for in family child care homes and by relatives (Hofferth, Brayfield, Deich, & Holcomb, 1991). Thus, similar to the NCCSS, it was important to investigate quality in general and the factors associated with variations in quality among home-based child care programs. The Study of Family Child Care and Relative Care was conducted in North Carolina, Texas, and California during the early 1990s (Kontos et al., 1995). What distinguished this study was that a mix of 226 regulated, unregulated, and relative home-based providers participated. They were visited at home, observed for the CIS and the FDCRS, and completed a paper-and-pencil survey covering a range of personal, professional, and child-related topics.

The results indicated that higher-quality child care and more caregiver sensitivity were associated with several program-level and individual factors. For example, quality was significantly higher in regulated home programs than it was in unregulated or relative care arrangements. Additionally, higher levels of global program quality were associated with less caregiver harshness and detachment, and with more sensitivity as well as more years of formal schooling. Individuals who operated regulated home-based child care programs were more likely to have relevant training, to participate in professional activities and inservice training, and to be engaged in their chosen career. Among the 124 participants who charged fees for their services, those who were regulated charged higher fees and earned more money than unregulated providers and relatives.

Across-state comparisons revealed few meaningful differences in caregiver–child interactions and the global quality of the child care environment. Furthermore, despite variation in state regulations, the providers under study did not vary widely on key structural variables, such as adult-to-child ratios. For the purposes of system building and performance assessment, this study's contribution concerns the licensing status of home-based programs. That is, research suggests that when children attend licensed home child care programs, they have better experiences as compared with children attending unlicensed home programs or who are in the care of a relative.

The Cost, Quality, and Child Outcomes Study. Similar to the NCCSS (Whitebook et al., 1989) and Kontos et al. (1995), the Cost, Quality, and Child Outcomes Study (CQCO Team, 1995) investigated the person, program, and state-level factors associated with variation in child care quality. What made the CQCO unique was its careful attention to the economics of child care and the relationship between cost and quality. About 400 child care centers in regions of four states (CA, CO, CT, and NC) were recruited and intensively studied. The states were carefully selected to represent different child care regulatory regimes and demographic contexts. Although the project also repeatedly observed and assessed a large sample of children from the participating centers, those findings will not be discussed here.

For the CQCO, child care quality was represented by a single variable that summarized scores from the ECERS or the ITERS, and from measures of lead teacher behavior, including the CIS. The actual center quality index was computed by averaging the summary scores from two classrooms, with additional weighting based on center enrollment for different child ages. Results indicated that child care center quality was positively linked with adult-to-child ratios, staff educational attainment, and program administrator experience. Specifically, center quality scores were higher when ratios favored children; staff had more formal, child-related education; and center directors had more years in the field. Staff wages, educational attainment, and specialized training also distinguished levels of overall program quality in anticipated ways. Additionally, the strictness of state child care regulations was linked with overall quality. Fewer low-quality programs were found in states with stricter adult-to-child ratios and stronger staff educational requirements.

The CQCO reported several notable findings about the economics of child care and program quality. For example, even in programs that offered mediocre services, child care was costly to provide. Labor costs alone constituted about 70% of a program's operating budget. Furthermore, about 25% of estimated operational costs were met by donations and forgone wages. Recall that child care providers earn less than comparably educated female members of the labor force. These forgone wages are part of the hidden costs of child care. Similar hidden costs are covered by donations of space and materials, rental subsidies, and volunteer efforts. In the CQCO, about 72% of program revenue was generated by parent fees and the remaining 28% came from state, federal, and philanthropic sources. Whether these economic findings about cost and quality hold in today's child care market is not known. Nonetheless, the CQCO replicated several findings from the NCCSS (Whitebook et al., 1989) and Kontos et al. (1995)—specifically, the multiple factors required to produce quality child care, including the significance of ratios, staff education, and wages. The CQCO also highlighted the critical role played by center directors in creating quality.

In summary, these multistate studies effectively identified the numerous inputs needed to produce quality child care services. In particular, they illustrated the relationship between structural characteristics of child care (e.g., licensing status, adult-to-child ratios, provider preservice and ongoing training) and important processes of caregiver interaction style (e.g., sensitivity, harshness, detachment). Follow-up studies with the NICHD SECC data showed similar findings among favorable staff-to-child ratios, higher level of caregiver education, more sensitive caregiving, and concurrent measures of child social-emotional well-being and school readiness (NICHD ECCRN, 1999, 2002a). Furthermore, it was also determined that "good caregivers" alone are not enough for quality to be produced. Child care providers in center- and home-based programs need to earn livable wages and receive employment-related benefits that are commonly associated with other professions.

Pioneering Child Care Quality Improvement Strategies

Two primary approaches to improving child care quality emerged from the research reviewed above. First, due to the significant role of training and education in predicting the quality of care that children received, states were urged to strengthen their educational and professional development requirements and opportunities for child care providers. Additionally, because the research indicated that numerous structural and process factors were necessary to create quality, the second approach to quality improvement centered on multifaceted program-level quality rating systems (QRS).

Making a Career of It:
A Study of Career Development in Early Care and Education

In 1991, a groundbreaking study was conducted of states' regulations for individuals employed in family child care, child care centers, school-based child care and preschool programs, and before-/after-school care (Morgan et al., 1993). Data were carefully compiled about child care training rules and regulations, teacher certification, higher education opportunities for child care practitioners, state financing for child care training, and the type and amount of child care training offered. The study's findings indicated great need to improve state child care regulations, create professional development plans, and influence child care quality. For the broader purpose of system building, the focus here is on the nature and extent of exemptions from state child care licensure and requirements for child care provider preservice and ongoing training.

Exemptions. The study identified many categories of exemption from child care licensing and regulation for child care centers and family child care homes (Morgan et al., 1993). For example, of the 50 states plus Washington, DC, and New York City (which at the time had its own regulations) surveyed, 38 did not require home-based programs with "small numbers of children" to comply with licensing standards. States varied in their definition of "small numbers," which ranged anywhere from two to seven children. This meant that in a given state, until the threshold number of children was met, small family child care homes were exempt from state licensure and regulation. Furthermore, although all states licensed child care centers, states varied in which centers were exempt from licensure. For example, in 23 states, no standards were applied to part-day, private nursery schools. In seven states, child care centers that identified themselves as "educational" were also exempt from licensure, regardless of the programs' hours of operation. Child care programs operated by faith-based organizations were exempted in nine states.

These exemptions and thresholds are noteworthy for several reasons. The concern is that very little is known about what transpires in unregulated and license-exempt facilities. Although basic public health and fire safety inspections might occur, other structural indicators of baseline quality are not mandated by law. For example, individuals who work in license-exempt programs may not be required to meet any preservice or ongoing training requirements.

Preservice and Ongoing Training Requirements. A summary of the states, Washington, D.C., and New York City preservice and training regulations for workers in licensed facilities is presented in Table 4.2. What follows is a description of the requirements for center teachers and directors and family home child care providers (Morgan et al., 1993). In 1991, all states regulated child care center staff in licensed facilities and 42 states regulated licensed, home-based providers.

Table 4.2. State Workforce Regulations: Preservice (i.e., prior to employment) and Annual Ongoing Clock Hours of Training Requirements

	Making a Career of It[a] (as of 1991)			National Child Care Information and Technical Assistance Center (NCCITAC) Compilation of State Licensing Requirements[b] (as of 2011)		
	Preservice (ECE-related)	*Annual Ongoing Clock Hours of Training*	*Both Preservice and Ongoing Training*	*Preservice (ECE-related)*	*Annual Ongoing Clock Hours of Training*	*Both Preservice and Ongoing Training*
Child Care Centers						
Teachers (1991, *n* = 52; 2011, 51)	16 states	43 states *Requirements:* 1–12 hrs: 29 13–19 hrs: 7 ≥ 20 hrs: 7	12 states	16 states	48 states *Requirements:* 1–12 hrs: 21 13–19 hrs: 16 ≥ 20 hrs: 9	15 states
Directors (1991, *n* = 52; 2011, 51)	30 states (*n* = 10 states with Admin. Requirements)	31 states *Requirements:* 1–12 hrs: 20 13–19 hrs: 4 ≥ 20 hrs: 7	18 states	ECE = 40 states Admin = 14 states	Gen = 45 states Admin = 11 states *Requirements:* General 1–12 hrs: 16 13–19 hrs: 14 ≥ 20 hrs: 13 Other: 2	ECE/Gen = 36 states Admin = 3 states

(continued)

Table 4.2. (continued)

Provider	Making a Career of It[a] (as of 1991)			National Child Care Information and Technical Assistance Center (NCCITAC) Compilation of State Licensing Requirements[b] (as of 2011)		
Small Family Child Care Homes						
Provider	13 states (of 42 that regulate role)	19 states *Requirements:* 1–12 hrs: 17 13–19 hrs: 1 ≥ 20 hrs: 1	7 states	11 states (of 42 that regulate role)	39 states *Requirements:* 1–12 hrs: 30 13–19 hrs: 7 ≥ 20 hrs: 2	10 states

a. Morgan et al. (1993).
b. Retrieved from occ-archive.org/topic/licensing/staff-requirements.

Notes:

CT and MN require percentage of hours worked for ongoing training (1% teachers; 2% directors).

In this table, preservice specifies early childhood–related credentials, post–high school education, and relevant training.

As shown, other than a high school diploma, GED, or "experience," states reported minimal requirements for child care–related preservice and ongoing training. Some amount of relevant preservice prior to employment was required of center teachers in 16 states. For center directors, 30 states required relevant preservice and 10 states mandated preservice that focused specifically on the administrative role. Of the 42 states that regulated home-based programs, 13 required relevant preservice for licensed home-based providers. For all roles, required preservice took many forms, including completion of first aid/CPR training, early childhood clock hours of training, college credits, or a credential or college degree.

More common were state requirements for annual clock hours of training (i.e., time spent in training). Forty-three states required ongoing training for center teachers, and 31 for center directors; 19 states required ongoing training for home-based child care providers. Table 4.2 also lists the range of ongoing training hours mandated by states for center teachers, directors, and home-based providers. As part of their licensing rules, some states required these roles to have both preservice and ongoing training. Twelve states required both for center teachers, 18 states required the same of center directors, and seven states required relevant preservice and ongoing training for home-based providers. Although "orientation" was required in 27 states for center teachers and in 19 states for center directors, the linkages were unclear between workforce development and this form of one-time training.

Quality Control in Professional Development. A careful examination of how training requirements were conceptualized and delivered revealed numerous opportunities for improvement (Morgan et al., 1993). For example, training activities were frequently implemented with little quality control. States exercised limited oversight of trainer qualifications and training content. Furthermore, very few states incorporated behavioral competencies into their training requirements for workers. Additionally, most training was limited to entry-level workers and was not systematically linked to higher education. With such minimal preservice requirements, it makes sense that the bulk of training emphasized entry-level skills and knowledge. The discovery that most training did not accumulate to something more, like college credits, was especially concerning. It revealed how child care provider training requirements and provisions operated on a parallel track to higher education's teacher certification programs. That is, whereas access to employment in publicly funded preschool programs required teacher certification, employment in child care required next to nothing, thus reflecting U.S. society's longstanding devaluation of care work (Folbre, 2001).

States also reported how they financed these activities. The authors noted that the recently allocated federal Child Care Development Block Grant (CCDBG) monies were restricted in their use across all of the settings where child care took place. Overall, there were limited funding sources designated specifically to meet the ongoing and diverse training needs and professional development of the child care workforce. Similar to the "hidden costs" of child care services identified by the CQCO Team (1995), the authors concluded that the costs associated with these requirements were shouldered primarily by training entities and child care providers. The research that was under way about worker education and child care quality would soon provide compelling evidence to increase preservice requirements and improve professional development opportunities. Indeed, some states had already taken notice.

State-Level Initiatives. Morgan et al. (1993) also described a range of creative initiatives to improve professional development opportunities for members of the child care workforce. These "promising practices" included, for instance, state efforts to link provider educational progression and wage enhancements. Other entities offered specialized training content associated with diverse child care provider roles and introduced progressive levels of training (i.e., entry, advanced). To advance career development opportunities, some states established articulation agreements among 2- and 4-year degree-granting institutions and between community-based noncredit training and higher education. This particular strategy allowed for the substantive accumulation of ongoing training hours and had great potential for developing and improving professionalism and career development.

Making a Career of It (Morgan et al., 1993) also showed that most state workforce development systems were not designed or implemented to cultivate child care professionals or to encourage career advancement. These insights explained the "revolving door" of child care employment that was identified by the NCCSS (Whitebook et al., 1989) and viewed as a major contributor to the child care workforce crisis. Child care employment was easy to enter and easy to leave. Moreover, because of the limited incentives and rewards, it was hard to stay motivated for the job. Nonetheless, states were encouraged to implement multifaceted career development systems for their child care workforce.

NAEYC Conceptual Framework for
Early Childhood Professional Development

Shortly after the release of *Making a Career of It* (Morgan et al., 1993), the National Association for the Education of Young Children (NAEYC, 1993) adopted the Conceptual Framework for Early Childhood Professional Development. NAEYC's objective was to advance a professional and career development system that would meet the needs of *all* individuals who worked with children from birth through age 8, regardless of setting. It was a bold effort to bring coherence to what was an increasingly fragmented and diverse landscape of child care and early education programs.

Inclusive. NAEYC's framework was both idealistic and grounded in several realities of child care and early childhood education. It fully acknowledged the extraordinary diversity of the combined workforce and embraced everyone working in full-day child care centers and family child care homes, part-day nursery schools, Head Start, and the newly emerging public prekindergarten programs. At the time, each setting had its own rules and expectations concerning staff educational preparation and ongoing training. Federal law mandated a child development associate (CDA) credential for at least one teacher per Head Start classroom by 1994, whereas child care centers and family child care homes required minimal preparation to enter employment. Such distinctions were evidence of the deep-seated tension between child care and early education that had been in place for decades. NAEYC (1993), however, recognized that "the essential nature of the service varies little when done in an appropriate manner for an individual child" (p. 3).

Career Lattice. NAEYC proposed a career lattice that facilitated movement both horizontally (e.g., over time) and vertically (e.g., by role and level of responsibility). The goal here was a framework that could meet the professional development needs of a diverse workforce with numerous roles and expectations. Also advanced was the common core of knowledge and behavioral competencies for all workforce members. This was essential because what distinguishes a profession is that its members share a specialized body of knowledge and skill (Abbott, 1988). The core competencies touched on several key areas such as knowledge of child development, skills of observation and assessment, and ability to plan and implement age-appropriate activities that foster all areas of child development. Other critical areas included the ability to form positive relationships with children and families and understanding the role of family, society, and culture in children's development. In the ideal sense, the full set of competencies distinguished the provision of child care and early education services as a profession. In practical terms, they functioned as a valuable tool for states that were creating professional development systems and other institutions involved in formally preparing early childhood professionals.

NAEYC's position statement also acknowledged the larger problem of system financing: "NAEYC believes that parents and early childhood professionals have borne a disproportionate burden in the provision of early childhood programs" (1993, p. 9). Consequently, NAEYC proposed that all members of the workforce with comparable credentials, experience, and role responsibilities should earn comparable wages, regardless of program auspices or setting.

Quality Rating Systems

Quality Rating Systems were introduced in the late 1990s as a strategy to measure child care quality and to pursue ongoing quality improvement. They integrate multiple structural and process domains of the child care ecology into a single tool for quality assessment that yields an easily interpreted outcome. Unlike program accreditation (e.g., NAEYC), which is guided by national standards, QRS are state-specific and aligned with state child care regulations and policies. The first QRS, Oklahoma's Reaching for the Stars, is a four-level tiered quality system, where the lowest star rating signifies that a program meets minimum licensing standards, and the highest level indicates that a program meets minimum licensing standards plus additional state-specific quality criteria, and is nationally accredited (www.okdhs.org/programsandservices/cc/stars/).

QRS were conceptualized to have multiple functions (Mitchell, 2005). Within a given state, they can serve as a multilevel metric for program quality that can be applied across a range of child care settings. They yield valuable descriptive data about a state's child care market and its landscape of quality in different counties and regions. QRS also have great potential as policy tools. For instance, they can be used to target training and technical assistance in areas lacking in high-quality child care. Additionally, QRS can be linked with child care subsidies. Specifically, as child care programs achieve higher levels of quality, they become eligible for enhanced subsidy reimbursement rates. For low-income families, linking subsidy reimbursement rates with quality ratings could improve access to better services. As a supply-side intervention, this outcome ideally would benefit all families who utilize child care. QRS can also provide much-needed information about child care quality for parents. By the start of the 21st century, three states were implementing quality rating systems (Oklahoma, starting in 1998; New Mexico and North Carolina starting in 1999) as part of their state child care licensing process (Tout et al., 2010).

Child Care Quality Indicators in 2012

Fast forward to December 2012. How has research about the structural and process factors needed for quality informed child care policy and practice over the past 2 decades? Several topics will be discussed, including an update on state exemptions from licensure and thresholds for small family child care homes, regulations for adult-to-child ratios and group size, and requirements for child care relevent preservice and ongoing training.

Licensing Exemptions and Thresholds

The concerns with licensing exemptions and thresholds identified by Morgan et al. (1993) were recently reiterated by the National Association for Regulatory Administration (Payne, 2011). Similar to the 1993 report, NARA recommended that states work to reduce the number of categories for exemption. From a system-building perspective, increasing the number of center- and home-based child care programs that are required to meet minimum standards will by itself improve quality. Moreover, if the goal is to link program participation with child outcomes, it makes more sense to have as many children as possible attending programs about which something is known. Furthermore, for families who utilize child care subsidies, it could increase access to quality services. As of 2010–2011 (USDHHS, 2010), more than half of states permit child care subsidies to pay for care in unlicensed programs.

Child Care Centers. As of 2008 (NCCITAC & NARA, 2010), states continued to exempt certain categories of child care centers from licensure. The most common exemptions were for centers with "small numbers of children" in care ($n = 27$ states), facilities that operated part-day ($n = 24$ states; e.g., Head Start, nursery schools), public school–operated preschool programs ($n = 19$ states), and programs run by religious organizations ($n = 12$ states). Although some license-exempt programs comply with other standards or regulations, such as federal Head Start performance standards, other centers meet only basic public health regulations. For example, in Missouri, license-exempt child care centers, such as those operated by religious organizations, are inspected once a year for the purpose of evaluating fire safety and sanitation. However, as per the Missouri Department of Health (n.d.), license-exempt programs are not required to meet state licensing rules for adult-to-child ratios, staff training, or food and nutrition. Thus, per NARA's recommendation (Payne, 2011), states must strive to reduce the number of programs that they exempt from state licensure, especially for those "free-standing" programs that have no affiliation with a larger public entity.

Family Child Care Homes. As of 2011, six of the 50 states plus Washington, DC, did not regulate and license home-based child care programs (NCCCQI & NARA, 2011). Compared with Morgan et al. (1993), who reported that 10 states did not regulate home-based programs, this is a modest improvement. The threshold at which regulation and licensure of home-based programs begins still varies greatly among states. In 2008, thresholds ranged from one child (10 states) to six children (4 states), with the most common threshold set at four children (11 states) (NCCITAC & NARA, 2010). For these states, the maximum number of children allowed in a licensed small family child care home ranged from four children to

16 children. Although these figures indicate some progress in the regulation and licensure of home-based programs, room for improvement is still present.

Several other concerns with how home-based programs are regulated emerged in NARA's report (Payne, 2011). One addresses state regulations for the child-age composition in family child care homes. If a state allows up to 16 children in a licensed family child care home, are requirements in place that define the number of children allowed by age? These are important considerations for both child safety and general quality in the home-based child care setting. Another thorny issue for the regulation of these programs concerns "related" children. As of 2008, 39 of the 44 states that licensed family child care included the providers' own children, or children living in the home, without specifying child age, as part of the maximum group size (NCCICTAC & NARA, 2010). Payne (2011) recommended that family child care providers' own children under age 12 be officially counted. At the time, 11 states stipulated this regulation. In states that do not count related children in allowable group size, how is "related" defined? In Missouri, related is defined as "any of the following relationships by marriage, blood or adoption between the provider and the children in care: parent, grandparent, great-grandparent, brother, sister, stepparent, stepbrother, stepsister, uncle, aunt, niece, nephew or first cousin" (Missouri Department of Health, 1999, p. 3). With such inclusive definitions of "related," what is the upper limit of child group size in Missouri-licensed, home-based child care programs?

Ratios and Group Size

Table 4.1 presents adult-to-child ratios and group-size requirements from several sources. There are two sets of "best practices" shown, the first from the 1980 Federal Interagency Day Care Requirements (Whitebook et al., 1989) and the second from the *Caring for Our Children* (CFOC) recommendations (American Academy of Pediatrics et al., 2011). The table also includes state child care regulations from 1989 (Phillips et al., 1990) and from 2011 (NCCCQI & NARA, 2011).

The table shows several trends. For example, the 2011 CFOC recommendations for best practice are somewhat more favorable for adults and children than the 1980 FIDCR standards. In particular, the recommended group size for 27-month-olds and the ratios and group sizes for preschoolers are lower. Examination of actual state licensing regulations indicates considerable variability among states for both ratios and group sizes, especially for 2011. When the most common ratios are compared with those from 1989, the ratios have worsened for toddlers and improved for 4-year-olds. However, because Phillips et al. (1990) presented medians and not the full range, as appears in the 2011 data, it is difficult to say with certainty whether and where change has occurred.

Nonetheless, when the ratios and group sizes of 2011 are compared with the CFOC goals (American Academy of Pediatrics et al., 2011), some differences appear. Although there are minimal differences for infants, the gaps are greater for 18- and 27-month-olds, and not in the favor of adults or toddlers. For 3- to 5-year-olds, the gaps are notable only for 5-year-olds. The differences between best practices and regulations for adult-to-child ratios have considerable bearing on maximum group size. This is apparent for 18-month-olds. CFOC recommends ratios of 1 adult to 4 toddlers, with a maximum group of 8. Most common among states is a ratio of 1 adult to 6 toddlers, with a group size of 12. In light of the developmental capabilities and needs of toddlers, especially for adult help with communication, self-regulation, and fruitful peer interaction, these differences are worrisome.

Child Care Licensing Standards for Staff Preservice and Ongoing Training

State child care regulations for provider preservice and ongoing clock hours of training from 1991 (Morgan et al., 1993) and from 2011 (NCCITAC, 2011) appear in Table 4.2. For child care center teachers, the figures show no change in the number of states with preservice requirements relevant to child care. In 1991, 16 states required such professional preparation for teachers in licensed centers; in 2011, the number of states is the same. However, a modest increase is evident in the number of states requiring ongoing annual clock hours of training (from 43 states to 48 states) and the number of states requiring both preservice and ongoing training (from 12 states to 15 states).

For child care center directors, the number of states with early childhood–oriented preservice requirements increased from 30 states in 1991 to 40 states in 2011. Four additional states (from 10 to 14) also require administratively oriented preparation for directors. Furthermore, an increase is evident in the number of states requiring ongoing clock hours of training for directors, from 31 to 45, with a marked increase in the number that stipulate ongoing administrative training. These changes are highly favorable and reflect the specialized nature of the child care center administrator role in creating program quality (CQCO Team, 1995; Jorde-Bloom & Sheerer, 1992). For both center teachers and directors, the median number of ongoing training hours has increased from 12 to 15 (NCCCQI & NARA, 2011).

In 1991, of the 42 states that regulated the role of family child care home provider, 13 required preservice. By 2011, the number of states that required preservice decreased to 11, although more states were regulating the role. This decrease might be offset by the number of states requiring ongoing clock hours of training for this group. The table shows an increase, from 19 states to 39 states, for licensed home-based providers' ongoing training.

Despite the increase in preservice requirements for center directors and the growing number of states that require ongoing clock hours of training for all three roles, it is not clear how these changes are improving workforce development and child care quality. The requirements to enter the field are still minimal at best, and the continued reliance on "clock hours" of training suggests little movement toward credentials or college degrees. Despite research indicating that formal education and specialized training predict higher-quality care, teacher certification and child care provider training continue to run on parallel tracks. Consequently, in this category of quality indicators, many of the concerns raised by Morgan et al. (1993) still resonate.

Quality Improvement Activities in 2012

States are presently engaged in numerous activities focused on improving child care quality. These efforts reflect notable public investments in the workforce and considerable expansion of program-level quality assessment. This section describes current state professional development activities and provides an update on quality rating and improvement systems.

Professional Development Activities

Despite modest changes in requirements for preservice and ongoing training, state professional development activities have expanded considerably. These activities are funded in part by the minimum 4% quality set-aside from the federal Child Care Development Fund (CCDF) established in 1996. A recent GAO report (2012) described states' professional development activities between 2007 and 2010. Although only 37 of 51 states responded, those that did are home to upward of 87% of the child population ages 5 and younger. Over the 4-year period, all states provided inservice training, coaching, and mentoring to members of the child care workforce. These activities accounted for about 61% of the state and federal funds expended. Other common investments included teacher scholarships, financial aid, and wage supplements.

Additional strategies to develop and improve the workforce included train-the-trainer programs, state certification or credentialing programs, career counseling, efforts to establish articulation agreements, and apprenticeship programs. Twenty-seven states reported investments in state workforce registry systems. These systems gather data about members of the child care workforce and track their employment, educational attainment, ongoing training, and other demographic characteristics. Altogether, the states that reported spent about $1.4 billion of state and federal funds over the 4-year period to foster child care providers' competencies, establish infrastructure for these efforts, and enhance child care quality overall.

The most recent CCDF report of state and territory plans (USDHHS, 2010) similarly indicates that all states and territories are engaged in workforce professional development activities. Per earlier recommendations (Morgan et al., 1993; NAEYC, 1993), 96% of states are implementing career lattices, 75% are creating or supporting a professional development system, 75% are implementing quality control measures with training and training approval, and 46% are utilizing core knowledge standards. Although there is considerable state activity focused on the workforce, the ongoing reliance on informal "training" opportunities is problematic. Together with the still minimal state preservice requirements, it keeps the preparation of child care and early education professionals on separate tracks. If a coordinated system is to be built, this needs to be addressed.

Quality Rating and Improvement Systems

Quality rating systems, now commonly referred to as quality rating and improvement systems, have also experienced notable expansion. An in-depth review indicated that 26 states or local areas were in various stages of QRIS development or implementation in 2009 (Tout et al., 2010). Before the year 2000, three states (NC, NM, and OK) had mandatory QRIS in place; as of 2010, three QRIS were partially mandatory and the remaining 20 QRIS were voluntary. For example, Maine's partially mandatory QRIS requires programs that care for CCDF-subsidized children to participate. All QRIS yield multiple tiered ratings, typically ranging from three to five levels that reflect increasing levels of program quality.

Program Eligibility. QRIS developers set criteria for who is eligible to participate, and eligibility criteria vary across systems (Tout et al., 2010). All 26 QRIS are available to licensed child care centers, and 23 are open to licensed family child care homes. Additionally, in 24 QRIS, Head Start and Early Head Start programs are eligible, and three QRIS permit legally unlicensed and license-exempt family child care homes to participate. Prekindergarten programs are welcome in 18 QRIS. Twenty-four QRIS provide training to child care programs interested in participating, and all systems provide on-site technical assistance to support participation.

Assessment and Content Areas. QRIS standards are evaluated and scored using a combination of paper-and-pencil surveys and observational methods (Tout et al., 2010). Most systems use the ECERS, ITERS, or FDCRS, respectively (Harms & Clifford, 1989; Harms et al., 1990; Harms, Clifford, & Cryer, 1998), and some also observe caregiver–child interaction, using the CIS (Arnett, 1989) or the Classroom Assessment Scoring System (CLASS; La Paro et al., 2004). Not all systems require on-site observations; Vermont and New Hampshire allow programs to submit self-assessments. Although there is considerable variation across QRIS, most include quality standards, or indicators, associated with licensing history and compliance, measures of the physical environment and staff credentials, strategies for family engagement, program leadership and administration, and national accreditation (Tout et al., 2010). Less common standards include, for instance, use of curriculum, ongoing child assessment, meeting the needs of diverse peoples (cultural, linguistic, and children with special needs), and community involvement.

Links with State Child Care Licensing. Twenty-three QRIS require state licensure for participation, and in 16, licensed status is the first tier of quality (Tout et al., 2010). For home-based programs, 13 QRIS similarly set program licensure as the first tier of quality. Improvement above state licensing rules for adult-to-child ratios and group size, by child age, is included in 13 QRIS for centers and in six QRIS for home-based programs. Four QRIS endorse the adult-to-child ratios and group-size requirements of NAEYC.

The education, ongoing training, and professional experience indicators for center directors, teachers, and family child care providers are very complex (Tout et al., 2010). Because licensing regulations for these indicators vary by state, QRIS baselines sit at different levels. For the many forms of education that child care workers can attain, ranging from a high school diploma to a PhD, QRIS can define unique indicators for the quality ratings in question. For instance, it is possible that state X requires center directors to have a bachelor's degree for the middle tier of quality, whereas state Y includes the bachelor's degree for center directors at the highest-quality rating, and state Z does not include the bachelor's degree as an indicator for center directors at any level. The same idea applies to ongoing clock hours of training and professional experience. Consequently, although these workforce-related indicators are common in all QRIS, they are difficult to summarize or compare across systems.

Workplace Environment. Using documentation from Tout et al. (2010), Austin et al. (2011) conducted an in-depth review of the QRIS indicators associated with child care program staff. They determined that although all systems address staff education and training, and most provide financial incentives for ongoing professional development, there is much less attention to improving worker compensation, benefits, and conditions of the adult work environment. Only three QRIS, all of which are voluntary, include specific guidelines for worker salary and benefits, and 11 QRIS include a menu from which to select benefit options. Staff meetings, staff professional development plans, and personnel policies or program goals were far more common (21 QRIS) than features of the adult learning environment that required a financial investment. For instance, only five QRIS included paid professional development opportunities and/or paid planning time, and three systems specified collaborative features of program planning.

   Incentives to Participate. How do states and local areas encourage QRIS participation? There are several strategies, primarily involving financial rewards via different mechanisms (Tout et al., 2010). The most common approach is to link quality ratings with the child care subsidy system. Some systems maintain a flat reimbursement level that increases with quality, whereas others implement tiered reimbursements that consider program type, region of the state or county, and child age. For example, when calculating reimbursement rates, Kentucky considers the percentage of children using subsidies in a program's total enrollment. Other approaches to encourage enrollment in QRIS involve one-time bonuses at the time a rating is determined or annual payments to programs that are based on the quality rating and the percentage of subsidized or at-risk children enrolled. Incentives for staff, such as access to scholarships, wage supplements, and retention bonuses, are other strategies to encourage program involvement in QRIS.

   QRIS continue to have great potential as state-level policy tools for supply-side interventions to improve families' access to quality services. From a systems-building perspective, however, because each state or local area designs its own QRIS, evaluating the level of quality needed for enhanced child outcomes could be tricky. The highest level of quality in one QRIS is not necessarily the highest level of quality in another QRIS.

The Child Care Workforce in 2012

> *The irreducible core of the environment of early development is people.*
> —Ross Thompson in Zigler, Marsland, and Lord, 2009, p. 82

Because child care providers are the vital link between program characteristics and children's child care experiences, snapshots of the workforce often serve as proxies for the quality of child care nationwide. Recent reports suggest that we know less than ever about today's workforce (NRC & IOM, 2012; Rhodes & Huston, 2012). Although it comprises many individuals with widely varying roles and responsibilities (Ryan & Whitebook, 2012), the focus here is on those who work in licensed child care facilities and who have primary responsibility for children. It is important to recognize that the data systems intended to count and characterize the multimillion-member child care and early education workforce are also plagued by the fragmentation and diversity of our current system (NRC & IOM, 2012). For example, size estimates of the paid workforce do not adequately distinguish by sector. How many workers are employed in licensed and unlicensed centers and homes? Furthermore, issues of ambiguity of purpose are present in these data-gathering systems. Specifically, child care and education are separate "industries." Individuals can have child care worker occupations in the child day care services industry or the elementary or secondary school industry (e.g., before- and after-school care). And, for those members of the "care" workforce, current data systems do not distinguish the age of children in a worker's care (i.e., birth to 5 years versus school-aged children). Nonetheless, what follows is the most recent knowledge available, drawn from reputable, national-level data sources, including the U.S. Census and the U.S. Bureau of Labor Statistics.

Educational Attainment and Wages. A 2005 report confirmed what the National Child Care Staffing Study forecast (Whitebook et al., 1989) and many in the field suspected: The child care workforce is not replacing itself with equally educated, career-committed workers (Herzenberg et al., 2005). With data from the U.S. Census Bureau's Current Population Survey, a bleak picture was painted of child care center teachers' and directors' educational attainment and wages from 1979 to 2004. Over time, the educational credentials of the center-based workforce declined, with fewer college-educated workers and more with a high school degree or less. The child care workforce of the early 1980s was, on average, better educated than the general civilian workforce (Whitebook et al., 1989). By 2004, this was no longer the case. Considering worker age further illuminated the problem. The decline in educational attainment was most pronounced among the youngest workers. In other words, those members of the workforce older than 50 years were the most highly educated. As discussed in Chapter 3, this trend runs against the educational attainment of young women in general.

Table 4.3 presents the educational qualifications of the child care workforce, including before- and after-school care providers, from an analysis of the Census Bureau's 2009 American Community Survey (GAO, 2012). Based on estimates of nearly 1.8 million "early child care and education" workforce members, the numbers show the educational attainment for different worker categories. To generate these percentages, the GAO (2012) carefully examined combinations of occupational codes and different industries. Because of how the data are collected and subsequently categorized, public school preschool teachers and family, friend, and neighbor care providers are not included in these figures. As the numbers show, the large majority of workers with direct responsibility for children have not earned an associate's or a bachelor's degree.

Low wages have been a detriment to the child care workforce for decades. In 1984, a college-educated center teacher earned $9.76 per hour compared with $15.14 earned by other female college graduates (Herzenberg et al., 2005). Similar trends were reported by the NCCSS (Whitebook et al., 1989). In 2002–2004, similar comparisons were $13.35 per hour and $19.23 per hour, respectively. At that time, 26% of center-based teachers and administrators and 35% of family child care home providers had incomes below 200% of the federal poverty line (Herzenberg et al., 2005). Since 2000, the hourly wage of child care center staff has increased 0.5%. Although this varies little from the 0.7% rate increase for all other workers, all other workers earn an hourly wage double that of child care workers (Blau, 2011)! The Bureau of Labor Statistics (2012) estimate of child care workers' median income in 2010 was $19,300 per year, or $9.28 per hour. This occupational category includes those employed in child day care services, private households, elementary and secondary schools (i.e., before- and after-school care), and religious or civic organizations. Those employed as kindergarten and elementary school teachers (a USDL, BLS occupational category that includes preschool teachers who work in public schools) earn a median annual income of $51,380 (USDL, BLS, 2012).

The vastly different requirements for entering the child care or the education industry play a critical role in the problem of poor wages for child care workers. U.S. society views care work as unskilled labor that does not require specialized training or education (Folbre, 2001). Decades of child care research show these beliefs to be unfounded, and state requirements for child care provider preservice and ongoing "clock hours" of training keep these perceptions alive. Only when professional preparation for these jobs is better aligned with teacher education and certification programs will compensation improvements be possible (Phillips et al., 1990).

Workforce Retention and Turnover. The National Child Care Staffing Study (Whitebook et al., 1989, 1998) identified workforce retention as a notable barrier to the provision of quality services for children and families. Every year, upward of 30% of child care workers change jobs or leave the field (Kagan et al., 2008), and about 18% of center-based staff leave the field entirely (Whitebook, Sakai, Gerber, & Howes, 2001). Although no recent multistate data are available to bring these trends up-to-date, a single-state, longitudinal study provides additional insights into the complexity of this phenomenon.

The data are from an evaluation of a cash incentive program for center staff and home-based child care providers (Gable, Rothrauff, Thornburg, & Mauzy, 2007). The intervention group received biannual cash payments, the amount determined by baseline educational attainment, for staying in their jobs and for completing annual training requirements. Over the course of the evaluation, turnover rates varied by initial group assignment (i.e., cash or no-cash), role, education, experience, and hourly wage. Turnover was highest among center-based providers with the least education and who earned the lowest wages. For example, 53% of the no-cash center providers with a high school diploma (three quarters of the control group at enrollment) left their positions by the end of the 20-month evaluation. A slightly worse rate of turnover occurred among the center providers

Table 4.3. Current Workforce Educational Attainment

Category of Worker[a]	% of Workforce	EDUCATIONAL ATTAINMENT			
		High School Graduate or Less	Some College But No Degree	Associate's Degree	Bachelor's Degree or Higher
Center-based Child Care Workers[b]	32%	48%	34%	7%	11%
Preschool Teachers[c]	24%	20%	33%	15%	32%
Family-based Child Care Workers[d]	23%	48%	29%	9%	14%
Private, Home-based Child Care Workers[e]	11%	48%	33%	5%	13%
Teaching Assistants[f]	6%	40%	40%	8%	13%
Program Directors[g]	5%	11%	26%	17%	46%

Head Start Staff[h]	No Degree in ECE or Child Development	CDA or State Equivalent Credential	Associate's Degree in ECE or Child Development	Bachelor's Degree or Higher in ECE or Child Development
HS/EHS Teachers	4%	17%	34%	44%
HS/EHS Teaching Assistants	49%	31%	14%	6%

a. GAO (2012). Excluded from ECCE workforce size estimates: public school–based preschool teachers, and family, friend, and neighbor care providers.

b. Center-based child care workers. Industry: child day care services or elementary/secondary school; occupation: child care worker.

c. Preschool teachers. Industry: child day care services; occupation: preschool or kindergarten teacher, or special education teacher.

d. Family-based child care workers: self-employed. Industry: child day care services; occupation: child care worker or education administrator.

e. Private home-based child care workers. Industry: private household ; occupation: child care worker.

f. Teaching assistants. Industry: child day care services; occupation: assistant teacher.

g. Program directors. Industry: child day care services; occupation: education administrator or under director of religious activities and education.

h. Head Start Program Information Report (PIR, 2008–2009, as cited in GAO, 2012).

who earned $7.20 or less an hour (about one-third of the original sample), regardless of initial cash or no-cash group assignment.

Workforce turnover remains a major problem and greatly undermines child care quality. The alarming rates should surprise no one, however. Chronic low wages and limited educational expectations and career opportunities make staying in the field a gamble (Kagan et al., 2008). How can a knowledgeable and skilled workforce be developed under these conditions? Head Start and state-funded prekindergarten show that it does not have to be this way.

Head Start and State Pre-K Teaching Staff. Indeed, professional expectations for select segments of the workforce that care for and educate young children have improved. Specifically, individuals employed by Head Start and state-funded prekindergarten programs have been subject to increased requirements for formal education and specialized training. With Head Start reauthorization in 1998, at least half of Head Start classroom teachers were to earn, at minimum, an associate's degree in early childhood education (or related field) by September 2003. If this was not possible, the child development associate (CDA) credential (or an equivalent) was a possible alternative. Since that first mandate, the requirements for teaching staff have steadily increased. Currently, the goal is that by September 2013, half of Head Start teachers will have completed a bachelor's degree in early childhood education or child development. All teaching assistants will have the CDA, be enrolled in an associate's or a bachelor's degree program, or be enrolled in a CDA program. Staff working in Early Head Start were required to have the CDA or equivalent as of September 2010, and by September 2012, the requirements included specialized training in infant/toddler development. Table 4.3 presents the most recent program information about Head Start and Early Head Start classroom staff's actual educational attainment. As reported by the GAO (2012), Head Start teachers earned, on average, $28,000 annually and teaching assistants earned $18,000.

Similar strengthening of teacher educational requirements appears in public prekindergarten standards. Per the National Institute for Early Education Research's ten program quality standards and indicators, four apply specifically to classroom staff: (1) teacher degree (at or above the bachelor's), (2) teacher specialized training (specializing in pre-K), (3) assistant teacher degree (CDA or equivalent), and (4) teacher inservice training (at least 15 hours annually). From the 2001–02 school year, when 37 states had 42 prekindergarten programs (Barnett et al., 2003), to 2010–11, when 39 states had 51 programs (Barnett et al., 2011), several improvements have occurred. The percentage of programs requiring teachers to have a bachelor's degree increased from 49% to 57%. Similarly, requirements for assistant teachers to have at minimum a CDA or equivalent climbed from 23% to 31% across the 10-year span. Such progress also appeared in the number of programs requiring specialized training in early childhood education (67% to 88%) and at least 15 clock hours of annual professional inservice (51% to 84%).

Coincidentally, with greater demand for formal education and specialized training among the early education segment of the workforce, teacher preparation programs (Early & Winton, 2001; Kagan et al., 2008; Whitebook & Ryan, 2011) and approaches to professional development (Howes, Hamre, & Pianta, 2012) are receiving considerable attention. Moreover, a flurry of activity is occurring to establish linkages among state QRIS, professional development systems, and early learning standards (Howes & Pianta, 2011). Many of these initiatives (and improvements) have been motivated by education policy linked with improving disadvantaged children's school readiness and reducing the achievement gap (Pianta et al., 2009).

Summing Up. In the meantime, the career development recommendations from Morgan et al. (1993) and NAEYC (1993) to build an inclusive early care and education workforce are stuck. Very little has taken place, at the state or the federal level, to improve the preservice requirements or working conditions for members of the child care workforce (Bellm & Whitebook, 2006). Indeed, millions of public dollars are being spent on quality improvement activities and, to date, there is little evidence of stronger credentials or improved compensation to account for these investments. The mostly voluntary initiatives for programs and providers are especially troubling. Although this is a common strategy toward motivating statutory change in state regulations—that is, incentivize participation and improvement and when a critical mass of volunteers is reached, pursue statutory change (Mitchell, 2005)—for how long can public funds be spent in this manner without some indication of progress? Furthermore, from a research perspective, when quality improvement efforts are voluntary, selection bias can undermine evaluation results. In other words, this form of bias raises the question, how do child care providers and programs that volunteer to participate differ from those that do not? What do we really *know* about the quality of child care services available to families?

HOW PRECIOUS ARE THE EARLY YEARS?

If we did not know how to provide good-quality child care to children of all ages, then it would be understandable that our nation has not moved forward to solve the problem. However. . . . we have all the knowledge that is needed. . . . I find it tragic that policy is not incorporating what we know.

—Zigler et al., 2009, p. xv

A fragmented approach to nonparental care, coupled with ongoing ambivalence about maternal employment and devaluation of care work, has fueled competing policy agendas for child care and early education. Recent trends indicate that an exclusive segment of the current system is garnering more resources and attention because of its promise to improve academic outcomes. States cannot be blamed for this, however. The current strategy is neatly aligned with federal investments in standards, testing, and child outcomes that have spanned two presidential administrations. Nonetheless, this is a strategy of avoidance that skirts the deep-seated issues that have plagued U.S. child care for decades. Investing in compensatory education without equal attention to child care has detrimental implications for everyone involved. Aligning the two policy streams is a far better way to support children and families (Rhodes & Huston, 2012). Moreover, integrating workforce preparation and professional development systems for child care and early education is a sensible place to begin.

During a 2011 workshop about the early childhood care and education workforce, discussion touched on how to effectively convey the value of the workforce to the general public (NRC & IOM, 2012). It was suggested that it might be necessary to "let go of some sacred cows" (p. 77) and that "Maybe the word 'care' should be dropped, because 'care doesn't say we should be paid a lot of money'" (p. 78). To hear this and later read it was heartbreaking (and infuriating). Care distinguishes the profession of child care and early education. Early education cannot take place without care, and sensitive, responsive child care includes education (Caldwell, 1990). This quality of the first 5 years of life is what makes them so very precious. The college students surveyed for Chapter 2 understood this principle. Perhaps, then, it is not the general public that needs to understand the value of the early childhood care and education workforce. Rather, it is those at the highest levels of state and federal government who set agendas, advance policy, and provide leadership who would benefit.

CHAPTER 5

A Shining Star

North Carolina's
Early Childhood System

WITH **JOANNA LOWER**

North Carolina is the envy of many child care advocates, especially those who believe that child care *systems* are possible. The standard characteristics and clichés of effective systems certainly apply. Throughout its history, NC's system has responded effectively to change, accommodated new initiatives, turned potential challenges into opportunities, and grown in scope and quality. The North Carolina child care community has succeeded primarily because its system is guided by a shared vision, relies on leadership and engagement at all levels, is inherently flexible, and follows familiar early childhood "best practices," such as reflection and intentional behavior. All together, the whole of North Carolina's early childhood system is much greater than the sum of its parts.

What makes NC's system particularly unique is that it has been able to achieve something that is not common in U.S. child care. As noted by Sue Russell, President, Child Care Services Association, "We've been a state that . . . could pride itself on collaboration and strategic and systemic thinking, . . . those kinds of things that have gotten us to where we are." For some time, North Carolina has been a national leader and role model in early childhood workforce development, wage enhancements, and quality rating and improvement systems. These approaches to early childhood system development enhance the knowledge and skills of the workforce, reduce turnover, and improve early childhood program quality for all children and families.

INVESTIGATING THE NORTH CAROLINA SYSTEM

To learn about the evolution of NC's system, in July 2009 we conducted a guided discussion with key early childhood leaders (hereinafter referred to as the NCDG, for North Carolina Discussion Group), some who had been involved since the late 1970s and others who were relatively new to the state. (A list of participants and the discussion guide appear in Appendix D.) Several follow-up discussions also took place to bring the chapter up to the present time. Our primary goal was to learn about the process of change that resulted in NC's system. As a side benefit, we also learned about the "eras" of early childhood in NC, which coincided with various federal child care priorities, research discoveries, and other state early childhood initiatives. Ultimately, we wanted to hear the story firsthand, from those who were and still are a part of early childhood in NC. From their experiences and insights, we sought to distill the elements of their success that could be useful to other states engaged in child care system development.

Toward that end, direct quotes from the NCDG and relevant background information are utilized to construct a case history of NC's early childhood system development. (All quotes are from July or November 2009.) Our approach takes two directions: The first is a temporal overview of the eras of early childhood since the late 1970s, and the second is an examination of the characteristics that underlie NC's progress and success. As discussed in Chapter 1, because the United States has virtually no national policies and standards for child care, states are free to chart their own course. Some states, such North Carolina, have established effective early childhood systems and have much to offer, by way of "lessons learned," to other states.

ERAS OF EARLY CHILDHOOD IN NORTH CAROLINA

A major milestone in NC's early childhood system, the passage of Smart Start (1993), was selected as a starting point for the discussion. However, several key informants took us back further, to an earlier and less promising time in NC's early childhood history. From there, the story unfolds.

The "Dark Ages"

As NCDG participant Dick Clifford recalled:

> I consider the 1980s in North Carolina the dark ages of child care when I
> felt like we lost a lot of what we had done with the Federal Inter-Agency Day
> Care Regulations. And we had a group of about a quarter of the centers that
> were really of very high quality or pretty high quality.

This quote refers in part to the consequences of prevailing federal child care policy during the 1970s and 1980s, when several national-level efforts to improve child care were stopped (Michel, 1999; J. R. Nelson, 1982). In 1971, President Nixon vetoed the Comprehensive Child Development Act, legislation that would have promoted child development services for all children and facilitated integration of different groups of children at younger ages. The 1970s also heralded the rise of the New Right, a group opposed to universal child care and more committed to child care policy as a vehicle for moving poor parents into the workforce. Although the FIDCR, which established minimum safety and health standards for federally supported child care programs, were somewhat functional in 1980, Title XX, signed into law by President Reagan in 1981, effectively undermined them. In addition to drastic funding cuts, Title XX established the practice of block-granting federal social welfare funds, including provisions for "workfare" to states. Consequently, child care programs that received federal funds no longer needed to comply with the FIDCR. Thus, as more families needed two incomes to stay afloat, the child care policies of the 1970s and 1980s ultimately handed off the regulation of child care to states.

The following account, from NCDG member Sharon Mims, a long-term member of the early childhood workforce, represents an appropriate baseline from which NC began its early childhood system development. At the time, NC's system was without a clear vision and, like most if not all states, provided fragmented services. Moreover, the state's early childhood workforce commanded little respect.

> I graduated in '78 . . . . Regarding attitudes, when I first came out [of college] . . . I was a county employee. At that time the center was licensed separately. There was the licensure and then there were subsidized centers that only took subsidized [low-income] children. And I was in one of the centers for subsidized children. It had a very impressive name, the blah, blah, blah child development center. In the local economy at the time you had to state your place of employment when you wrote a check. I remember doing this experiment where I would go in. I would be asked for my employment. And I varied it by saying I worked in a child care center. At another time I might say the blah, blah, blah child development center. And then I could also say I was a county employee. And I remember the different response I got back. It was "Oh," when I was a county employee. The respect for the field was very different . . . I think that the value we place on young children, while it still has some room to grow, it's definitely changed in 30 years. That's the perspective on working in those times.

As Ms. Mims distanced herself, step-by-step, further from "day care," the respect she received from local businesses increased. Around the same time, early childhood advocates in the state realized that to transition out of the "dark ages," they needed to try a different approach. This is when NC's present-day early childhood system was conceived. According to Dick Clifford:

> We had gone through three legislative sessions in which child care, Head Start, school pre-K had basically all gone to the legislature with proposals for increases. And we had basically all killed each other off. None of us got anything. They used the differences between those groups to say we can't do one without the other. They ended up doing essentially nothing for three sessions in a row. . . . We finally realized we can't keep doing this. So a group came together to form the NC Child Care Coalition.

From a pragmatic perspective, this "lesson learned" resulted in an early childhood advocacy arm that would prove crucial to the success of the eras that followed. Additionally, around the same time, a group began to focus on issues associated with the early childhood workforce. According to Sue Creech, "Sometime in the '80s we went to an NAEYC conference in California. There were 12 people from North Carolina there, and . . . we met and we formed over a period of years what is now the North Carolina Institute for Early Childhood Professional Development." This move toward workforce development coincided with research from the 1980s on child care and children's experiences that identified the public health factors and program characteristics associated with quality that could be regulated by states (e.g., Whitebook et al., 1989). Several easily measured (i.e., structural) predictors of quality were identified, including caregiver education and ongoing training, and to this day play an important role in the quality of caregiver–child interactions and children's adjustment to child care. By the end of the 1980s, NC's early childhood system was headed in the direction of coordinated efforts to advocate for young children and engagement with the workforce to both extend respect and encourage (and reward) professional development. Indeed, NC's innovative professional development program, T.E.A.C.H. (Teacher Education and Compensation Helps) Early Childhood® scholarships, was in place by 1990 and still serves as a model for other state systems.

Era of Success

At the beginning of the 1990s, North Carolina's early childhood system transitioned into an era of remarkable growth and success. In some ways, NC got lucky. A gubernatorial candidate, James Hunt, (re)appeared on the scene, and brought with him exceptional leadership skills and personal interest in the topic. As NCDG member Peggy Ball saw it, "He came along at that moment in time with great inspirational and consensus-building abilities and an interest in young children.

And there was an opportunity to cultivate that interest. He could have been interested in something else and been as successful at promoting something different." Furthermore, Hunt was a known quantity with relevant past experience. According to Sue Creech:

> We were fortunate to have Jim Hunt as governor for two terms. After he left government service the first time, he became a grandfather and naturally became more interested in programming for young children. He was inspired to run for governor again, using early care and education issues as an integral part of his political platform.

During Hunt's first administration (1977–1985), he campaigned on and established kindergarten for the state. "He had done kindergarten," Clifford explained, "and then there had been a lot of the same sort of discussion, . . . 'we need to get to kids earlier. We'll solve this problem if we get to kids earlier.'" After his election, he promptly found allies in the state legislature and together they set about to conceive of and draft comprehensive early childhood legislation. Sue Russell explained:

> People always talk about the Smart Start legislation. Well, embedded in that . . . was legislation beyond Smart Start. It was to raise [improve] ratios for infant and toddler care. It was to do rates. It was to do tax credits for families. It was T.E.A.C.H. And so we often talk about that moment as one moment, but it was this huge early childhood agenda that happened in the '93 session. And it really was a change.

As described earlier, research had been conducted during the 1980s that provided sound, empirical evidence for proposing structural and regulatory changes intended to produce better child care. The bill, "Early Childhood Education and Development Initiatives" (SB 27), was sponsored by Representatives Ruth Easterling, Edd Nye, and W. Dickson, and Senators William Richardson, Herbert Hyde, and Russell Walker. The bill's preamble is stunning in its clarity of purpose and neutral, objective position on early childhood:

> The General Assembly finds, upon consultation with the Governor, that every child can benefit from, and should have access to, high-quality early childhood education and development services. The economic future and well-being of the State depend upon it. To ensure that all children have access to quality early childhood education and development services, the General Assembly further finds that:

1. Parents have the primary duty to raise, educate, and transmit values to young preschool children;
2. The State can assist parents in their role as the primary caregivers and educators of young preschool children; and
3. There is a need to explore innovative approaches and strategies for aiding parents and families in the education and development of young preschool children.

Unlike so much fragmented U.S. child care policy, North Carolina's system was designed, from the beginning, to support all children and families. Rather than initially targeting low-income or at-risk children, NC's system was grounded in principles that applied uniformly to all parents raising young children. From a broader societal perspective, this was a bold move away from cultural ideologies about what makes a "good mother" (e.g., Arendell, 2000; Hays, 1996) and experts seemingly determined to establish causal relationships between maternal employment and poor outcomes for children (e.g., Barglow et al., 1987). Furthermore, it acknowledged that regardless of household income status or other family demographic characteristics, parents are children's primary caregivers and educators. From a systems perspective, it set in place a common ground and shared vision from which to build NC's early childhood system.

The passage of SB 27 represented a major success and huge leap forward for NC's system-building efforts. Smart Start established county-level early childhood boards and facilitated a real connection between the state and the front line of early childhood programs (i.e., the workforce). As NCDG member Peggy Ball reflected, "You talk about the dark '80s and not winning anything. And then you get that first taste of being able to move things forward . . . and that fed the fire of all of the advocates. The advocacy base . . . just exploded because Smart Start put . . . all those local boards in place." After the bill's passage, 12 pioneer partnerships, representing 18 counties, were established; as of 2010, all 100 of North Carolina's counties were represented by 77 partnerships (Smart Start & the North Carolina Partnership for Children, 2010).

Thus, in addition to new leadership in the governor's office, this era, more formally than any before, engaged communities and the workforce and connected them with state policymakers. Furthermore, the creation of the local partnerships positioned NC to make the most of the next large-scale federal initiative that had implications for child care: welfare reform.

Welfare Reform (Mid-1990s)

Also during Governor Hunt's administration, federal welfare reform created new challenges and opportunities for states. Several big changes were put in place that had a direct bearing on state child care systems. Specifically, time limits were set for welfare recipients' access to federal aid, and states were charged with reducing their caseloads by moving individuals from welfare to work (GAO, 1997). This combination put enormous pressures on states to get people employed, and child care clearly played a vital role. Indeed, as caseloads were reduced, states received increased funding for child care subsidies. However, as straightforward as this may sound, states were confronted with critical decisions about how best to allocate child care subsidies and keep low-income parents working. According to NCDG participant Sue Russell:

> With welfare reform states could make the decision to allow the focus to only be on family or they could make the harder decision to say no, this is about quality for kids and families going to work. And there was a moment in time where that conversation had to be held at the very highest levels. And we opted, thank heavens, for the right approach. And that approach means we don't have [subsidized] kids in unregulated care, or very few, less than 1%. . . . I think that sort of integration of child and family, . . . that was a moment . . . where it could have all gone a different direction. . . . [Welfare reform] was one of those hard battles that . . . helped us with our system.

Because SB 27 advanced a vision for NC's early childhood system, this same vision guided the implementation of welfare reform as far as child care was concerned. Furthermore, with early childhood workforce development programs already in place (e.g., T.E.A.C.H.) and increased funding from the Child Care Development Fund, North Carolina was able to undertake a new quality initiative, the rated license, better known as the quality rating and improvement system. The QRIS was put into place in 1999 with two primary goals. First, the initiative established a star-based metric for parents to use when searching for child care. On a scale of one to five, more stars are associated with higher quality. Second, by paying higher child care subsidy rates to those programs that achieved more stars, the QRIS encouraged child care programs to improve their overall quality. Because NC child care subsidy dollars can be utilized only in licensed and rated programs, the QRIS benefits all of NC's working parents and their young children.

In September 2009, upon the 10th anniversary of North Carolina's QRIS, an advisory committee was convened to offer recommendations for the future. The committee's final report was released in August 2012 (NC QRIS Advisory Committee) and, in part, proposed strategies for restructuring advancement through the star ratings. Specifically, two- and four-star programs will be considered as "in process" toward the next star level, with the intent that this strategy will encourage ongoing efforts to improve quality. Other recommendations included establishing areas of specialization for programs to pursue within the framework of the QRIS (e.g., the arts, caring for children with special needs, infant/toddler care) and requiring individualized health plans for children with chronic health conditions.

Embracing New (and Existing) Programs

The era that began following Governor Hunt's administration was distinguished by system expansion and engagement with existing programs. As the 2000 election approached, Mike Easley, a gubernatorial candidate who was little known to the early childhood community, announced his run for governor with, in part, a pre-K agenda. At the time, pre-K was on the radar for many states, a trend that can be loosely attributed to the release of "new" brain development research, made possible with advanced imaging technology, and the "I Am Your Child" public awareness campaign of the late 1990s. "So when Easley won the primary," Dick Clifford noted, "there was a little contact [with the early childhood community] but not a whole lot until the election. He won in November 2000." After Easley won the election, the work of devising and launching More at Four (now known as NC Pre-K) began.

More at Four was carefully placed in the hierarchy of North Carolina's state government. John Pruette explained the course of events:

> It was in the governor's office, and that was the place where he always said he would incubate the program with the intention of eventually moving it to a permanent department. . . . In 2005, the Office of School Readiness was created, which brought pieces of early childhood from the Department of Public Instruction . . . into the governor's office; the Title 1 prekindergarten program, the exceptional children's prekindergarten program, Even Start Family Literacy . . . the Head Start State Collaboration office . . .

Situating More at Four in this manner allowed the program to stabilize before it was integrated with other pre-K programs. The existing early childhood infrastructure was also called on to support More at Four and willingly rose to the occasion. According to Peggy Ball:

> There was this explicit agreement among all the players in the early childhood world in North Carolina that we were going to support More at Four within the existing system. . . . There were scholarships needed for teachers in the More at Four programs. So instead of creating a separate scholarship program, we put more funding into the existing T.E.A.C.H.

scholarship program. . . . There was a need to do the environment rating scale assessment in More at Four classrooms. So the existing contract to do the assessment for the rated licensing [QRIS] was adjusted to accommodate the increased needs in More at Four. And we built the More at Four classrooms on the rated license. We said, we already have a set of standards, let's make this efficient. Let's free up the prekindergarten office so they don't have to do the basic standards. They'll be done through the rated license. And they can focus on the added standards. We started using all the current resources to support pre-K so we could make it roll out fast, be successful, and also weave [it] into the existing system.

The implementation goals of More at Four also created the opportunity for partnering with existing programs, in this case, Head Start. "This is the first time we really fully integrated Head Start into this system," Clifford noted. "With More at Four there's been a huge difference. And Head Start is a fully integral part and vital to that." More at Four called for system expansion, and those in charge pursued the new opportunities pragmatically and with a focus on relationships. According to Pruette, "One of the important things that we've done with Head Start . . . we didn't compete. . . . We weren't going to set up a classroom across the street from Head Start and run Head Start out of business. . . . We were very clear from the very beginning that we want to partner. . . . It was a long-term effort of building trust . . . ." In today's complex and mostly fragmented system of child care and early childhood, such efforts are noticed and deeply appreciated. NCDG participant Khari Garvin added:

I'll just jump in to underscore the point . . . two points I want to make that we have to be very sensitive to. One is Head Start, love them or hate them, they've been around since 1965. This is an entity that's been around a long time and does not necessarily enjoy being, I guess, the appearance of being lectured to about what is or what should be or whatever. Because in the minds of many they've been maybe the trendsetters or that kind of thing. . . . So the fact that the state pre-K program comes on the scene and extends a very loving hand was very, very good to help make this work. So that's the first thing. The second thing, too, is I think that what we've been able to get out of it is something very good. When you look at, again, the comprehensive services of Head Start and then the quality initiatives of More at Four, the marriage between the two produces a depth of service that really just does not independently exist in either one. And I think that's critical.

The Recession of 2008

At the time of the key informant discussion in July 2009, the implications of the recession for NC's early childhood system had not yet fully emerged. Two years later, in June 2011, the NC legislature proposed a 20% budget cut to More at Four, now called NC Pre-K (Webley, 2011). The legislature's actions were not unusual; during the 2009–10 budget year, state funding for prekindergarten programs declined nationwide for the first time in a decade (Barnett et al., 2010). However, then-Governor Beverly Perdue vetoed the budget; her veto was then overridden by the NC state legislature. On a separate track, several low-income school districts organized and sued the state, calling on legal precedent from *Leandro v. the State* (1997) to support their case. They claimed that their children's state constitutional right to "equal opportunity to receive a sound basic education" was being violated (i.e., a child's *Leandro* right). Judge Howard Manning, who presided over *Leandro v. the State*, also ruled in this case. He found that the legislature's actions with the Pre-K budget were unconstitutional. Indeed, in July 2011 he ruled that all NC preschoolers at risk for school problems because of disability or low-income status have a constitutional right to this educational opportunity. Governor Perdue then directed the state agencies to determine how they would serve all eligible preschoolers who applied to NC Pre-K. Also in 2011, NC Pre-K was moved to the Division of Child Development and Early Education (DCDEE). In the meantime, the NC legislature appealed Judge Manning's decision and, as of August 2012, the NC Court of Appeals upheld Judge Manning's ruling (Blythe, 2012). At the time of this writing, the case is under appeal by the NC General Assembly to the NC Supreme Court.

The fiscal challenges faced by NC Pre-K were not unique in the state. NC DCDEE also administers the child care subsidy program for low-income children, and during a recession, a time of high unemployment *and* underemployment, the demand for such supports only increases. Underemployment can reduce household income and the ability to pay for child care, and, for most families, child care is required in order to successfully transition from unemployment to employment. Meeting these needs in today's U.S. child care policy regime requires careful blending of various federal and state funding sources and is an object lesson in the illogic of our current child outcomes–driven system. An individual preschooler's child care fees can be paid for by any combination of common funding sources, such as state Pre-K funds, Head Start, child care subsidies, and parent co-pays. Moreover, that child's peers could have their child care costs covered by an entirely different constellation of sources. When it comes to assessing that child's school readiness, how is credit, or blame, assigned for the outcomes?

A Silver Lining: The Early Learning Challenge and NC Ready

In August 2011, North Carolina applied for federal funding via the Race to the Top Early Learning Challenge (NC, 2011). This funding was made possible via the ARRA, President Obama's economic policy initiative intended to reinvigorate the national economy via targeted, one-time investments in key components of public infrastructure. The state proposed an exciting plan, *NC Ready*, that showcased its established early childhood system and was linked with then-Governor Beverly Perdue's *Career and College: Ready, Set, Go!* initiative and NC's earlier funded Race to the Top plan for fundamental reform of K–12 education (NC, 2010). To meet the objectives of the request for applications, NC put forth three general strategies: (1) to "strengthen standards, assessment, and capacity for data collection and analysis to inform quality and ongoing improvement," (2) to "invest in people and relationships to increase teacher and system effectiveness and sustain change," and (3) to "target high-intensity supports and community infrastructure building efforts to turn around poor outcomes for young children in the state's highest need counties" (defined in the application as a Transformation Zone) (NC, 2011, pp. 66–67). NC identified ten goals, focused mostly on improving inputs for quality services, as performance indicators. The goals targeted gains in program quality ratings and workforce credentials; more developmental screenings of at-risk infants, toddlers, and preschoolers; a rigorously tested Kindergarten Entry Assessment; a functional data system; impact assessments in the targeted Transformation Zone; and realistic plans for sustainability.

Additionally, with the Early Learning Challenge funding, the state plans to increase the quantity and quality of infant and toddler care for families in the Transformation Zone. Many NC infants and toddlers from low-income families are unable to access licensed and quality-rated child care because of the wait for subsidized slots. Consequently, *NC Ready* will provide technical assistance to existing programs, grant funding to create new infant/toddler slots in four- and five-star programs in the Transformation Zone, and enhanced subsidy payments to high-quality programs for infant/toddler care. These are promising strategies to better serve a population that seems to be lost in national discussions about prekindergarten and school readiness.

NC Ready also proposed an ambitious, multi-activity plan for workforce development. Using already established infrastructure (e.g., community colleges; coaching, mentoring, and technical assistance; child care resources and referral), the activities focus broadly on workforce preparation, ongoing professional development and support, recognition and compensation, career development opportunities, and research on the early childhood workforce. Several of the proposed activities are intended primarily for workforce members in the

Transformation Zone. For example, new training and technical assistance opportunities will be available to support classroom teachers' ability to positively manage children's challenging behaviors.

Embodied in the state plans for *NC Ready* is a vision for a national system of child care. From a developmental perspective, the emphasis on the whole child is especially appealing, with equal attention to child health, social-emotional well-being, cognitive development, and school readiness. From a broader perspective, the state illustrates how its current early childhood system, designed to meet the needs of all children and families, is inherently flexible and can be deployed to address the greater needs of at-risk children and families. Although this expectation is grounded in *Leandro*, because of how NC's system was originally conceived, it is actually possible. It was no surprise that North Carolina's Early Learning Challenge application received the highest score among those states that applied in the first round. As *NC Ready* unfolds, the state's experiences will likely inform other states with similar visions of an early childhood system.

CHARACTERISTICS OF NORTH CAROLINA'S EARLY CHILDHOOD SYSTEM

North Carolina's eras of early childhood are useful for demarcating the distinct stages of growth and change in its system. The chapter now turns to the underlying characteristics that transcend the eras and, at heart, illustrate how NC has been able to accomplish so much. These attributes explain how the state's early childhood system first came into existence, how it operates, and why it has evolved.

A Shared Vision

The thread that connects North Carolina's different stages of early childhood is its shared vision of quality for all children and their families. Having a shared vision is valuable for many reasons. For instance, a shared vision can be used to engage and educate interested parties. It also gives system advocates the ability to stay on point when telling the story. For individuals at all levels, a shared vision serves as the guide for day-to-day decision making and long-term planning, and allows for reflecting on successes and persistent challenges. And lastly, a shared vision positions the system to be "poised and ready" when new opportunities present themselves. These functions of a shared vision are alive in the leadership and routine operation of North Carolina's early childhood system.

The eras of early childhood in NC, reviewed in the previous section, reveal how the state's vision emerged and became institutionalized. In the future, *NC*

Ready will extend the system's reach to touch even more children. For instance, to increase participation in the QRIS, NC will reach out to license-exempt programs and offer supports and incentives to get them involved (NC, 2011). At present, public school–located and religiously affiliated early childhood programs are exempt from licensure and thus are not required to participate in the QRIS. The state will also explore the feasibility of licensing part-day early childhood programs (i.e., those that operate less than 4 hours per day) and home-based child care programs that enroll fewer than three unrelated children. Because licensure is the door to the state's QRIS, these efforts will increase the number of licensed and rated programs, connect more programs and workforce members to quality enhancement infrastructure supports, and raise fundamental safety and quality of early childhood services for families.

Several aspects of NC's shared vision are appealing to child care system advocates. First, the state's vision reflects how contemporary families operate. As Dick Clifford observed:

> This shift in our society about how we care for young children is a very pervasive change in the way families are organized. And we're trying to figure out how to deal with it still. We're not through with that. But we have made a huge amount of progress in North Carolina.

The second is its inclusive nature: quality for *all* children and families. Peggy Ball explained it this way: "It's always about being flexible . . . [focusing on] what you're trying to achieve . . . being in agreement about it and *to always realize it's the same group of kids we're all serving* . . . ." U.S. child care policy has a long history, evident in NC's "dark ages," of a priori dividing groups of young children on the basis of their families' income. While some of these issues are certainly relevant, especially in terms of targeted system financing, they need not be evident in the choices available to parents or in the overall quality of those choices.

Leadership and Engagement

Successful systems are also characterized by effective leadership and, equally important, engagement with the people who are most directly affected by system-level decisions. Indeed, such relationships are critical to the system's ongoing success. NCDG participant Khari Garvin described some of what transpired during the design and implementation of More at Four:

> On the one hand you have this state-level policy, meaning that there were people who decided on the state level that this would be an okay way

to go and so it became policy. But the second thing that had to support that was people pounding the pavement on the local level to help foster relationships. . . . The policy itself didn't do it. It was the relationship building that helped to do it.

On the Ground. NC began its system building with a clear commitment to the workforce. During the 1980s, the state was among the forerunners into the realm of professional development systems and wage enhancements. These efforts had a much greater likelihood for success because the workforce was already engaged and represented in meaningful ways. As noted by Sue Russell: "We have a really effective advocacy arm for early childhood . . . the coalition. . . . We have a full-time paid lobbyist. And we have a network of organizations and individuals who are completely wired together, and we've had that for a long time."

This was especially critical to the state's level of readiness for someone with the leadership skills and interests of Governor Hunt. As recalled by Sue Russell, the local early childhood communities were primed and ready when he announced his candidacy:

> Because what happened then was when he publicly said, "I'm running, and I'm running on an early childhood platform," what the early childhood community did, which I don't think it's ever done since then, is it formed political groups in local communities to raise money for Hunt. That had never happened. And so there were parties and receptions and other things that were happening all over the state on his behalf. Everybody knew it was on their own time and all of that, but it was like this is our chance. I thought that was another sort of coming-of-age moment for the early childhood community that hadn't ever been done. It wasn't that early childhood people had a lot of money. It was just the notion that they were going to be engaged, and they did it labeling this as an early childhood event and we're doing it. So I thought that was pretty phenomenal.

Organizing in this manner paid off; the local boards associated with SB 27 and Smart Start were more likely to be effective because those on the ground were already engaged. Someone in a position of power was taking them and their work very seriously.

At the Top. The individuals who participated in the NCDG are all early childhood leaders in their own right, at the state, the national, and, for some, the international level. Their collective wisdom and experiences made this case history possible. What is especially impressive about them as a group is how each person routinely navigates several worlds of early childhood. The NCDG members were early childhood policymakers, national and state agency leaders, researchers, and current or former early childhood practitioners. It is this multifaceted perspective that has given them such remarkable insight into the history and business of North Carolina's early childhood system development. Furthermore, having such talented leaders and child development experts gave another remarkable leader exactly what he needed to take NC's early childhood system into the future. Indeed, early childhood in North Carolina had a winner in Governor James Hunt.

From the start, he was very strategic and pragmatic about his desire to run with an early childhood platform. Said Sue Russell, "In the very beginning he had to see if this was going to fly. He was very pragmatic." Dick Clifford elaborated: "Yes, he did want to win. . . . And they did these focus groups with typical people in North Carolina and access to child care was very high on their list. Fortunately for us it was, because he embraced that and campaigned on that for 9 years."

By going to the people and finding out what was on their minds, Hunt learned about the importance of early childhood for most NC citizens and was thus able to confidently pursue his campaign goals. In essence, he established a direct line to those who ultimately would benefit from the changes and improvements he was proposing.

After he won the election, Governor Hunt jumped into action, which was possible because so much work had already been done. He established a state-level entity, the Division of Child Development, and staffed it with experts. NCDG participant Dick Clifford was the first division director. Governor Hunt also announced a new early childhood initiative, which would become SB 27, and immediately funded those crucial workforce development programs that were already in place (e.g., T.E.A.C.H.). It is important to bear in mind, however, that Smart Start and the other changes proposed in Governor Hunt's early childhood initiative didn't just happen; SB 27 needed a passing vote. As recounted by NCDG members, Governor Hunt's desire to improve and expand NC's early childhood system became everyone's business.

> *Mr. Clifford:* . . . And then the job was to get the legislation through. A critical event in that process was Hunt got the legislature to convene a joint session. It essentially was supposed to be the appropriations from House and Senate, but what it really was, it ended up being pretty much everybody from both houses came together. And he orchestrated this. He brought in . . . the CEO of Bellsouth, Bank of America.
> *Ms. Russell:* Wachovia.
> *Mr. Clifford:* . . . Duke Power was there. And . . . Julius Chambers. . . . He argued before the Supreme Court for desegregation. . . . Larry Schweinhart came from HighScope, and he brought a Head Start parent.

Ms. Russell: It was unbelievable.

Mr. Clifford: It was televised. . . . For me that was the thing that solidified the passage of the bill. Because it was your business. People said this is something we need to do. This is part of infrastructure. We have to do this long term.

Governor Hunt also viewed the content matter seriously. Most people think that they know something about kids because they once were a child and because they have interacted with children, whether as parents or in a relative or caregiving role. However, for those who have formally pursued the study of child development and early childhood education, "knowing about kids" is a scholarly discipline, complete with theories, research, and best practices. This category of knowing is fundamentally different from personal experience and folk wisdom. Sue Russell explained the governor's approach:

He embraced learning about it. He just wanted to soak it all up, and that was what made him such a phenomenal leader. . . . He used his role as governor to consistently educate and bring people together around early childhood. . . . He'd have private breakfasts with the religious community, with the business community. He'd have public events all around early childhood. He just kept doing it over and over. He'd have legislators in for breakfast, "Here's what I need to get done in terms of early childhood." It was unbelievable to have that kind of leadership.

By appointing content experts, engaging in self-education, and using his position as governor to educate others, Hunt honored child development as an academic discipline. Such actions conveyed the ideal that quality early childhood services require a workforce with specialized knowledge and training, programs that implement best practices, and government-funded infrastructure to support the people and the programs. His leadership was vital, and although his term came to an end in 2000, his legacy lives on because of the state's shared vision and the people and "best practices" that are the foundation of North Carolina's early childhood system.

The Processes, or "Best Practices"

Throughout our guided discussion, several organizational processes stood out as especially critical to the growth and development of NC's early childhood system. These characteristics were evident in the description of how NC transitioned out of the "dark ages" with the intentional decision of the early childhood community to join forces when approaching the state legislature.

Reflection and Intentionality

Whether about policy, "telling the story," or issues of leadership, North Carolina recognizes and enacts the basic principles of quality practice—reflection and intentional behavior—that we strive to impart to those who constitute the early childhood workforce. Indeed, transitioning away from legislative failures, just like creating engaging lesson plans or redirecting a child's problematic behavior, requires reflecting on past experiences or new knowledge as part of intentionally charting a different course of action. Reflection and intentional behavior are hallmarks of how NC has built its early childhood system.

Reflection. Reflection is a valuable exercise for many reasons. Looking to the past helps guide future activities, permits setting baselines to evaluate progress, aids future planning, allows for celebration, and creates a safe space to examine unsuccessful efforts. During our discussion, evidence of reflection emerged on several occasions. Some comments were positive and concerned system growth and stabilization. For example, NCDG participant Deb Cassidy reflected: "But I think we have had maybe an opportunity for some of our initiatives to stabilize, like the rated license [QRIS]; we've had it for 10 years now and it feels so much safer and secure than it felt to me early on."

Other remarks centered on the implications of the still-somewhat-new recession. Recall that the first group discussion took place in July 2009. The economic recession of 2008 has placed extraordinary strains on state budgets, as evident in the recent court battles over NC's Pre-K funding, and difficult funding decisions need to be made among what many view as discretionary programs. Dick Clifford commented: "I do think the current financial crisis has really put a strain on this system, on this effort to hold together. And we're struggling to keep it together. I think we will, but it is a struggle."

The position of early childhood emerges in state budget priorities. Indeed, the challenges of embedding a state early childhood system into an even larger one, specifically, U.S. society and its ambivalent stance toward child care, working mothers, and universal social services, are noted in this remark from Sue Russell:

> I think this whole legislative session has said to me that as hard as we've worked and as well as we've done, we've failed to embed early childhood education in the fabric of our society in the most fundamental way. When legislators can cut early childhood at rates far in excess of what they're doing for education or human services, it says as good as we've been, we've failed at that key piece of embedding. . . . We haven't done that yet.

Intentionality. Intentional behavior similarly has useful functions for system building and routine operations. It suggests a more conscious, calculated, and strategic approach to solving problems or meeting goals. As explained by Deb Cassidy:

> And the second piece that I think we've done really well at . . . is using carrots first and sticks second. That is, seeing the change we want to have happen, figure out ways to incentivize that change. And then when we reach critical thresholds finishing it up with the stick . . . a regulatory stick.

Furthermore, intentional behavior often flows from ideals or standards. In the case of North Carolina, this typically involves upholding the state's shared vision for early childhood and how the state literally builds its system and integrates new parts. Sue Russell describes the process in the following:

> What we've done is try to weave things together in ways that make them hard to pull apart. But that comes from a systemic view that I think we keep trying to have over and over again and to figure out if there's a new piece that needs to happen. How do you weave that in so that you strengthen the whole and then it becomes the next piece you can't pull apart because it's all woven together?

"Weaving" and "embedding" were mentioned frequently in a metaphorical sense as desired outcomes of intentional system development.

The idea of institutionalizing change so as to strengthen the system overall also requires intentional behavior. Deb Cassidy shared the following about her then-new position:

> When I took this job [Director, Division of Child Development], which has only been 2 months ago, one of my colleagues said to me, "Whatever you do, Deb, whatever changes you make, institutionalize them. You don't want it to be that it's dependent on you being there." It's about building a system and building programs that are not easily taken away with the ebb and flow of state dollars.

North Carolina has also undertaken several intentional efforts to strengthen existing higher education infrastructure so as to guarantee access for members of the early childhood workforce. Because of the North Carolina early childhood and administration credentials, which require college credit–bearing preservice requirements for lead teachers and administrators in state-licensed child care programs, access to higher education is crucial. During Governor Hunt's administration, he made sure that all 58 of NC's community colleges offered this curriculum.

As Deb Cassidy described: "Once we had that minimum requirement that included college credits, then we saw our community college system . . . wildly expand. Governor Hunt was governor when early childhood was expanded to all of the community colleges, because he was such an advocate."

Since then, the Division of Child Development and Smart Start have invested funds in supporting the community college programs to become accredited by the National Association for the Education of Young Children. And recently, a portion of the Early Learning Challenge funds will go toward increasing access to the early childhood degree programs at community colleges and to further supporting these higher education programs to pursue NAEYC accreditation. Deb Cassidy explained the state's rationale for this approach:

> The Division of Child Development has put a lot of money into community colleges. And so has Smart Start. Not as much into the 4-year schools, because that's not where our workforce is. For example, right now the division is offering an incentive for ten more community colleges to be accredited by NAEYC. Now some people would say, "Should that be the role of the Division of Child Development?" We see it as our role because we want the workforce educated . . . and not just any old education will do. We really want the best. We want it to be that these are programs that are accredited by NAEYC. So we are assured that they [the community college programs] are developmentally appropriate in their approach and the students are getting what we want them to get. . . . A couple of years back we paid for . . . community college instructors to receive the PITC [Program for Infant-Toddler Care] training, which is the infant/toddler training . . . because we wanted to really put a focus on improving the quality of infant/toddler care. And one way of doing that, that gives us rewards exponentially, is to give it to those [community college] instructors who pass along that information to the students [members of the early childhood workforce]. . . . We have put a lot of money into that. Smart Start has funded instructors, full lines, at community colleges.

NC's early childhood workforce has benefited greatly from the intentional investments made in the higher education infrastructure that prepares and supports the workforce. Furthermore, as a result of the state's professionalizing the early childhood workforce and improving working conditions, families have benefited via greater access to quality early childhood services.

Institutionalizing change can also take the form of intentionally structuring (and, ideally, changing) how and what those in positions of authority think about state investments in early childhood. As Peggy Ball recounted her agency's strategy:

The state agency always did this pie chart that would go to the legislature every session . . . that showed the sources of money for child care, showed the big pie. . . . We started putting [in the picture] how much families contributed with their co-pay. And we consistently did that, because that was part of the story we wanted to tell over and over again. And it was not down in a little bitty footnote. . . . But the point was that we wanted them to remember over and over again . . . [that the child care subsidy] is not a giveaway program. Parents contribute and they contribute a lot.

The need to intentionally cultivate the next generation of leaders was also discussed. In developmental terms, this is called generativity, that is, guiding and preparing the younger generation to take up the reins and lead in the future. The early childhood workforce is made up of many people, including those who direct early childhood programs, those who work with children, and leaders such as the individuals who participated in our discussion. It is highly probable that the same structural forces that plague the child care workforce (Bellm & Whitebook, 2006; Herzenberg et al., 2005) also plague the leadership and staffing of early childhood administrative and infrastructure systems. During the discussion, the key informants reflected on this leadership challenge and the need for more intentional efforts to address it. Sue Creech described it as follows: "The biggest need for us is to have people who can sit around this table 10 years from now . . . not us. We have not done a good job of bringing younger people to this table who can sustain what we have accomplished so far."

Calculated Risk-Taking

Committing to a shared vision requires some calculated risk-taking in the service of system building. During the mid-1990s, when federal welfare reform called on states to make critical decisions about child care and reducing caseloads, North Carolina took a calculated risk in choosing quality for children *and* getting parents to work. The risk came not so much with the state's vision but rather with the details of program implementation. States were at liberty to set family income levels for the receipt of subsidy dollars and to decide which child care providers and programs were eligible to receive those monies. When the time came, NC set family income levels high, the implication being that more families would be eligible for (and in need of) subsidies, and they allocated child care subsidy dollars only to state-licensed child care centers and family child care homes. NCDG participant Peggy Ball was at the Division of Child Development then.

There were a couple of [administrative functions] that were not as visible. . . . At the same time we blended the funds . . . we set one eligibility [level] for all families who received child care . . . and allocated the money to the counties. We said, "You don't [need to] make any decisions about which kid is paid for with which fund. . . . We will do that at the state level. And our goal at the state level is to spend every single penny we have to serve families. So we're moving that money if you don't spend it. And, by the way, you as a county have a [welfare] caseload reduction goal that you have to meet." So suddenly the counties were speaking up and saying child care was really important for them to be able to reduce the caseloads. . . . And we talked about why it was important to get those kids into quality child care so those parents would continue to work.

The calculated risk came at several decision points. First, because these decisions were set against getting parents to work, it wasn't just about the state's child care system. Other state agencies were also involved. Second, by setting the income eligibility level high, NC created a demand that it may, or may not, be able to meet. Indeed, blending sources of state and federal funding and allocating the right amount of money to counties to cover subsidy costs was a big risk. As Dick Clifford recounted:

That was a big risk for the Division of Child Development, because then it was their fault. It took the blame so that the locals didn't have to bear that burden of making that decision and being liable if the Feds came back and said that was a wrong decision. The state division took that on. And that freed up the locals to be able to provide the care that was needed.

The risk, however, was in the service of further developing the state's early childhood system. And, as Peggy Ball remarked, "It was a challenge too, but it was a really big opportunity. And we were willing to take the risk to build that kind of system."

North Carolina also set parameters on parent choice by paying subsidies only to state-licensed early childhood programs. This decision, too, was a calculated risk that was guided by the state's shared vision of quality for all children and families. NCDG member Sue Russell noted, "Our mantra was 1 year of high-quality child care is better than lots of years of poor-quality child care for our children." In some states, the employment-related objectives of welfare reform were (and still are) achieved by spending child care subsidy dollars in the legally unlicensed child care market. For a state like NC that was firmly committed to early childhood system development and quality for all children, investing child care subsidies in the family, friend, and neighbor market was not an option. Peggy Ball explained the rationale:

It's not that I don't care about those children [who attend family, friend, and neighbor care] and that I don't think that they deserve quality, but I have yet to see a strategy that's going to raise quality during the short period of time that they're caring for those kids and that will show a result from your investment. And so when I tell them [other state child care administrators] that almost all of our [subsidized] kids are in centers, [that] we have very little family, friend, and neighbor care that we fund with subsidy, they just think you must be very oppressive. "Why aren't you spending your money on developing family, friend, and neighbor care?" We're spending our money on developing a system that will be around. And when parents have the option, they choose center and regulated family care.

Indeed, for low-income families, quality (i.e., formal, state-licensed child care) matters a great deal, both for children's well-being and for employed parents who need reliable services. NC's decision making and program implementation associated with welfare reform exemplify calculated risk-taking for the benefit of system development. The state approached welfare reform strategically and as an opportunity to improve the system. By setting income eligibility high, it created a maximum level of demand for child care subsidies, and by allowing subsidy dollars to purchase only regulated child care, it communicated the vision of quality for all children and families (while also increasing demand in the formal, state-licensed child care market). And with the QRIS, the state created an incentive for early childhood programs to improve quality for all children and families. Indeed, as of July 1, 2012, child care subsidy dollars can no longer be used in one- or two-star programs.

Willingness to Manage Controversy

Early childhood system development in North Carolina was not always smooth sailing. It had its fair share of controversy. Another benefit to having a shared vision is the ability to confront and manage controversy and opposition. For example, when Governor Hunt was trying to advance SB 27, religious forces made their opposition to the legislation widely known. Dick Clifford recalled the controversy:

Jerry Falwell's group flooded North Carolina with tens of thousands of letters opposing Smart Start during this passage. So Hunt went to the North Carolina Council of Churches, got them to say it's not an issue about Christian values. And they supported improved services for young children. . . . You argued that these are conservative values. Welfare of our children, what's more conservative than saying we need to protect our children?

Because the language of SB 27 was so neutral (and inclusive), confronting the opposing forces in reasonable terms was possible.

Another controversy arose when members of the state legislature voiced disapproval of incorporating an "anti-bias" curriculum into the taxpayer-supported rated license (i.e., QRIS). The colorful episode was described by several members of the NCDG.

> *Ms. Russell*: We really did have some ugly fights.
> *Ms. Ball*: . . . about the rated license and the NAEYC curriculum.
> *Ms. Russell*: . . . This one legislator was horrified, this came out of the anti-bias curriculum. . . . He was horrified that teachers would teach children the correct names of body parts. And Ruth [Easterling] got up on the floor . . . we were sitting in the gallery . . . and she talked about how her mother had taught her the correct names of body parts and she believed in teaching children that.
> *Mr. Clifford*: "Can't you say these words? Are you afraid to say these words?"
> *Ms. Russell*: She just [stopped this man in his tracks].

Ruth Easterling was among the original sponsors of SB 27 and, from what the key informants said about her, a deeply devoted advocate for young children. She was a priceless ally in the legislature who could be trusted to support the state's vision for early childhood.

Poised and Ready

Over and over, the concept of "poised and ready" presented itself during the discussion. North Carolina's early childhood system was poised and ready for the day, and poised and ready for the future. Deb Cassidy put it this way: ". . . But I'm really very positive, very optimistic. North Carolina is, I feel like in spite of some bumps along the way recently, I think we're poised. That is the word I would use." Being poised and ready is another trait of North Carolina's early childhood system. It characterizes how they have conducted themselves over the past 30 years and exists because of the vision, the people, and the "best practices" described and discussed throughout the chapter. As Dick Clifford remarked:

> I think as a state we've done an incredible job of finding those right moments and acting quickly to take advantage of them. So I think we've not been too rigid in saying what needs to be done today. We all have ideas about the most pressing needs, but sometimes you have to take advantage of things that aren't necessarily the most pressing needs

because you can do it now rather than fighting a battle that you can't win now. So you have to find some balance between those. And I think we've done a pretty good job at that.

The state's top-ranking Race to the Top Early Learning Challenge application, funded during the first round, is more than sufficient evidence of its being poised and ready. In fact, the funding was awarded in 2011, 2 years after our first key informant discussion occurred!

The discussion ended on a humorous note, when an anecdote was shared by two NCDG members about Governor Hunt's communication style and how he influenced others committed to NC's early childhood system:

> *Ms. Ball:* . . . [His] having the same message, being on the same page, being on the same talking points, constantly, which goes back exactly to what Hunt used to do. . . . And he was a master at listening to you. He always listened to you, and he could translate what he heard into how he would use it.
>
> *Ms. Russell:* Unless it was when he picked up the phone and called you. . . . "Find the children in the ditch."
>
> *Ms. Ball:* He said, "I just discovered there are kids we are not serving, kids in the ditch, I saw them as we drove past."

With his very public commitment to young children and families, Governor Hunt was free to be on the lookout for ways to make the system stronger, to extend its reach to more children and families, and to make sure that no child was overlooked. Although his political acumen and interest in early childhood seemed to be a stroke of luck for the state, the advocacy, engagement, and leadership that were in place when he appeared and that live on after him are the true testament to the early childhood *system* that NC has established. North Carolina has a long and contentious political history of racial divisions and inequality—it is a Southern state, after all—characteristics that clearly were transcended to achieve unity among the state's early childhood leaders and policymakers in order to guarantee quality for all children and families. These realities of NC should be a source of hope and inspiration to others invested in creating early childhood systems. As Sue Russell put it:

> That's why we believe you can do this in any state. If we can do it here given all of those kinds of pressures, we fought every kind of battle, with every kind of attitude about it that you can imagine, and we were able to flip our system.

CHAPTER 6

It's Time for New Approaches

In this book, I have examined a range of relevant topics associated with the ecology of U.S. child care at the start of the 21st century. In part, I provide a unique perspective on several chronic barriers that have forestalled the vision of a national system for child care. Chapter 1 presented necessary background on federal child care policy since the 1960s and described the myriad of current sources of funding for child care and compensatory education programs. Combined with the ongoing economic challenges faced by families with young children, the chapter suggested that maintaining the status quo of child care in the United States may not be a wise course of action.

Chapter 2's examination of today's child care marketplace illustrated the amount of ingenuity that goes into the naming of child care centers and the description of their services. The chapter also highlighted the wide chasm between perceptions of what the names convey and what is known to occur behind closed doors. Where can affordable, quality services be found? At Children's World Learning Center, Lola's Day Care LLC, or Juz Kidz Nursery and Preschool? Very few states provide universal, quality-related information to let consumers know.

Chapter 3's heartfelt and insightful discussions revealed the private fulfillment and dissatisfaction shared by working women and mothers. Ambivalence played a starring role in this chapter. It colors women's issues, is ubiquitous in media depictions of modern women, and underlies much about child care in the United States.

Chapter 4 synthesized decades of rigorous, thoughtful, and highly informative child care research and advocacy efforts, only to reveal how little has been translated to meaningful policies that touch all U.S. children and families. Especially disconcerting is the chronic devaluation of the child care workforce and the lax professional expectations associated with employment.

However, in this book I never intended to offer only doom and gloom. The case history of North Carolina's early childhood system presented in Chapter 5 shows what is possible for a national system of child care. Since the 1980s, the state has been intentionally building the system it envisions for children, families, and

144 The States of Child Care

the workforce. As recounted, it all began when the state's early childhood entities coordinated their requests to the state legislature and thus acted as a unified force, not as competitors vying for limited funds. They next went on to implement what are now widespread models of workforce development that, at the time, were fresh and forward-thinking.

As the national economy falters, income inequality grows (Greenhouse, 2013), and child poverty is at historic rates, the stakes for continued policy fragmentation at the federal level keep escalating. Employment is more necessary than ever for parents and, if poverty rates worsen, more young children will qualify as at risk for academic problems. Thus, as both "traditions" of nonparental care are in demand—the mostly privatized and minimally regulated services to support parental employment, and compensatory education and child development programs for at-risk children—the national debt and slow growth of the U.S. economy suggest that fewer funds will be available to meet these needs (e.g., Schulman & Blank, 2012).

It is hard to fathom what more is needed to spark real action. Major education reforms, such as No Child Left Behind (2001), are driving a great deal of state policy and funding to improve preschoolers' academic outcomes. However, it remains to be seen whether the downward extension of these reforms will be universally implemented for 4-year-olds and extended even further, to infants and toddlers. Chapter 3's discussion of women's life-course trajectories of simultaneous employment, childbearing, and parenting show the ever-present need for infant and toddler care, not to mention parental leave programs. Furthermore, from a developmental perspective that honors children as active agents of their learning (Falk, 2012; Hirsch-Pasek, Golinkoff, Berk, & Singer, 2009), the potential long-term costs of directing resources to produce test gains—a shaky goal at best—are very real. It is time for new approaches in U.S. child care policy. Here I offer three recommendations for incremental progress toward a national, coordinated system of child care.

RECOMMENDATION 1:
RESOLVE FRAGMENTATION WITH INTEGRATION

The first recommendation calls on national leaders to resolve system fragmentation with policy integration. To begin the process of change, a vision for policy could be adopted that integrates child care for parental employment with compensatory education for school readiness. Similar to North Carolina's system, the new tradition would focus on family support and assistance with child development. As demonstrated throughout this book, the current, fragmented approach does not guarantee all families access to the full range of quality child care and early education. To meet the challenges and opportunities of the 21st century, more inclusive strategies for human capital formation during the early years of life are warranted. One can only imagine where the nation's child care system would be today had the Comprehensive Child Development Act of 1971 been enacted. Recall that this piece of legislation sought to integrate policy traditions, expand and improve services for all families, and integrate children from different backgrounds at younger ages (Michel, 1999; J. R. Nelson, 1982).

Long-Term Goal

Quality matters for all children. Does it matter more for some children than for others? Yes. Does that mean that a separate set of services should be developed for those who need "more" quality? The answer to this question depends on who is asked. The arguments presented in this book suggest no. Instead, I advocate that a system of quality services first be developed for all children and families and then be tailored to meet the greater needs of some children and families. North Carolina's system of early childhood, especially as depicted in the recently funded *NC Ready*, is a model for such an approach.

Distinguishing family support as the new policy focus follows from what is known about the primary influences in children's lives. The action begins at home, with parents. The NICHD SECC reported that parents and the home environment were the strongest and most consistent predictor of children's overall development (NICHD ECCRN, 2006). In addition to debunking the myth that day care and maternal employment are bad for children, this is among the study's principal findings. Indeed, actively fostering program–parent partnerships on behalf of children's well-being (e.g., Knoche, Cline, & Marvin, 2012), an essential component of quality child care (Frede, 1995), seems to be getting lost in the race to improve child outcomes.

Federal involvement in resetting policy about nonparental care would legitimize child care with the highest endorsement in the land. Without such leadership, the needs of young children and working families appear unimportant. Recent recognition of the child care problem at the highest levels of national politics is heartening. In 2011, Nancy Pelosi, past Speaker and current Minority Leader of the U.S. House of Representatives, vowed to "do for child care" the type of comprehensive change that was accomplished for health care (Henneberger, 2011). During her travels throughout the nation, women everywhere told her about the challenges of finding "reliable care that would make their family lives calmer and work lives more productive." Minority Leader Pelosi understands. She is the mother of five and has maintained an active, lifelong career in public service. If parental leave programs and government-supported, affordable, quality child care were available, all parents would be better equipped to balance work and family responsibilities (Drago, 2007).

To achieve the long-term goal of access to affordable, quality child care that supports all families, several short- and intermediate-term goals are proposed. Because this subject is rife with political over- and undertones, it will be essential to institutionalize any changes in such a way that they are independent of the political process. National leadership is crucial.

Short-Term Goals

The short-term goals are intended to generate actionable knowledge that will inform the implementation of intermediate goals. The first goal is to carry out a comprehensive accounting of all public funds used for child care and early education. This includes the state and federal investments listed in Table 1.1, revenue expenditures produced by the IRS tax credits, and funds expended for quality improvement initiatives. It will be especially important to "follow the money" to a level of analysis that reflects a child's day. How much money does the United States invest in the average child, by age, in child care and early education programs? These data, combined with forthcoming data from the National Survey of Early Care and Education (National Opinion Research Center, 2012), will be vital to describing current trends and to estimating future resource needs.

The second short-term goal is to commission a case history of the Comprehensive Child Development Act of 1971 and any other related legislation that has proposed a coordinated system of nonparental care. There is much to be learned from the past and from many experts and scholars who can bring these lessons into the present. This history would provide knowledge of how the federal government proposed to make quality services available to all families. Of course, issues of scale would differ at the start of the 21st century, but notes on planning and details of implementation could offer clues for translation.

Intermediate-Term Goal

The proposed intermediate-term goal involves taking action on the current parameters of public funding for child care. Specifically, a plan would be implemented whereby public funds could no longer be used for the purchase of legally unregulated forms of child care or for voluntary quality improvement activities. In particular, quality set-aside dollars associated with the Child Care Development Fund would be restricted to child care workers' mandated child-relevant preservice training or to support their attainment of a credential or a college degree.

Chapter 1 reported that 78% of child care subsidies are spent in regulated child care centers and homes (Blanchette, 2012). This figure shows that there is room for improvement. Less is known about how quality set-aside dollars are expended for system-building activities. Nonetheless, as discussed in Chapter 4, there is cause for concern associated with the nonintersecting professional preparation tracks for child care workers and teachers (Morgan et al., 1993). To achieve the long-term goal of quality for all, funding could be linked with child care facilities and settings about which something is *known* and with strategic efforts to *develop* a workforce. Most states do not require child-relevant preservice for workers in licensed programs, and about half of the workforce has, at most, a high school diploma. Public funds are not well invested when used for professional developmental activities that do not accumulate and lead to a recognized credential or degree.

RECOMMENDATION 2:
REPLACE AMBIVALENCE WITH WORKFORCE DEVELOPMENT

The second recommendation respectfully asks state and national policymakers to agree, once and for all, that the provision of child care and early education is a profession. In today's fragmented system, only one segment of the workforce has the "professional" distinction. These professionals, a.k.a. "teachers," have emerged from the policy tradition of compensatory education. As discussed in Chapter 4, with the recurrent interest in enhanced academic outcomes, the educational qualifications associated with these positions have been strengthened in the recent past. In the case of Head Start, these workforce improvements have been mandated, not merely recommended. Similar gains in expectations and professionalism have not been realized among the child care workforce.

Long-Term Goal

Thus, aligned with the new approach proposed in Recommendation 1, all members of the child care workforce should be subject to increased preservice and education requirements. As Chapter 4 illustrated, decades of sound research indicates that caring for infants, toddlers, and preschoolers in group settings requires competency-based, specialized training and education. Furthermore, Chapter 5 recounted how NC initiated its early childhood system building with a strategic focus on developing the workforce. If families are to feel supported and children are to have positive child care experiences and be ready for kindergarten, they need to be in the company of individuals with relevant child development and early education qualifications and credentials.

A more systemic approach to workforce development will also address ongoing problems associated with compensation, benefits, and workplace conditions. Chapter 3's discussions with members of the child care workforce show the inequities associated with this tradition of nonparental care. For licensed home-based providers, the days are long and paid time off is exceedingly rare. Center-based providers work for meager wages and receive mixed messages about what is required for the job. Both groups encounter situations that elicit feelings of low worth in the complex ecology of parental employment, child care, and child development.

People are the thread that connects child care across settings of all kinds. As shown in Table 1.2 and throughout Chapter 2, infants, toddlers, and preschoolers receive nonparental care in a variety of programs and facilities. Targeting policy and resources at the person level is a feasible strategy to achieve Recommendation 1. Implementing small and incremental changes for required preservice and educational attainment is a step in the right direction. As presented in Chapter 4, there is no shortage of background material to draw from in developing and implementing such a system. Head Start was able to mandate changes and, as shown in Table 4.2, some states also require child-relevant preservice for members of their child care workforce.

Consequently, the long-term goal associated with Recommendation 2 is to establish a system of individual licensure that is linked with common child care roles and that complements existent child care facility regulation and licensure. Similar to Recommendation 1, several short- and intermediate-term goals are proposed as steps toward meeting the long-term goal.

Short-Term Goals

The first short-term goal is to commission an independent study of Head Start's experiences (past and present) with improving teacher credentials. This report would provide valuable information about the challenges and opportunities faced by Head Start grantees and staff in meeting these mandates. Particular attention should be given to actual per-person costs, by role and requirement, and how staff managed work, school, and personal life. Additionally, inquiry is necessary into how higher education has responded to the challenge (or not) and the role played by technology and online coursework. Head Start is the country's early childhood laboratory for taking evidence-based policy changes to a national scale. There are surely many insights to be gained from its workforce development experiences.

The second short-term goal will be to identify common child care roles, by facility type, and to define skill- and knowledge-based competencies for each role. There are many roles involved with the provision of child care and early education. For this particular goal, the emphasis first should be on those roles that have primary responsibility for children's care and early education. For instance, the roles might include center-based classroom teacher, assistant teacher, and aide, and home-based program director/teacher and assistant.

Intermediate-Term Goal

For Recommendation 2's intermediate-term goal, several states should undertake pilot projects to create and implement systems of individual licensure for the child care roles defined above. Federal funds should be awarded to states from different regions and that represent different child care policy regimes. In addition to planning and implementation, these projects should provide extensive, per-license cost data, including the financial resources necessary to align compensation with credentials and educational attainment.

It is likely that individual licensure systems can be built, in great part, from already existing systems of credentialing (e.g., the CDA) and higher education. For instance, the recurrent emphasis on child outcomes has brought considerable attention to the bachelor's degree (e.g., Early et al., 2006, 2007). There are pros and cons to such scrutiny. Higher education is an already established system with an existing infrastructure and capabilities to serve many, especially with new educational technologies. Furthermore, higher education and other established workforce preparation systems will likely respond flexibly as changes are implemented (Bredekamp & Goffin, 2012). However, because approximately half of the currently employed child care workforce has no child-relevant educational qualifications, it will be necessary to identify realistic "entry points" for these individuals, such as the child development associate credential. The CDA is especially attractive because it can be delivered to yield college credits and typically includes an observational assessment of students' behavioral competencies. For pilot states, the goal will be to create a flexible system, similar to the career lattice proposed by NAEYC in 1993, that recognizes current workers and welcomes those of the future. Current systems for "ongoing clock hours" of training can be redeployed to deliver early employment orientation, rapid response training (e.g., "Back to Sleep," disaster preparedness), and conferences for advanced professionals.

RECOMMENDATION 3:
REMEMBER OUR AUDIENCE

The final recommendation differs from the first two. It has no specific short-, intermediate-, or long-term goals. Instead, Recommendation 3 is a gentle reminder to remember our audience. Ultimately, all child care policies directly touch U.S. infants, toddlers, preschoolers, and their families. In the ideal sense, these policies reflect what is best for young children when they are outside of their parents' immediate care. They also prepare young children and their families for what comes next (Crosnoe, Augustine, & Huston, 2012; Folbre, 2001). There is a cumulative quality to a national system of child care for all families that is missing from the current policy landscape.

The focus on preschool education and academic outcomes concentrates attention and resources in a way that overlooks the fundamental nature and process of development during the first 5 years of life (Falk, 2012; Hirsch-Pasek et al., 2009). It sidesteps the long-understood and recently confirmed (e.g., Grindal, Hinton, & Shonkoff, 2012) significance of routine adult–child interactions. These interactions establish the foundation that is crucial for adaptive functioning and optimal learning during all stages of early development. Knowledgeable, skilled, and professional workers recognize developmental progression and understand the role of individual differences when building this foundation. A national system of quality, affordable child care and early education will similarly acknowledge infants', toddlers', and preschoolers' age-related needs, capabilities, and unique attributes of personality. Furthermore, it will provide much needed support to young families striving to manage the challenges of work life and home life in the 21st century.

Child Care Program Names
Study Methodology

DEVELOPMENT OF THE LIST

The list of program names for our study was obtained from the Missouri Department of Health and Senior Services, Bureau of Child Care. It included 3,881 child care centers, Head Start programs, public school preschools, home-based child care programs, and before- and after-school programs. To keep the focus on children ages birth through prekindergarten, programs that served only school-aged children were removed and 3,521 center- ($n = 1,778$) and home-based ($n = 1,743$) programs remained.

The list was further reduced when a decision was made to remove home-based programs. At the time that the list was generated, 97% of home-based child care programs were identified by operator name as listed on the state certificate of licensure (e.g., Jane Doe). Since studies have shown that parents who seek home-based child care programs do so because of the personal connection they want for themselves and for their children (Johansen et al., 1996; Kontos et al., 1995), we reasoned that a person's name on the official license was sufficient to indicate the desired personal connection, with no further analysis of consumer appeal needed. Thus, the final list of names for analysis included 1,778 child care centers, Head Start programs, religiously affiliated centers, and public school–operated preschools.

DATA CODING AND REDUCTION

Two goals guided the time-consuming process of coding the center names. The first goal was to summarize the different labels used to describe child care services (e.g., day care, learning center, preschool). Next, common themes were identified that could potentially convey information and influence consumer decisions.

The process began by moving all Head Start programs and nationally recognized child care chains, such as La Petite Academy and Kinder Care Learning Center, to separate databases. The names that remained were written on 3 x 5 cards and sorted on the basis of common words and messages, separate from how services were described. As the piles took shape and themes emerged, a coding system was developed that captured global themes and subthemes present in the names. Every effort was made to avoid purely subjective reactions to the names, although at times it was difficult not to chuckle (e.g., Wee Care Learning Center) or grimace (e.g., Ivy League Preschool).

To ensure the reliability of the coding decisions, the full list of program names (including Head Start and national chains) was sorted to the lowest level of coding—by service descriptors and subthemes—and repeatedly reviewed. After the review was completed, the final codes were entered into Excel and imported into SAS 9.1 for data cleaning, quality control, and, later, descriptive analysis.

Employed Mothers and Child Care Workers

Focus Group Research Methodology

THE FOCUS GROUPS

Women were recruited to participate in the focus groups because of their connection with child care. One group (HB) comprised 11 home-based child care providers and another group (CC) included seven individuals (six women and, unexpectedly, one man, with a gender-neutral name) who worked in community child care centers. These participants were recruited via phone calls to randomly selected licensed child care programs in a single county of a Midwestern state. We sought individuals who worked directly with children for at least 30 hours per week, 12 months of the year, and had at least 1 year of experience and no children of their own younger than prekindergarten age. The third group (WM) included 14 working mothers who worked at least 30 hours per week, 12 months per year, and had been in their current position for at least 1 year and had at least one child of preschool age in full-time child care. They were invited to participate via a Midwestern university's weekly faculty and staff electronic information newsletter.

The eligibility criteria were set to minimize variations in structural aspects of the participants' current employment status (i.e., all were full-time employees who had been in their current positions for at least 1 year). Similarly, we excluded child care providers who were simultaneously caring for their own preschool-age children in the home or who were working in child care programs where their own children were in attendance, as these arrangements could be linked with unique motivations for employment. Each participant received $25 for taking part in the focus groups, and the child care providers also received 2 hours of state-approved training toward their annually required 12 clock hours of professional development. Appendix C contains demographic information about the participants.

Overview of the Discussion Guide

The discussion guide for the focus groups was developed using recommendations from Morgan (1998). The *funnel approach* was adopted, which begins with broad, general questions about the central topic—in this case, women and work—and then moves to more specific questions. Discussions began with introductions, followed by a general discussion of women and work (defined as *paid employment activity*) and the reasons that women have for working. The remaining questions asked about what supports women's work, what gets in the way of women's work, and the benefits and downsides of women's work. The questions were phrased in the third person; that is, they focused on the experience of women in general and did not specifically query individual women about their own experiences. Participants approached this differently; some spoke exclusively about their own experiences, others kept to the generalized perspective of "working women," and, most commonly, discussion vacillated between the two. Furthermore, because all but three of the participants were mothers, the discussions focused primarily on working mothers. No efforts were made to correct or guide participants to a particular perspective during discussion. Each group followed the same discussion guide, presented below, and discussions, which were audio recorded, lasted for approximately 1 hour and 40 minutes. The audio recordings were transcribed verbatim and used for analysis.

Transcript Coding

Two primary goals guided the coding process. The first was to portray the conditions associated with maternal employment at the start of the 21st century and involved identifying global and secondary themes (e.g., Strauss & Corbin, 1998). The second goal was to illustrate cultural anxiety and ambivalence regarding maternal employment and nonmaternal care. Passages of individual dialogue and multiparticipant conversation that evidenced opposing perspectives or emotions on a topic were identified. Coding was completed primarily by the author.

DISCUSSION GUIDE:
INTRODUCTION OF PARTICIPANTS AND QUESTIONS

1. Let's first go around the room for introductions. Please tell us your name and your current job title or position. [5 minutes]

2. To begin, I'd like us to warm up and start our thinking processes by going around the room again and asking each of you, "When you think about women and work—and by work, we mean paid employment activities—what comes to mind?" [10 minutes]

3. Next, I'd like us to think about what motivates women to work. What reasons do women have for working? (Make list on easel pad.) [15 minutes]

PROMPTS

    a. For instance, there could be forces inside of women that motivate them to work ... ?
    b. There could also be forces outside of women that motivate them to work ....

4. Now, I'm going to hand out a sheet of paper. I'd like you to put one of your code number labels at the top. Then, I'd like you to look over the list that we have made on the easel and write down the most important reasons women have for working. Please write down the top three reasons in order from the most important to the least important. [10 minutes]

    Okay, let's briefly discuss what you have written. Someone mention the top item on their list and tell us how it ended up in the most important spot. (Collect papers after discussion.) [5 minutes]

5. Now, we're going to talk about what supports women's work. What people, or things, or even personal qualities, help women participate in paid employment? [10 minutes]

PROMPTS

    a. For instance, are there certain people who support women's work activities? If so, who are they and what do they do?
    b. Are there particular resources or things? If so, what are they and how do they support women's work?
    c. And finally, are there any private or personal qualities that support women's work? If so, what are they and how do they support women's work?

6. This next question is the opposite of the one we just discussed. What gets in the way of women's working? That is, what people, or things, or even personal qualities, challenge, or make difficult, women's work activities? [10 minutes]

7. Now, we're going to talk about the benefits of women's work. For women, what are the benefits or rewards of working? [10 minutes]

8. And, on the flip side, what are the downsides, or disadvantages, of women's work activities? [10 minutes]

9. This is our last question: What role models do women have for working? (Be sure to elicit a response from everyone in the group; make list on easel pad.) [10 minutes]

    I'm going to hand out another sheet of paper. Again, I'd like you to put one of your code number labels at the top. *Then, I'd like for you to write down who your role models are (or were).* Please write down one to three role models, in order from the most important to the least important. And, be sure to describe who the person is/was, not just their name (in fact, you can give a fake name or use initials if you'd like, but please make sure to describe who the person is/was). Briefly discuss responses. [5 to 10 minutes]

    Okay, that completes the discussion part of our group! But before you leave, I'd like to ask you to complete two brief questionnaires. (Distribute questionnaires.) Please put a code label at the top of each sheet. The first questionnaire asks if you think that our discussion adequately captured your thoughts about women and work and if you'd like to add anything else. The second questionnaire asks about your background.

Demographic Characteristics of Focus Group Participants

The following tables present the focus group participants' demographic characteristics, by group and individual. At the conclusion of the discussions, each participant completed a brief demographic questionnaire. They reported their age, race, current occupation and title, and several facts about their membership in the paid labor force (e.g., years since age 18 in the workforce overall, years in current position, and average hours worked per week in current position). Participants also used pre-defined categories to indicate the highest level of education that they had completed and the composition of their household. The focus group members also reported their personal income and their household income before taxes. The survey was designed so that income data could be reported as an hourly wage, a monthly amount, or annual income. Finally, using a five-point scale, where *1* = highly dissatisfied, *2* = dissatisfied, *3* = neutral, *4* = satisfied, and *5* = highly satisfied, participants indicated the level of satisfaction they felt with their current work situation. Please note that empty cells in the tables indicate that the information was not reported.

Appendix Table C-1. Home-Based Child Care Providers (Fall 2008)

Number	Age	Race	Family Structure	Occupation & Title	Yrs. in Workforce	Yrs. in Current Position	Hours /week	Education (highest level)	Pers. Income$	House. Income$	Job Satisfaction
1	44	White	2 parents, > 1 child	Preschool Teacher/Owner	26 yrs.	14	55	Some College	5,000– 5,835/ Month	8,335– 12,500/ Month	Satisfied
2	50	White	1 parent, 1 child	Child Care Provider/Owner & Operator	32 yrs.	3	55	Graduate or Professional Coursework	30,000– 35,000/ Year	Same	Neutral
3	53	White	2 parents, > 1 child	Home Day Care Provider/Owner	35 yrs., 10 mos.	26 yrs., 9 mos.	53	Graduate or Professional Coursework	30,000– 35,000/ Year	50,000– 60,000/ Year	Satisfied
4	57	African American	1 adult, no children	Day Care Provider/ Provider	40	20 yrs., 11 mos.	70	Master's Degree	2,500– 2,915/ Month	Same	Dissatisfied
5	43	Hispanic	2 parents, > 1 child	Family Child Care/Owner Director	25 yrs.	8	60	Vocational Program	50,000– 60,000/ Year	80,000– 90,000/ Year	Highly Satisfied

#	Age	Race	Household	Job Title				Education			Satisfaction
6	41	White	2 parents, > 1 child	Preschool Teacher/Child Care Provider	23 yrs., 6 mos.	19 years, 3 mos.	57.5	Vocational Program & some college	—	3,750–4,165/ Month	Highly Satisfied
7	42	White	2 parents, > 1 child	State Licensed Day Care Provider/Owner	27 yrs.	19	50	Vocational Program	15,000–20,000/ Year	70,000–80,000/ Year	Satisfied
8	45	White	2 parents, > 1 child	Home-Based Child Care Provider/Owner & Director	27 yrs.	16	65	Bachelor's Degree	35,000–40,000/ Year	45,000–50,000/ Year	Highly Satisfied
9	55	White	1 adult, no children	Child Care Provider/Owner	34 yrs.	19	50–55	Vocational Program/ Associate's Degree	—	30,000–35,000/ Year	Satisfied
10	48	White	2 parents, > 1 child	Preschool Teacher/Owner & Director	30 yrs., 10 mos.	25	50+	Associate's Degree/ working toward Bachelor's	4,165–5,000/ Month	>12,500/ Month	Highly Satisfied
11		African American	1 parent, > 1 child	Child Care Provider/ Director & Owner	29 yrs.	11 +	40+	9th to 12th grade	—	2,085–2,500/ Month	Neutral

Appendix Table C-2. Working Mothers (Fall 2008)

Number	Age	Race	Family Structure	Occupation & Title	Yrs. in Workforce	Yrs. in Current Position	Hours per / week	Education (highest level)	Pers. Income$	House. Income$	Job Satisfaction
1	31	White	2 parents, > 1 child	Sr. LPN-Nurse	13 yrs.	3 yrs.	40–45	Some College	——	40,000–45,000/ Year	Neutral
2	39	White	2 parents, > 1 child	RN/Nurse Clinician	20 yrs.	3 yrs.	40–42	Bachelor's Degree	4,165–5,000/ Month	90,000–100,000/ Year	Satisfied
3	30	White	2 parents, 1 child	Residential Life Administrator	12 yrs.	3.5 yrs.	40–50	Master's Degree	40,000–45,000/ Year	80,000–90,000/ Year	Satisfied
4	35	White	2 parents, 1 child	Executive Staff Assistant	17 yrs.	3 yrs.	40	Some College	15.01–17.25/ Hour	>17.25/ Hour	Satisfied
5	32	White	1 parent, 1 child	Office Support	12 yrs.	2 yrs.	40	Bachelor's Degree	12.76–15.00/ Hour	Same	Dissatisfied
6	44	White	2 parents, > 1 child	Administrative Associate	26 yrs.	12.5 yrs.	40	Graduate Coursework	35,000–40,000/ Year	90,000–100,000/ Year	Highly Satisfied

#	Age	Race	Family	Job Title			Hours	Education	Salary	Salary	Satisfaction
7	30	White	2 parents, 1 child	Geographic Information Systems Specialist	12 yrs.	6 yrs.	40	Master's Degree	40,000–45,000/ Year	80,000–90,000/ Year	Neutral
8	34	White	2 parents, > 1 child	Project Director for Research	16 yrs.	5.5 yrs.	40–50	Bachelor's Degree	50,000–60,000/ Year	80,000–90,000/ Year	Satisfied
9	26	White	2 parents, 1 child	Patient Service Representative, Level	8 yrs.	4 yrs.	45–50	Some College	10.50–12.75/ Hour	45,000–50,000/ Year	Satisfied
10	28	White	2 parents, 1 child	Office Support Staff Level IV	8 yrs.	7 yrs.	40	Bachelor's Degree	12.76–15.00/ Hour	70,000–80,000/ year	Satisfied
11	31	White	2 parents, 1 child	Academic Advisor II	12 yrs.	2 yrs.	40	Bachelor's Degree	30,000–35,000/ Year	60,000–70,000/ Year	Satisfied
12	38	White	2 parents, > 1 child	Administrative Associate	20 yrs.	2 yrs.	40+	Associate's Degree	35,000–40,000/ Year	90,000–100,000/ Year	Satisfied
13	37	White	2 parents, > 1 child	Web Development, Marketing Specialist	19 yrs.	2 yrs.	40	Bachelor's Degree	3,750–4,165/ Month	100,000–150,000/ Year	Neutral
14	36	White	2 parents, 1 child	Healthcare, Coordinator Guest Services	—	1.5 yrs.	50+	Master's Degree	>12.75/ Hour	80,000–90,000/ Year	Highly Satisfied

Appendix Table C-3. Child Care Center Providers (early Spring 2009)

Number	Age	Race	Family Structure	Occupation & Title	Yrs. in Workforce	Yrs. Current Position	Hours per week	Education (highest level)	Pers. Income$	House. Income$	Job Satis-faction
1	24	White	1 adult, no children	Lead Preschool Teacher	5 yrs.	4 yrs., 5 mos.	40+	Bachelor's Degree	10.50–12.75/ Hour	Same	Neutral
2	28	White	2 parents, > 1 child	Head Teacher, Pre-K Class	10 yrs., 10 mos.	9 yrs., 3 mos.	40	Some College	10.50–12.75/ Hour	Same	Highly Satisfied
3	29	White	2 parents, > 1 child	Child Care, Teacher	10 yrs.	1 yr.	40	High School	6.85–7.51/ Hour	Same	Satisfied
4	36	White	1 parent, > 1 child	Child Care, Lead Teacher	18 yrs.	2 yrs.	40+	9th to 12th grade	8.50–9.44/ Hour	Same	Neutral
5	35	White	2 parents, > 1 child	Teacher (preschool), Lead Teacher	17 yrs.	2 yrs., 3 mos.	40	Associate's Degree	1,665–2,085/ Month	40,000–45,000/ Year	Satisfied
6	68	White	Other	Assistant Staffer	43 yrs.	2 yrs., 8 mos.	40	Some College	8.50–9.44/ Hour	2,500–2,915/ Month	Highly Satisfied
7 (male)	30	White	1 adult, no children	Primary Care Provider, Assistant Teacher	12 yrs.	2 yrs.	40	Bachelor's Degree	7.52–8.49/ Hour	Same	Satisfied

North Carolina Discussion Group Participants and Discussion Guide

Key Informants (Titles and Affiliations on July 31, 2009)

Peggy Ball, formerly Deputy Director and Director of the NC Division of Child Development

Deb Cassidy, PhD, Professor, Human Development and Family Studies, University of North Carolina, Greensboro, and Director, Division of Child Development

Richard Clifford, PhD, Senior Scientist Emeritus, Frank Porter Graham Child Development Institute, University of North Carolina at Chapel Hill

Sue Horne Creech, former director of the NC Institute for Early Childhood Professional Development

Khari Garvin, Director, NC Head Start State Collaboration Office

Sharon Mims, Director, University of North Carolina, Greensboro, Child Care Education Program and PhD candidate in Human Development and Family Studies, University of North Carolina, Greensboro

John Pruette, Executive Director, NC Office of School Readiness

Sue Russell, President, Child Care Services Association

Discussion Guide: Getting Started and Discussion Questions

1. To get started, let's go around the room and have everyone say their name, affiliation, and something special about a current project (personal or professional). Among other things, this exercise will aid the transcription process.

2. To begin, I'd like us to warm up and start our thinking processes by going around the room and asking each of you, "When you think about early care and education in North Carolina *today*, what comes to mind?"

3. Next, I'd like for you to *take yourself back*, to the early 1990s . . . what were you doing then?

4. Think about early care and education in North Carolina before the passage of the 1993 Smart Start legislation . . . what comes to mind? Bear in mind that I view this as a starting point; I recognize that other activities, especially early childhood workforce development initiatives, were also on the radar.

5. Now, we're going to talk about *the process of change* from 1993 until today. [As much as possible, facilitators will elicit information to put responses into a timeline, such as dates, names, agencies, etc.]
   a. What barriers or challenges do you recall?
   b. What opportunities?
   c. What alliances (both likely and unlikely) formed?
   d. What factions (both likely and unlikely) formed?
   e. What magic (those "I can't believe this is happening" moments) can you recall?

6. Anything else?

This concludes our discussion. Thank you for your participation!

References

Abbott, A. (1988). *The system of professions: An essay on the division of expert labor*. Chicago: University of Chicago Press.

Advisory Committee on Head Start Research and Evaluation. (2012). *Final report: Submitted to the secretary of the U.S. Department of Health and Human Services*. Retrieved from www.acf.hhs.gov/programs/opre/resource/advisory-committee-on-head-start-research-and-evaluation-final-report

Ainsworth, M. D. S., Blehar, M. C., Waters, E., & Wall, S. (1978). *Patterns of attachment: A psychological study of the strange situation*. Hillsdale, NJ: Erlbaum.

American Academy of Pediatrics, American Public Health Association, & National Resource Center for Health and Safety in Child Care and Early Education. (2011). *Caring for our children: National health and safety performance standards: Guidelines for early care and education programs* (3rd ed.). Elk Grove Village, IL: American Academy of Pediatrics; Washington, DC: American Public Health Association. Retrieved from nrckids.org

Arendell, T. (2000). Conceiving and investigating motherhood: The decade's scholarship. *Journal of Marriage and the Family, 62*, 1197–1207.

Arnett, J. L. (1989). Caregivers in day care centers: Does training matter? *Journal of Applied Developmental Psychology, 10*, 541–552.

Austin, L. J. E., Whitebook, M., Connors, M., & Darrah, R. (2011). *Staff preparation, reward, and support: Are quality rating and improvement systems addressing all of the key ingredients necessary for change?* Berkeley: Center for the Study of Child Care Employment, University of California, Berkeley.

Barbarin, O. A., McCandies, T., Early, D. M., Clifford, R. M., Bryant, D., Burchinal, M., Howes, C., & Pianta, R. (2006). Quality of prekindergarten: What families are looking for in public sponsored programs. *Early Education and Development, 17*(4), 619–642.

Barglow, P., Vaughn, B. E., & Molitor, N. (1987). Effects of maternal absence due to employment on the quality of infant–mother attachment in a low-risk sample. *Child Development, 58*, 945–954.

Barnett, W. S., Carolan, M. E., Fitzgerald, J., & Squires, J. H. (2011). *The state of preschool 2011*. New Brunswick, NJ: National Institute for Early Education Research, Rutgers University.

Barnett, W. S., Epstein, D. J., Carolan, M. E., Fitzgerald, J., Ackerman, D. J., & Friedman, A. H. (2010). *The state of preschool 2010.* New Brunswick, NJ: National Institute for Early Education Research, Rutgers University.

Barnett, W. S., Robin, K. B., Hustedt, J. T., & Schulman, K. L. (2003). *The state of preschool 2003.* New Brunswick, NJ: National Institute for Early Education Research, Rutgers University.

Bellm, D., & Whitebook, M. (2006). *Roots of decline: How government policy has de-educated teachers of young children.* Berkeley: Center for the Study of Child Care Employment, Institute of Industrial Relations, University of California, Berkeley.

Belsky, J. (1990). Parental and non-parental child care and children's socio-emotional development: A decade in review. *Journal of Marriage and the Family, 52,* 885–903.

Belsky, J., & Rovine, M. (1988). Nonmaternal care in the first year of life and the security of infant–parent attachment. *Child Development, 59,* 157–167.

Belsky, J., & Steinberg, L. (1978). The effects of day care: A critical review. *Child Development, 49,* 929–949.

Belsky, J., Vandell, D. L., Burchinal, M., Clarke-Stewart, K. A., McCartney, K., Owen, M. T., & NICHD Early Child Care Research Network. (2007). Are there long-term effects of early child care? *Child Development, 78*(2), 681–701.

Blanchette, E. (2012, June 18–20). *Child Care and Development Fund (CCDF): Overview and reform agenda.* National Head Start Research Conference, Washington, DC.

Blau, D. (2011, February 28). *The economics of early childhood care and education: Implications for the child care workforce.* Presentation to the Early Childhood Care and Education Workforce Workshop, Washington, DC.

Blythe, A. (2012, August 21). Court lifts cap on poor children in Pre-K program. Retrieved from www.newsobserver.com/2012/08/21/2282524/court-lifts-cap-on-poor-children.html

Bowlby, J. (1969). *Attachment: Attachment and loss* (Vol. I). New York, NY: Basic Books.

Bramlett, M. D., & Mosher, W. D. (2002). Cohabitation, marriage, divorce, and remarriage in the United States. *Vital Health Statistics, 23*(22), 1–93.

Brandon, R. N., & Martinez-Beck, I. (2006). Estimating the size and characteristics of the United States early care and education workforce. In M. Zaslow & I. Martinez-Beck (Eds.), *Critical issues in early childhood professional development* (pp. 49–76). Baltimore, MD: Brookes.

Bredekamp, S., & Goffin, S. G. (2012). Making the case: Why credentialing and certification matter. In R. C. Pianta et al. (Eds.), *Handbook of early childhood education* (pp. 584–604). New York, NY: Guilford Press.

Bronfenbrenner, U. (1986). Ecology of the family as a context for human development: Research perspectives. *Developmental Psychology, 22*(6), 723–742.

Bub, K. L., & McCartney, K. (2004). On childcare as a support for maternal employment wages and hours. *Journal of Social Issues, 60*(4), 819–834.

Caldwell, B. (1990). "Educare": A new professional identity. *Dimensions, 18*(4), 3–6.

Campbell, F. A., & Ramey, C. T. (2010). Carolina Abecedarian project. In A. J. Reynolds & J. A. Temple (Eds.), *Childhood programs and practices in the first decade of life* (pp. 76–98). New York, NY: Cambridge University Press.

Capizzano, J., Adams, G., & Sonenstein, F. (March, 2000). *Child care arrangements for children under five: Variation across states* (Series B, No. B-7). Washington, DC: Urban Institute.

Chaudry, A. (2004). *Putting children first: How low-wage working mothers manage child care.* New York, NY: Russell Sage Foundation.

Chaudry, A. (2012, June 18–20). *Demographics of America's children and families: The changing face of Head Start.* Plenary session at National Head Start Research Conference, Washington, DC.

Child Care Aware of America. (2012). *Child care in America: 2012 state fact sheets.* Arlington, VA: Author.

Correll, S. J., Benard, S., & Paik, I. (2007). Getting a job: Is there a motherhood penalty? *American Journal of Sociology, 112*(5), 1297–1339.

Cost, Quality, and Child Outcomes Study Team. (1995). *Cost, quality, and child outcomes in child care centers, public report* (2nd ed.). Denver: Economics Department, University of Colorado at Denver.

Cotter, D., England, P., & Hermsen, J. (2007). *Moms and jobs: Trends in mothers' employment and which mothers stay home.* A fact sheet from Council on Contemporary Families. Retrieved from www.contemporaryfamilies.org/work-family/momsjobs.html

Crittenden, A. (2001). *The price of motherhood.* New York, NY: Metropolitan Books, Henry Holt.

Crosnoe, R., Augustine, J. M., & Huston, A. C. (2012). Children's early child care and their mothers' later involvement with schools. *Child Development, 83*(2), 758–772.

Cryer, D., & Burchinal, M. R. (1997). Parents as child care consumers. *Early Childhood Research Quarterly, 12*(1), 35–58.

Dillaway, H., & Paré, E. (2008). Locating mothers: How cultural debates about stay-at-home versus working mothers define women and home. *Journal of Family Issues, 29,* 437–464.

Drago, R. W. (2007). *Striking a balance: Work, family, life.* Boston, MA: Dollars & Sense, Economic Affairs Bureau.

Early, D. M., Bryant, D. M., Pianta, R. C., Clifford, R. M., Burchinal, M. R., Ritchie, S., Howes, C., & Barbarin, O. (2006). Are teachers' education, major, and credentials related to classroom quality and children's academic gains in pre-kindergarten? *Early Childhood Research Quarterly, 21,* 174–195.

Early, D. M., & Burchinal, M. R. (2001). Early childhood care: Relations with family characteristics and preferred care characteristics. *Early Childhood Research Quarterly, 16,* 475–497.

Early, D. M., Maxwell, K. L., Burchinal, M. R., Alva, S., Bender, R. H., Bryant, D., . . . Zill, N. (2007). Teachers' education, classroom quality, and young children's academic skills: Results from seven studies of preschool programs. *Child Development, 78*(2), 558–580.

Early, D. M., & Winton, P. J. (2001). Preparing the workforce: Early childhood teacher preparation at 2- and 4-year institutions of higher education. *Early Childhood Research Quarterly, 16,* 285–306.

Edwards, M. E. (2001). Uncertainty and the rise of the work–family dilemma. *Journal of Marriage and Family, 63,* 183–196.

Edwards, M. E. (2005). Occupational structure and the employment of American mothers of young children. *Journal of Family and Economic Issues, 26*(1), 31–53.

Falk, B. (2012). Introduction. In B. Falk (Ed.), *Defending childhood: Keeping the promise of early education* (pp. 1–10). New York, NY: Teachers College Press.

Feree, M. M. (2010, June). Filling the glass: Gender perspectives on families. *Journal of Marriage and Family, 72,* 420–439.

Folbre, N. (2001). *The invisible heart: Economics and family values.* New York, NY: New Press.

Frede, E. C. (1995). The role of program quality in producing early childhood program benefits. In R. E. Behrman (Ed.), *The future of children: Long-term outcomes of early childhood programs* (Vol. 5, pp. 115–132). Los Altos, CA: Center for the Future of Children.

Freeman, C. E. (2004). *Trends in educational equity of girls and women: 2004* (NCES 2005-016). U.S. Department of Education, National Center for Education Statistics. Washington, DC: U.S. Government Printing Office.

Fuller, B., Holloway, S. D., & Liang, X. (1996). Family selection of child-care centers: The influence of household support, ethnicity, and parental practices. *Child Development, 67,* 3320–3337.

Gable, S., & Cole, K. (2000). Parents' child care arrangements and their ecological correlates. *Early Education and Development, 11*(5), 549–572.

Gable, S., & Hansen, J. (2001). Child care provider perspectives on the role of education and training for quality caregiving. *Early Child Development and Care, 166,* 39–52.

Gable, S., Rothrauff, T. C., Thornburg, K. R., & Mauzy, D. (2007). Cash incentives and turnover in center-based child care staff. *Early Childhood Research Quarterly, 22,* 363–378.

Galinsky, E. (1992). The impact of child care on parents. In A. Booth (Ed.), *Child care in the 1990s: Trends and consequences* (pp. 159–171). Hillsdale, NJ: Erlbaum.

Gilliam, W. S. (2005). *Prekindergartners left behind: Expulsion rates in state prekindergarten systems.* New Haven, CT: Yale University Child Study Center, Yale University.

Goffin, S. G., & Washington, V. (2007). *Ready or not: Leadership choices in early care and education*. New York, NY: Teachers College Press.

Graff, E. J. (2007). The opt-out myth. *Columbia Journalism Review*, pp. 51–54.

Greenhouse, S. (2013, January 12). Our economic pickle. *The New York Times* Week in Review, p. 5.

Grindal, T. A., Hinton, C., & Shonkoff, J. P. (2012). The science of early childhood development: Lessons for teachers and caregivers. In B. Falk (Ed.), *Defending childhood: Keeping the promise of early education* (pp. 13–23). New York, NY: Teachers College Press.

Harms, T., & Clifford, R. M. (1980). *Early childhood environment rating scale*. New York, NY: Teachers College Press.

Harms, T. & Clifford, R. M. (1989). *Family day care rating scale*. New York, NY: Teachers College Press.

Harms, T., Clifford, R. M., & Cryer, D. (1998). *Early childhood environment rating scale—revised edition*. New York, NY: Teachers College Press.

Harms, T., Cryer, D., & Clifford, R. M. (1990). *Infant/toddler environment rating scale*. New York, NY: Teachers College Press.

Hayes, C. D. (Ed.). (1982). *Making policies for children: A study of the federal process*. Washington, DC: National Academy Press.

Hays, S. (1996). *The cultural contradictions of motherhood*. New Haven, CT: Yale University Press.

Heckman, J. J. (2011). Effective child development strategies. In E. Zigler, W. S. Gilliam, & W. S. Barnett (Eds.), *The pre-K debates: Current controversies and issues* (pp. 2–8). Baltimore, MD: Brookes.

Helburn, S. W., & Howes, C. (1996). Child care cost and quality. In R. E. Behrman (Ed.), *The future of children: Financing child care* (Vol. 6, pp. 62–82). Los Altos, CA: Center for the Future of Children.

Helms-Erikson, H., Tanner, J. L., Crouter, A. C., & McHale, S. M. (2000). Do women's provider-role attitudes moderate the links between work and family? *Journal of Family Psychology, 14*(4), 658–670.

Henneberger, M. (2011, November 17). "Princess Nancy" Pelosi calls Cain "clueless"; vows to do more for child care. *Washington Post*. Retrieved from articles.washingtonpost.com/2011-11-17/lifestyle/35282356_1_child-care-care-for-low-income-parents-drew-hammill

Herzenberg, S., Price, M., & Bradley, D. (2005). *Losing ground in early childhood education*. New York, NY: Economic Policy Institute in conjunction with the Foundation for Child Development and the Keystone Research Center.

Hirsch-Pasek, K., Golinkoff, R. M., Berk, L. E., & Singer, D. G. (2009). *A mandate for playful learning in preschool: Presenting the evidence*. New York, NY: Oxford University Press.

Hochschild, A. R. (1989). *The second shift: Working parents and the revolution at home.* New York, NY: Viking.

Hofferth, S. L., Brayfield, A., Deich, S., & Holcomb, P. (1991). *National child care survey, 1990.* Washington, DC: Urban Institute Press.

Hofferth, S. L., & Phillips, D. A. (1987). Child care in the United States, 1970–1995. *Journal of Marriage and the Family, 49*(3), 559–571.

Holloway, S. D., Fuller, B., Rambaud, M. F., & Eggers-Pierola, C. (1997). *Through my own eyes: Single mothers and the culture of poverty.* Cambridge, MA: Harvard University Press.

Howes, C., Hamre, B. K., & Pianta, R. C. (2012). *Effective early childhood professional development: Improving teacher practice and child outcomes.* Baltimore, MD: Brookes.

Howes, C., Phillips, D. A., & Whitebook, M. (1992). Thresholds of quality: Implications for the social development of children in center-based child care. *Child Development, 63,* 449–460.

Howes, C., & Pianta, R. C. (2011). *Foundations for teaching excellence: Connecting early childhood quality rating, professional development, and competency systems in states.* Baltimore, MD: Brookes.

Howes, C., Whitebook, M., & Phillips, D. A. (1992). Teacher characteristics and effective teaching in child care: Findings from the National Child Care Staffing Study. *Child and Youth Care Forum, 21*(6), 399–414.

Hynes, K., & Habasevich-Brooks, T. (2008). The ups and downs of child care: Variations in child care quality and exposure across the early years. *Early Childhood Research Quarterly, 23,* 559–574.

Johansen, A. S., Leibowitz, A., & Waite, L. J. (1996). The importance of child-care characteristics to choice of care. *Journal of Marriage and the Family, 58,* 759–772.

Jong, E. (2010, November 6). Mother madness. *The Wall Street Journal.* Retrieved from online.wsj.com/article/SB10001424052748704462704555906035536742 96.html

Jorde-Bloom, P., & Sheerer, M. (1992). The effect of leadership training on child care program quality. *Early Childhood Research Quarterly, 7,* 579–594.

Kagan, S. L. (2012). Early learning and development standards: An elixir for early childhood systems reform. In S. L. Kagan & K. Kauerz (Eds.), *Early childhood systems: Transforming early learning* (pp. 55–70). New York, NY: Teachers College Press.

Kagan, S. L., & Kauerz, K. (2012). *Early childhood systems: Transforming early learning.* New York: Teachers College Press.

Kagan, S. L., Kauerz, K., & Tarrant, K. (2008). *The early care and education teaching workforce at the fulcrum: An agenda for reform.* New York, NY: Teachers College Press.

Kagan, S. L. & Neville, P. R. (1992). *Parent choice in early care and education: Myth or reality?* White Plains, NY: A. L. Mailman Family Foundation.

Knoche, L. L., Cline, K. D., & Marvin, C. A. (2012). Fostering collaborative partnerships between early childhood professionals and the parents of young children. In R. C. Pianta, W. S. Barnett, L. M. Justice, & S. M. Sheridan (Eds.), *Handbook of early childhood education* (pp. 370–392). New York, NY: Guilford Press.

Kontos, S., Howes, C., Shinn, M., & Galinsky, E. (1995). *Quality in family child care and relative care.* New York, NY: Teachers College Press.

La Paro, K. M., Pianta, R. C., & Stuhlman, M. (2004). The classroom assessment scoring system: Findings from the prekindergarten year. *The Elementary School Journal, 104*(5), 409–426.

Laughlin, L. (2011). Maternity leave and employment patterns of first-time mothers: 1961–2008. *Current Population Reports.* Washington, DC: U.S. Census Bureau.

Laughlin, L. (2013). Who's minding the kids? Child care arrangements: Spring 2011. *Household Economic Studies.* Washington, DC: U.S. Census Bureau.

Leandro v. the State, 488 S.E.2d 249 (NC 1997). Retrieved from law.duke.edu/childedlaw/schooldiscipline/attorneys/case summaries/leandrovstate

Luo, M. (2009, September 7). Out of work, and too down to search on. *The New York Times*, A1 & A11.

Macartney, S., & Laughlin, L. (2011). *Child care costs in the current population survey's annual social and economic supplement (CPS ASEC): A comparison to SIPP* (SEHSD Working Paper No. 2011-1). Washington, DC: U.S. Census Bureau.

Magnuson, K. A., Ruhm, C., & Waldfogel, J. (2007). Does prekindergarten improve school preparation and performance? *Economics of Education Review, 26*, 33–51.

McCall, R. (1977). Challenges to a science of developmental psychology. *Child Development, 48*, 333–344.

McMenamin, T. M. (2007, December). A time to work: Recent trends in shift work and flexible schedules. *Monthly Labor Review, 130*(12), 3–15.

Merriam-Webster. (2010). Ambivalence. Retrieved from http://www.merriam-webster.com/dictionary/ambivalence

Meyers, M. K., & Jordan, L. P. (2006). Choice and accommodation in parental child care decisions. *Community Development, 37*(2), 53–70.

Michel, S. (1999). *Children's interests/mothers' rights: The shaping of America's child care policy.* New Haven, CT: Yale University Press.

Missouri Department of Health. (1999, August 31). *Licensing rules for family day care homes (Chapter 61).* Division 30—Division of Health Standards and Licensure. Jefferson City, MO: Author.

Missouri Department of Health. (2000, July 31). *Licensing rules for group day care homes and child day care centers (Chapter 62).* Division 30–Division of Health Standards and Licensure. Jefferson City, MO: Author.

Missouri Department of Health. (n.d.). *General differences between licensed, licensed-exempt and unregulated facilities.* Retrieved from http://health.mo.gov/safety/childcare/pdf/Unregulated_facilities_general_differences.pdf

Mitchell, A. W. (2005). *Stair steps to quality: A guide for states and communities developing quality rating systems for early care and education.* [United Way Success by Six.] Retrieved from www.earlychildhoodfinance.org/downloads/2005/MitchStairSteps_2005.pdf

Morgan, D. L. (1998). *Planning focus groups.* (Focus group kit, Vol. 2; D. L. Morgan & R. A. Kreuger, Eds.). Thousand Oaks, CA: Sage.

Morgan, G., Azer, S. L., Costley, J. B., Genser, A., Goodman, I. F., Lombardi, J., & McGimsey, B. (1993). *Making a career of it: The state of the states report on career development in early care and education.* Boston, MA: The Center for Career Development in Early Care and Education, Wheelock College.

Morris, J. R., & Helburn, S. W. (2000). Child care center quality differences: The role of profit status, client preferences, and trust. *Nonprofit and Voluntary Sector Quarterly, 29*(3), 377–399.

Morrissey, T. W. (2008). Familial factors associated with the use of multiple child-care arrangements. *Journal of Marriage and Family, 70,* 549–563.

Morrissey, T. W. (2009). Multiple child-care arrangements and young children's behavioral outcomes. *Child Development, 80*(1), 59–76.

National Association for the Education of Young Children. (1993). *A conceptual framework for early childhood professional development: A position statement.* Washington, DC: Author.

National Center on Child Care Quality Improvement & National Association for Regulatory Administration. (2011). *Trends in child care center licensing regulations and policies for 2011* (Research Brief No. 999). Fairfax, VA: Author.

National Child Care Information and Technical Assistance Center. (2011). *Staff requirements.* Retrieved from occ-archive.org/topic/licensing/staff-requirements

National Child Care Information and Technical Assistance Center & National Association for Regulatory Administration. (2010). *The 2008 child care licensing study.* Fairfax, VA: National Child Care Information and Technical Assistance Center.

National Opinion Research Center. (2012). *National survey of early care and education.* Retrieved from www.norc.org/Research/Projects/Pages/national-survey-of-early-care-and-education.aspx

National Research Council & Institute of Medicine. (2001). *Getting to positive outcomes for children in child care: A summary of two workshops.* Washington, DC: The National Academies Press.

National Research Council & Institute of Medicine. (2012). *The early childhood care and education workforce: Challenges and opportunities: A workshop report.* Washington, DC: The National Academies Press.

Nelson, J. R. (1982). The federal interagency day care requirements. In C. D. Hayes (Ed.), *Making policies for children: A study of the federal process* (pp. 151–205). Washington, DC: National Academy Press.

Nelson, M. K. (1990). *Negotiated care: The experience of family day care providers.* Philadelphia, PA: Temple University Press.

Newcombe, N. S. (2003). Some controls control too much. *Child Development, 74*(4), 1050–1052.

NICHD Early Child Care Research Network. (1997). The effects of infant child care on infant–mother attachment security: Results of the NICHD study of early child care. *Child Development, 68*(5), 860–879.

NICHD Early Child Care Research Network. (1999). Child outcomes when child care center classes meet recommended standards for quality. *American Journal of Public Health*, 89(7), 1072–1077.

NICHD Early Child Care Research Network. (2002a). Child-care structure process outcome: Direct and indirect effects of child care quality on young children's development. *Psychological Science*, 13(3), 199–206.

NICHD Early Child Care Research Network. (2002b). Early child care and children's development prior to school entry: Results from the NICHD study of early child care. *American Educational Research Journal*, 39(1), 133–164.

NICHD Early Child Care Research Network. (2006). Child-care effect sizes for the NICHD study of early child care and youth development. *American Psychologist*, 61(2), 99-116.

No Child Left Behind: A New Era in Education Presentation. (2001). Retrieved from www2.ed.gov/nclb/overview/intro/presentation/index.html

North Carolina Quality Rating and Improvement System (QRIS) Advisory Committee. (2012, August). *Executive summary*. Raleigh, NC: Author.

North Carolina, State of. (2010). Race-to-the-Top application. Retrieved from www2.ed.gov/programs/racetothetop/phase2-applications/index.html

North Carolina, State of. (2011). Race-to-the-Top: Early Learning Challenge application. Retrieved from www2.ed.gov/programs/racetothetop-earlylearningchallenge/ awards.html

Obama, B. (2013). The State of the Union. Retrieved from www.whitehouse.gov/state-of-the-union-2013

Payne, A. L. (2011, May). *Strong licensing: The foundation for a quality early care and education system*. Lexington, KY: National Association for Regulatory Administration.

Perry-Jenkins, M., Repetti, R. L., & Crouter, A. C. (2000). Work and family in the 1990s. *Journal of Marriage and the Family*, 62, 981–998.

Personal Responsibility and Work Opportunity Reconciliation Act of 1996. Major provisions. Retrieved from www.acf.hhs.gov/programs/ofa/resource/law-reg/finalrule/aspesum

Phillips, D., Lande, J., & Goldberg, M. (1990). The state of child care regulation: A comparative analysis. *Early Childhood Research Quarterly*, 5, 151–179.

Pianta, R. C., Barnett, W. S., Burchinal, M. R., & Thornburg, K. (2009). The effects of preschool education: What we know, how public policy is or is not aligned with the evidence base, and what we need to know. *Psychological Science in the Public Interest*, 10(2), 49–88.

Pope, E. (1955, July). Front page: Is a working mother a threat to the home? *McCall's*, 82(19), 29.

Rabinowitz, D. (1990, May). From the mouths of babes to a jail cell: Child abuse and the abuse of justice: A case study. *Harper's Magazine*, pp. 52–63.

Raikes, H. (1998). Investigating child care subsidy: What are we buying? *Society for Research in Child Development, Social Policy Report*, 12(2) 1–19 .

Rampell, C. (2009, February 6). As layoffs surge, women may pass men in job force. *The New York Times*, p. A1.

Resnick, G. (2010). Project Head Start: Quality and links to child outcomes. In A. J. Reynolds, A. J. Rolnick, M. M. Englund, & J. A. Temple (Eds.), *Childhood programs and practices in the first decade of life* (pp. 121–156). New York, NY: Cambridge University Press.

Reynolds, A. J., Temple, J. A., & Ou, S. (2010). Impacts and implications of the Child–Parent Center preschool program. In A. J. Reynolds, A. J. Rolnick, M. M. Englund, & J. A. Temple (Eds.), *Childhood programs and practices in the first decade of life* (pp. 168–187). New York, NY: Cambridge University Press.

Reynolds, A. J., Temple, J. A., Ou, S., Arteaga, I. A., & White, B. A. B. (2011). School-based early childhood education and age-28 well-being: Effects by timing, dosage, and subgroups. *Science*, 333(6040), 360–364.

Rhodes, H., & Huston, A. (2012). Building the workforce our youngest children deserve. *Society for Research in Child Development, Social Policy Report*, 26(1) 1–31.

Rideout, V. J., Foehr, U. G., & Roberts, D. F. (2010, January). *Generation M2: Media in the lives of 8- to 18-year-olds*. Menlo Park, CA: Kaiser Family Foundation.

Ridgeway, C. L., & Correll, S. J. (2004). Motherhood as a status characteristic. *Journal of Social Issues*, 60(4), 683–700.

Riley, L. A., & Glass, J. L. (2002). You can't always get what you want—infant care preferences and use among employed mothers. *Journal of Marriage and Family*, 64, 2–15.

Rodham, H. (1977). Children's policies: Abandonment and neglect [Review of the book *The children's cause*, by G. Y. Steiner]. *Yale Law Journal*, 86(7), 1522–1531.

Rolnick, A. J., & Grunewald, R. (2011). The economic case for targeted preschool programs. In E. Zigler, W. S. Gilliam, & W. S. Barnett (Eds.), *The pre-K debates: Current controversies and issues* (pp. 22–26). Baltimore, MD: Brookes.

Rose, K. K., & Elicker, J. (2008). Parental decision making about child care. *Journal of Family Issues*, 29(9), 1161–1184.

Ruopp, R., Travers, J., Glantz, F., & Coelen, C. (1979). *Children at the center: Summary findings and their implications*. Cambridge, MA: Abt Books.

Ryan, S., & Whitebook, M. (2012). More than teachers: The early care and education workforce. In R. C. Pianta, W. S. Barnett, L. M. Justice, & S. M. Sheridan (Eds.), *Handbook of early childhood education* (pp. 92–110). New York, NY: Guilford Press.

Satkowski, C. (2009). *The next step in systems-building: Early childhood advisory councils and federal efforts to promote policy alignment in early childhood*. Retrieved from www.newamerica.net/files/Early_Childhood_Advisory_Councils_Nov_09_0.pdf

Scarr, S. (1998). American child care today. *American Psychologist*, 53(2), 95–108.

Schulman, K., & Blank, H. (2012). *Downward slide: State child care assistance policies 2012*. Washington, DC: National Women's Law Center.

Schweinhart, L. J. (2010). The challenge of the HighScope Perry Preschool study. In A. J. Reynolds, A. J. Rolnick, M. M. Englund, & J. A. Temple (Eds.), *Childhood programs and practices in the first decade of life* (pp. 157–167). New York, NY: Cambridge University Press.

Sears, W., & Sears, M. (2001). *The attachment parenting book*. New York, NY: Little, Brown.

Smart Start, SL93-321 (1993). Retrieved from hugh.ncsmartstart.org/wp-content/uploads/2010/05/1993legislation.pdf

Smart Start & the North Carolina Partnership for Children. (2010). *About Smart Start*. Raleigh, NC: Author. Retrieved from www.smartstart.org/category/smart-start-information/smart-starts-history and www.smartstart.org/category/smart-start-information/about-smart-start

Stipek, D., Milburn, S., Clements, D., & Daniels, D. H. (1992). Parents' beliefs about appropriate education for young children. *Journal of Applied Developmental Psychology, 13*, 293–310.

Strauss, A., & Corbin, J. (1998). *Basics of qualitative research*. Thousand Oaks, CA: Sage.

Swarns, R. (2009, May 28). On the homefront, a twist of candor. *The New York Times*, p. E1.

Szekely, A. (2011). *State early childhood advisory councils: An overview of implementation across the states* (Issue Brief). Washington, DC: National Governors Association.

Tout, K., Starr, R., Soli, M., Moodie, S., Kirby, G., & Boller, K. (2010). *Compendium of quality rating systems and evaluations*. Washington, DC: Mathematica Policy Research & Child Trends.

U.S. Census Bureau. (2011). *Who's minding the kids? Child care arrangements: Spring 2010*. Survey of Income and Program Participation (SIPP), 2008 Panel, Wave 5. Washington, DC: Author. Retrieved from www.census.gov/hhes/childcare/index.html; www.census.gov/sipp/top_mod/2008/topmod08.html

U.S. Census Bureau. (2012). Current population survey, annual social and economic supplements. Table F-10. Presence of children under 18 years old: All families by median and mean income: 1974–2011. Retrieved from www.census.gov/hhes/www/income/data/historical/families/index.html

U.S. Department of Health and Human Services. (2010). *Child care and development fund: Report of state and territory plans FY 2010–2011*. Washington, DC: Author.

U.S. Department of Health and Human Services. (2012a). 2012 HHS poverty guidelines. Washington, DC: Author. Retrieved from aspe.hhs.gov/poverty/12poverty.shtml

U.S. Department of Health and Human Services. (2012b). Head Start program facts fiscal year 2011. Washington, DC: Author. Retrieved from eclkc.ohs.acf.hhs.gov/hslc/mr/factsheets/2011-hs-program-factsheet.html

U.S. Department of Health and Human Services. (2012c). OCC fact sheet. Retrieved from www.acf.hhs.gov/programs/occ/fact-sheet-occ

U.S. Department of Labor, Bureau of Labor Statistics. (2011a, May 6). The editor's desk: Share of married couples with an employed mother at its lowest: 1994–2010. Retrieved from www.bls.gov/opub/ted/2011/ted_20110506.htm

U.S. Department of Labor, Bureau of Labor Statistics. (2011b, December). *Women in the labor force: A databook (2011 Edition; Report 1034)*. Washington, DC: U.S. Department of Labor.

U.S. Department of Labor, Bureau of Labor Statistics. (2012a). Economic news release: The American time use study. Retrieved from www.bls.gov/news.release/atus.toc.htm

U.S. Department of Labor, Bureau of Labor Statistics. (2012b). Employment characteristics of families: 2011. BLS News Release, USDL-12-0771. Retrieved from www.bls.gov/news.release/pdf/famee.pdf

U.S. Department of Labor, Bureau of Labor Statistics. (2012c). Occupational outlook handbook, 2012–2013 Edition, Child care workers. Retrieved from www.bls.gov/ooh/personal-care- and-service/childcare-workers.htm

U.S. Department of Labor, Bureau of Labor Statistics. (2012d). Usual weekly earnings of wage and salary workers: Third quarter of 2012. Retrieved from www.bls.gov/news.release/archives/wkyeng_10182012.pdf

U.S. Government Accountability Office. (1989). *Child care: Government funding sources, coordination, and service availability* (GAO/HRD-90-26BR). Washington, DC: Author.

U.S. Government Accountability Office. (1997). *Welfare reform: Implications of increased work participation for child care* (GAO/HEHS-97-75). Washington, DC: Author.

U.S. Government Accountability Office. (2012). *Early child care and education: HHS and Education are taking steps to improve workforce data and enhance worker quality* (GAO-12-2 48). Washington, DC: Author.

U.S. Internal Revenue Service. (2011). Ten things to know about the child and dependent care credit. Retrieved from www.irs.gov/uac/Ten-Things-to-Know-About-the-Child-and-Dependent-Care-Credit

U.S. Internal Revenue Service. (2012). Dependent care assistance. Retrieved from www.irs.gov/publications/p15b/ar02.html

Uttal, L. (2002). *Making child care work: Employed mothers in the new childcare market.* New Brunswick, NJ: Rutgers University Press.

Vandell, D. L., Belsky, J., Burchinal, M. R., Steinberg, L., Vandergrift, N., & NICHD SECC. (2010). Do effects of early child care extend to age 15 years? Results from the NICHD study of early child care and youth development. *Child Development, 81*(3), 737–756.

Vandell, D. L., & Wolfe, B. (2000). *Child care quality: Does it matter and does it need to be improved?* (SR #78). Madison: University of Wisconsin, Institute for Research on Poverty.

Waldfogel, J. (1997). The effect of children on women's wages. *American Sociological Review, 62,* 209–217.

Waldfogel, J. (2006, March–May). What do children need? *Public Policy Research,* pp. 26–34.

Wallis, C. (1987, June 22). Is day care bad for babies? *TIME Magazine,* pp. 54–63.

Webley, K. (2011, October 10). The preschool wars. *Time Magazine,* pp. 46–49.

Whitebook, M., Howes, C., & Phillips, D. (1989). *Who cares? Child care teachers and the quality of care in America.* Final report of the national child care staffing study. Oakland, CA: Child Care Employee Project.

Whitebook, M., Howes, C., & Phillips, D. (1998). *Worthy work, unlivable wages: The national child care staffing study 1988–1997.* Washington, DC: Center for the Child Care Workforce.

Whitebook, M., & Ryan, S. (2011). *Degrees in context: Asking the right questions about preparing skilled and effective teachers of young children* (Preschool Policy Brief 22). New Brunswick, NJ: National Institute for Early Education Research, Rutgers University.

Whitebook, M., Sakai, L., Gerber, E., & Howes, C. (2001). *Then & now: Changes in child care staffing, 1994–2000, technical report.* Washington DC: Center for the Child Care Workforce.

Willer, B., Hofferth, S. L., Kisker, E. E., Divine-Hawkins, P., Farquhar, E., & Glantz, F. B. (1991). *The demand and supply of child care in 1990.* Washington, DC: National Association for the Education of Young Children.

Williams, J. C., Manvell, J., & Bornstein, S. (2006). *"Opt out" or pushed out? How the press covers work/family conflict.* San Francisco: Center for Worklife Law, University of California, Hastings College of the Law.

Wong, V. C., Cook, T. D., Barnett, W. S., & Jung, K. (2008). An effectiveness-based evaluation of five state pre-kindergarten programs. *Journal of Policy Analysis and Management, 27*(1), 122–154.

Wrigley, J. (1995). *Other people's children.* New York, NY: Basic Books.

Yeung, W. J., Linver, M. R., & Brooks-Gunn, J. (2002). How money matters for young children's development: Parental investment and family processes. *Child Development, 73*(6), 1861–1879.

Zaslow, M., Tout, K., & Halle, T. (2011). Differing purposes for measuring quality in early childhood settings: Aligning purpose with procedures. In M. Zaslow et al. (Eds.), *Quality measurement in early childhood settings* (pp. 389–410). Baltimore, MD: Brookes.

Zigler, E., Marsland, K., & Lord, H. (2009). *The tragedy of child care in America.* New Haven, CT: Yale University Press.

Index

About the Author

Sara Gable has been engaged in practical and scholarly activity focused on children, families, and child care since the 1980s. In 1986, she completed an undergraduate internship at Syntex Corporation's employee child care program in Palo Alto, CA. During her master's degree studies, she was a lead teacher at Utah State University's Child Development Lab and conducted extensive in-home observations of mothers and their babies across the first year of life. At Penn State, her PhD research involved naturalistically observing first-born toddlers in two-parent homes before, during, and after dinner to characterize the co-parenting relationship. Upon completing her PhD, she was a post-doctoral project coordinator for a federally funded child abuse prevention demonstration project at the University of Missouri. From 1996 to the present, she has been on the faculty at the University of Missouri in Human Development and Family Studies and, more recently, as an associate professor and extension specialist in the Department of Nutrition and Exercise Physiology. During her tenure, she has conducted research with the child care workforce, created and taught educational programs for child care providers, and served on numerous local and state agency advisory boards related to child care. She also conducts research on the etiology and outcomes of childhood obesity and is currently working to integrate her child care and child health research.